How to Hire a Nanny

Your Complete Guide to Finding, Hiring, and Retaining Household Help

GUY MADDALONE
THE NATION'S HOUSEHOLD HR™ EXPERT

ISBN: 978-1-48358-628-1 (print)
ISBN: 978-1-48358-629-8 (ebook)

To my wife, Diane, who keeps it all together as we strive to achieve an effective work-life balance, and to household employers, who seek the same by hiring and retaining the best help possible.

Acknowledgments

...my children, Michael, Elise, and Jeffrey, who have helped me understand a unique aspect of household employment with Nanny Ester, Missy, Venus, Erin, and Sosan.

...my mother, Joyce, for our first entrepreneurial experience in home care, and to Henry, my father, who taught me commitment, responsibility, and determination.

...my management team and all the experts at GTM who give it their all in order to make a difference in our clients' lives.

...my good friends for all the years of support and encouragement.

...Bob Mark and no-nonsense seminars that inspired GTM's educational arm.

...the Growth Guy, Verne Harnish, and my MIT Birthing of Giants classmates, who challenged me to write this book.

...all referral partners who have sent their clients to GTM over the years.

...Colleen, Rob, Shelley, Loni, and Gloria at GE for your belief in GTM's work-family benefit program.

...my brothers, Todd and Michael, who strive to make GTM into a company we are all proud to share with others.

...household employers Maria Ascenzo, Jim Chaney, Rex Haberman, April Musson, Stephanie Oana, Zuzka Polishook, Denise Shade, and Gretchen Weisman, who shared their stories.

...household employment agency owners and managers Leann Brambach, Pat Cascio, Kim Cino, Denise Collins, Janet Cook, Sylvia Greenbaum, Hilary Lockhart, Judi Merlin, Ilo Milton, Arline Rubel, Mary Starkey, Lin Taylor-Pleiman, Susan Tokayer, and Candi Wingate, who shared advice and experience.

...household employees John Robertson and Bruce Reynolds, both of the International Butlers Guild, as well as Stephanie Doyle, Crystal Hinman, JoAnn Rogahn, Liz, Trish Stevens, and other household professionals who shared advice and experience.

...the GTM and A New England Nanny marketing teams, especially Gemma Lavender, who worked diligently to keep this project on track and researched the latest information for this edition, as well as Debbie Sgroi, who worked tirelessly interviewing and researching details for this book.

...employment attorneys Heather Diddell, Esq.; Ellen Bach, Esq.; and Leslie Theile, Esq., of Whiteman, Osterman & Hannah, and John Bagyi, Esq., of Bond, Schoeneck & King, who contributed to the federal, immigration, and New York legal aspects detailed within this book.

...the International Nanny Association (INA) and the Alliance for Premier Nanny Agencies (APNA) for giving their support.

...the thousands of household employers who allow GTM to serve their needs daily.

...anyone I may have unintentionally omitted.

Please note that all case studies represented in this book have been collated in the years 2004-2011 and have been published in previous editions. The stories told and information and advice given are still relevant today, so are included again.

Acclaim for How to Hire a Nanny*:* *First Edition*

"I believe that one of the most important ways to enact societal change is through education. The Domestic Worker Law that I passed in 2003 was aimed in part at educating workers and employers of their rights and responsibilities. The information in Guy's book is crucial to educating people who employ domestic workers and ensuring that they know and understand the relevant laws and regulations."

—Gale A. Brewer, New York City
27th Manhattan Borough President and former council member
(D-Manhattan), NY

"As an agency owner for more than 20 years, I have added *How to Hire a Nanny* to my list of essential guidance books for families. There is so little consistent information available today that provides good, sound advice in this arena. Thank you, Guy, for educating and informing household employers on effective household management!"

—Julie Biondi, founder, Choice Care
Nannies & Baby Nurses, Westfield, NJ

"Often we only see one side of the story—our own. Guy Maddalone pulls from a variety of viewpoints, bringing about a well-rounded glimpse of the domestic employment relationship. Often domestic relationships fail because of unreal expectations or a difference in value systems. Guy reveals the experiences from all involved and provides families with invaluable information."

—Leann Brambach, experienced agency owner,
Home Details, Inc., Seattle, WA

"Having been a nanny agency owner for the past 20 years, I understand that for most families obtaining and applying for tax and labor law information can be cumbersome and confusing. With this easy-to-follow instructional handbook, Guy Maddalone streamlines an otherwise complicated process for the domestic employer. I applaud his contribution, and I look forward to continuing to recommend the services of GTM knowing my clients will be in very good hands."

"After nearly a decade in the field of private service, I am thrilled to finally find the missing link in the employment process. Guy Maddalone's book elevates the employment relationships of the staffed homes of the world—from the servile nature of centuries past—into a functional likeness of today's corporate culture. Many, many thanks!"

"There is a saying that leaders lead! Guy Maddalone is a leader in the household staffing industry. His book is insightful, informative, and inspiring! Guy Maddalone and his superb team are motivated to find solutions and get results. I was fortunate to serve on the board of APNA (Association of Premier Nanny Agencies) with Guy for three years. Guy and GTM have been a major contributor to industry organizations. Guy is a farsighted businessman and always goes the extra mile to serve his clients and agencies nationwide. Guy Maddalone understands that you cannot take the 'human touch' out of the household staffing industry. GTM has been a sensational resource for Nannies & Housekeepers USA and many of our important clients use their payroll service. I encourage all agency owners, managers, and families to read this book."

"I commend Guy in his effort to educate and support our industry by writing and publishing this very valuable handbook. Employers and agencies will appreciate having this resource to turn to whenever questions arise."

"The household employment industry has needed such a book as this for a long time. And I can't think of a better person to have written it. Guy Maddalone is a visionary in the industry and a man of integrity who is very well respected by partners, clients, and competitors alike. Guy has greatly contributed to the professionalism and growth of the industry. Thank you,

Guy, for bringing these human resource issues to the attention of all and for always being a business partner that we can trust and count on."

—Denise Collins, CEO, In-House
Staffing at Aunt Ann's, San Francisco, CA

"Guy Maddalone has done it again. After many hours of hard work, he has created an important tool for household employers. Families should review the contents of this book before hiring an employee. They will find a wealth of information to help make the working relationship in their home a success."

—Annie Davis, president,
Annie's Nannies, Seattle, WA

"Guy Maddalone has an unsurpassed commitment to the in-home employment industry. His many years of experience assisting thousands of families, coupled with his personal experience as the eldest of thirteen and father of three, enabled him to have an unparalleled perspective and influence on the professional employment needs of today's American families."

—Betty Davis, experienced agency president,
In Search of Nanny, Inc., Beverly, MA

"There is arguably no person in the industry better equipped to write this book. As an agency owner, I have followed Guy Maddalone's success (and referred clients to his company) for nearly a decade. As an author, he has the rare combined insight of being a household employer himself and owning a business, which services clientele nationally. His commitment to trade-related organizations (and the sound influence he infuses to the many boards he serves on) immeasurably benefits the industry as a whole. In a sense, Guy has dragged this industry—sometimes kicking and screaming—to a new level of professionalism and recognition. This book is a must-read."

—Emily Dills, president, The Seattle
Nanny Network, Inc., Kirkland, WA

"Working with GTM as a partner has brought so much satisfaction to a number of our client families. We are continually given positive feedback about the high level of service and cutting-edge knowledge of household payroll and taxes. GTM has a marvelous way of answering tough questions and demystifying the complications of taxes and issues of employer vs.

employee responsibilities. It is such a relief to refer anxious parents to our prized experts, the kind people at GTM. I hope that they will be around for a long time."

"The legal complexities of human resources can be daunting to a non-professional hiring in-home child or house care. This book by Guy Maddalone should ease the burden considerably, as it ties together in a logical and understandable way of the employment process. It is a much-needed resource."

"As agency owners for 23 years, our association with Guy Maddalone has been a consistent source of comfort and support for both our staff and our client families. In the many years of referring our families to GTM for payroll support we have NEVER received a single complaint. Guy's ethical business practices underlie all that he oversees. His book, *How to Hire a Nanny* is a further reflection of how much Guy understands and genuinely cares about the relationships between families and nannies. We are proud to have GTM as our right-hand resource."

"I have worked with Guy Maddalone for many years and found him to be an expert in providing clear, concise, up-to-date, and valuable information to household employers and their staff. His new book will be a valuable resource to increase the knowledge and raise the standards for all household employers and our industry."

"We referred to Guy's book when building our business model and continue to use it to this day. He's spot-on with information that's important to our nannies, babysitters, and clients. Guy, and the GTM team, are an important partner to our company."

—*Georganne Hall, experienced agency president,*
Nannies of Kansas City, MO

"GTM is the leading provider of household employment HR and payroll services. It's easy to get sloppy in dealing with a nanny and often a spouse is left with the task of managing this person with very little experience—it's bad enough if you're having problems at the office!! Guy's book fills this important gap."

—*Verne Harnish, CEO of Gazelles, Inc. and*
author of Mastering the Rockefeller Habits, *Ashburn, VA*

"I believe strongly in educating my clients about all aspects of hiring household employees. I give Guy's book to all of our new clients. I find it to be an excellent tool to educate them on the benefits of using a quality placement agency, tax laws, and employer/employee expectations. Giving them the book shows our clients that we are confident that our level of service will match that suggested by Guy when choosing an agency. They know that they are making the right choice by coming to us and that we value having the answers to all of their questions regarding our industry."

—*Kathleen Heydorn, experienced agency owner,*
The Nanny Connection in Hudson, OH

"*How to Hire a Nanny* is a one-stop shop of very useful and often hard-to-find information related to household employees. Guy Maddalone's handbook provides a wealth of facts for every family in the process of staffing and trying to figure out those thorny areas of immigration, discrimination, termination, taxation, etc. This fact-packed book is a must-have for every household with employees."

—*Barbara Kline, president, White House Nannies Inc.,*
and author of White House Nannies, *Bethesda, MD*

"Guy has done it again! He is always working hard for the industry to help agencies and clients. GTM is an amazing resource and they continue to impress us!"

"Guy Maddalone has been a pioneer in the household human resource industry and has established the nanny industry with professional standards practiced from successful small businesses to Fortune 500 companies. In his book, Guy has defined confusing legal domestic employment tax issues in a simplified manner without sacrificing any details. *How to Hire a Nanny* is an immensely helpful guide for parents, nannies, and nanny placement agencies."

—*Gena James Pitts, former owner and director,*
Child Care Resources, Alpharetta, GA

"In a comprehensive guide, Guy Maddalone has compiled all the information a household employer needs to properly manage anyone working in the home. He covers the range of domestic help from hiring one nanny to employing a full staff. With practical information and accurate facts, *How to Hire a Nanny* will be a valuable resource and handy tool for all household employers and employees."

—*Wendy Sachs, president, The Philadelphia*
Nanny Network, Inc., Philadelphia, PA

"Most of our clients are extremely busy and are relieved to hear that there is a payroll tax service to help process legally mandated household employee payroll obligations. When we meet with our clients and give them a GTM brochure, a smile and look of relief returns to their face. GTM provides a 'real value' that eliminates a time-consuming activity a parent doesn't have to worry about when hiring and employing a nanny. GTM has been a consistent and exceptionally helpful resource for our clients."

—*Lorna and Courtney Spencer, owners,*
A Choice Nanny, Columbia, MD

"I'm delighted that Guy Maddalone and GTM have created a much-needed manual on household employment issues. It will bring focus and understanding of these most important issues to both employers and service staff. As Starkey International has long stood for the importance of education in the household, my sincere congratulations to GTM for positioning itself at the forefront of giving sound and pertinent advice on how to comply with labor laws and how to better manage household service employee(s). Mr. Maddalone's handbook should be an essential resource for all successful household employers."

"Caring for children is the most important profession there is. A handbook for household employers will be a tremendous help in ensuring adequate compensation for these valuable employees. I applaud Guy Maddalone for seeing and responding to this need."

"When considering hiring a nanny, a family can easily become overwhelmed by the complex and often conflicting employment laws and regulations that govern how they will relate to their nannies. A family may be hesitant to keep a lawyer and an accountant on the household payroll to ensure consistent compliance with these employment laws. Mr. Maddalone's book provides families with a cost-effective way of learning the basics of hiring a nanny."

TABLE OF CONTENTS

Introduction

Millions of American households strive to find that intricate work-life balance by employing household workers, including nannies, senior caregivers, housekeepers, gardeners, chauffeurs, personal assistants, and so on. (See Chapter 1 to read about the diverse types of household help.) Today, household employers include not only the wealthy but also established, dual-income households in which both parents cultivate their professions; young, dual-income families in which both parents must work to maintain the household; single-parent households dependent on one income; overburdened, sandwich-generation families tasked with simultaneously caring for both young children and ailing elderly relatives; and mature households that must hire a variety of senior care for one or more family members (most times an elderly spouse or parent).

To achieve an effective and practical balance between your work and your life—making your private and professional lives enjoyable, fulfilling, and manageable—and to smoothly operate your home, tend to your children, and/or care for your parents, you decided to become a household employer. From the start, the new household employer must see household employment as a legitimate profession. Nannies and household employees have long been held in high regard as genuine professionals outside the United States. In the past, Americans often stumbled by not considering nannies or other household employees as authentic professionals. Your nanny is entering your home and the private life within to tend to your children's needs. It is his or her career that just happens to be based in your home and just happens to involve your family. As his or her employer, it is your business—one recognized by the federal, state, and local government—so you must treat your household employment as the real profession it is. (Note: although this handbook discusses topics in terms of nannies, the content and most of the laws and legal mandates discussed herein cover all types of household employees.)

Offered throughout this handbook is information to help you professionally manage your household employee—whether he or she is your nanny, your parent's senior caregiver, your housekeeper, your gardener, etc.—just as you would professionally manage and treat employees at your place of business. As you read through this handbook, you will realize that effective household management relies on clear and open communication and on treating your household employees as professionals.

In the years since the first edition of this book went to print (2004), the household employment industry has progressed in establishing a more professional structure around a very informal and often customized situation. However, the American attitude toward household employment has remained the same, and many families still see the employment of help within the home as an informal relationship.

Although outright discrimination toward household help is not as rife as it once was, it is still very much a consideration of the industry, and there are still many employers who take advantage every day of the fact that most labor laws fail to protect domestic workers. Many states are seeking to improve the rights of domestic workers, and much more is being publicized about how families need to abide by legal and official practices when employing help. By reading this book, you are already one of the many families educating yourselves on how to hire household help successfully with a well-defined and well-compensated job, what legal considerations you need to adhere to, and how best to set up a mutually respectful relationship.

As household employment's continued growth throughout the United States helped to authenticate the household professional as a qualified, well-trained, career-minded specialist, the troubled economic times, rapid technological progress, and changing fiscal realities created several industry trends, such as online hiring, nanny sharing, and fluctuating pay and employment benefits. In addition, industry trends showed a marked increase in senior care provided in the home—an increase that will continue to grow—and new laws to benefit household employees.

The internet continues to change our lives in so many ways. Using the internet to help hire a nanny or other type of household employee makes sense to many families. The do-it-yourself attitude, the ability to search and hire employees any time of day or night, and the assumption that using the internet will save money are the main reasons people try to hire online. Thorough background checks; employment and education verification; and research into payroll, tax, salary, and insurance laws are musts for all hires, whether you are using the internet or standard hiring methods, to avoid potential problems and to help maintain the safety of your loved ones and your home (see Chapter 4 for information regarding online hiring).

Nanny sharing, first begun in the 1980s, has increased, particularly when economic times have taken a downturn. Nanny sharing is when a nanny is shared by more than one family (usually two families but sometimes more), and the families split the costs. (Each family is expected to pay its part of the nanny's salary, as well as its share of payroll taxes.) For instance, neighbors may join together to hire and retain a nanny who works for each family at one of the families' homes. Another nanny-share scenario occurs when a nanny is shared by two families who need only a limited set of regular hours. The nanny will work for one family for part of the workday or workweek and then work for another family the remainder of the workday or workweek in order to accumulate the hours needed for a full-time work week. A child care solution that falls between a traditional nanny and day care situation, nanny sharing is also known as shared care.

During difficult economic times, nannies and other household help can experience a decrease (or at least a fluctuation) in their annual salaries. Because household workers are dependent on individuals and not companies for their wages, nannies and other household workers then experience the same hard fiscal realities their household employers face. If one parent's firm is downsizing and he or she must take on a lower paying job, then the nanny may need to accept a lower annual salary. If a parent's company is foregoing another year of salary increases, then the nanny may need to deal with another year at the same salary and forfeit another cost of living increase. Yet nannies across the United States are reporting that they are being offered some benefits, such as paid time off, sick leave, and health insurance, which were unheard of several years ago. The federal government and some state legislation (such as the Domestic Workers' Bill of Rights for seven key states, see below) has begun to force the hand of household employers by influencing their behavior toward household help and attempting to ensure that they follow labor, tax, and insurance law to professionalize the industry. This type of intervention helps to improve the working conditions within the home for the 2.5 million domestic workers in the United States.

In 2010, New York State became the first state to enact a Domestic Workers' Bill of Rights that offers labor protections, such as overtime pay and paid time off, to nannies and other household employees who do not work for an agency, regardless of their immigration status. The law also provides protection against discrimination and harassment. This led to other states following suit: Hawaii, California, Massachusetts, Oregon, Connecticut, and Illinois.

Despite New York's precedent in enacting safeguards for household workers, the news still broadcasts scandals involving political and other well-known figures who willingly disregarded the labor and tax laws with respect to their household help. They not only risk jeopardizing their personal finances, reputation, and professional careers, but even face potential jail time. It is not new, but it is still surprising that people—even those well versed in the law—continue to evade their responsibilities when employing and paying their household help.

"Nannygate" was coined in 1993 after the infamous case of Zoe Baird. Baird—nominated by President Clinton as U.S. attorney general—had in the past employed two illegal aliens as a nanny and chauffeur and paid them under the table. Baird's deliberate disregard for U.S. law forced her to step down from consideration as a Clinton cabinet member. Just a month later, another Clinton selection, Kimba Wood as federal judge, was reported to have employed an illegal alien to care for her child in her home. While Wood paid Social Security taxes for her childcare worker and while media reports stated that during the time Wood employed the illegal alien it was legal to do so, the media attention was sufficient to cause her to be immediately removed from consideration. Nannygate brought an open secret and practice into the mainstream, highlighting the need for professionally managing household help and the need to protect household workers through fair employment practices and employment taxes.

Since Nannygate became a household catchphrase, many politicians and celebrities suffered media and public criticism of their household workers' mismanagement and illegalities. In 2001, Linda Chavez was nominated as President George W. Bush's secretary of labor. She withdrew from consideration after it was reported that she had given money to a onetime illegal immigrant who had lived in her home more than a decade earlier. In 2004, President Bush's nomination of Bernard Kerik as homeland security secretary was forced to be withdrawn after press reported Kerik, former New York City police commissioner, had unknowingly hired an undocumented worker and failed to pay payroll taxes.

Good human resources, as you will read in this handbook, can be quite involved. Yet thousands do it properly and are committed to it. GTM Payroll Services Inc. makes it easier with this book and its household HR counseling, insurances, and payroll and tax services (visit www.gtm. com). Education is vital for the household employment industry. While great advancements have been made, misconceptions, misunderstandings, and blatant tax evasion remain.

This handbook covers everything you will need to know about hiring and retaining household help: easy-to-access guidelines, real-life experiences, practices, procedures, handy samples of forms and letters, and up-to-date information on laws and regulations. It is your resource. Use it throughout your household employment experience—whether you are reading it through for the first time or referencing specific sections as issues arise. With it, you are well on your way to becoming a successful household employer.

You Can Be Successful Too!

This handbook is designed to help you prepare and maintain successful employer-employee relationships. It addresses many lessons learned by household employers throughout the United States. In a sense, you will learn from those who have been doing this for the last 30 years and who have mastered—sometimes the hard way—the best ways to handle issues like hiring, firing, writing work agreements, and managing payroll and taxes.

Once you realize that household employment *is* employment, a little bit of business experience and personal intuition will help guide you. You most likely are, or have been, employed somewhere in the United States and, therefore, know many of the requirements, guidelines, and laws that you need to follow and implement. Many first-time household employers worry about keeping abreast of the legal requirements and mandates issued by federal, state, and local governments. This can be a time-consuming and frustrating aspect of being a household employer. However, if you decide not to follow U.S. laws and regulations, you may find yourself in a much more time-consuming and frustrating situation. In fact, it could greatly cost you both monetarily and in the lifestyle your family and you presently enjoy. Legislatures and courts throughout America are no longer turning a blind eye and instead are enforcing laws and regulations pertaining to household employment at an aggressive rate. Just look to the New York Domestic Workers' Bill of Rights, which is now taken up by six other states (Hawaii, California, Massachusetts, Oregon, Connecticut, and Illinois).

Employing household help to care for your loved ones and for your home—what you hold most dear—takes careful thought and preparation—preparation that will help you when unexpected challenges arise, or even avoid those challenges altogether. Investing the time and effort from the start and treating your nanny (or other household employee) as the professional she or he is, will not only help you begin a successful working relationship with your nanny (or other household employee), but will also put you on course to achieve a comfortable work-life balance.

Much of the information in this book is kept up to date on GTM's website at www.gtm.com.

Disclaimer

The author hopes that you find the information provided herein helpful. However, the information should not be misinterpreted as a replacement for competent legal or accounting advice. Accordingly, use of this information is at your own risk. In particular, while the information herein is believed to be accurate, the applicable laws and regulations are complex and change from state to state. Therefore, the author cannot be held responsible for any errors or omissions in the text, or for any misunderstandings on the part of the reader. We strongly recommend that you consult an experienced employment law attorney or accountant to address any questions or issues that you may have. Furthermore, any references to outside sources provided herein do not indicate an endorsement of the services or products provided by those sources.

Preface

I have been working for over 30 years in the household employment industry. All those years of experience working with thousands of household employers throughout the United States is provided in this handbook to prepare you for employing a nanny or other household worker. The most important thing is to simply remember that your nanny is working for you. He or she is doing so to earn a living. It is your nanny's *livelihood*—your nanny's way of living and providing for self and family.

I first became involved in household employment soon after my grandfather became ill. My mother, Joyce, a registered nurse, and I began a home health care and hospital staffing agency. While running the agency, I met many people who juggled caring for their own families while attending to the needs of their ailing parents, much as many families face today with the increase in demand for senior care. Truly, these people were sandwiched between generations, with each demanding extensive care, time, and energy. To help these caregivers further, I knew I needed to add child care to the agency mix. Thus began my company, GTM,—which started as a nanny placement agency; then extended to payroll and tax services; and finally evolved to the household employment human resources service it is today, including benefits, HR tools, insurance services, and consulting. GTM Payroll Services Inc. is known throughout the United States as the leader in the industry, having built an impeccable reputation and gained complete client confidence by always providing accurate, timely, and extremely valuable services in a way that consistently yields a 99 percent client satisfaction rating. One of the goals I maintain for GTM is that it continually responds to clients' needs through innovation, new services, and excellent assistance to make the lives of household employers and their employees easier.

As I am one of 13 children, family has been, and always will be, extremely important to me. Naturally, when it came time to raise my own children, I wanted the very best for them. To me, home is where children tend to always feel more secure and comfortable. Part of that security and comfort means they are not forced to adapt to our work schedules. They are not woken up and sped off to the day care center in the morning or forced to nap at the direction of a day care worker, only to be disrupted, bundled up, and brought home in the evening. For Diane and I, there was one choice—employing a nanny to work in our home. Later, with a family of three children parented by two busy professionals, we found that we needed both a nanny and housekeeper.

We prepared for our nanny in many ways, but we have learned much, much more over the years. We entrust that our nanny will follow the standards and procedures we have developed—often with her input—for the daily challenges of our busy household. It really comes down to using common sense and good judgment to handle daily problems or issues. We, as parents, have provided our nanny with control of our children's day. If Grandma drops by unannounced to take the kids out for a treat, my nanny knows that she has the right to say no, or, of course, to call Diane or I if necessary.

Since we are working and try to keep phone calls to a minimum, our household policies clearly define what is and is not acceptable. Grandma cannot take the kids out for an ice cream at 4 p.m., so close to their dinner time. If a playmate visits for a scheduled playdate and unexpectedly brings another friend along to play, that is not okay, and takes advantage of our nanny. Use common sense and good judgment. Ask yourself, "Would you do that without making arrangements first?" and "How does this affect my nanny and what we have agreed that he or she is expected to do?"

An incident occurred in one of my client's homes that would have put their nanny on the spot if she had not been empowered to say no to unacceptable situations. Before leaving on a weekend trip, my clients gave their son permission to invite a friend over to play. As most would do, the young visitor's parents accompanied their son into the client's home. However, instead of leaving after making sure their son was in good hands, the parents sat right down in the family room and not only engaged the nanny in extensive conversation but even asked the nanny if they could have a drink. The nanny knew this was not okay, as it distracted her from watching the children, and she knew she could address the situation by politely but firmly asking the parents to come back later to pick up their child. She did not have to call her employers for advice, because she clearly knew where she stood in such situations. My clients did not have their trip interrupted, and their nanny was not overburdened in her workday.

In another incident involving one of our own nannies, a neighbor asked our nanny to watch her child for an afternoon. When our nanny learned that the neighbor had not spoken to Diane or me about this, she knew that it was her decision to make. We—working as a team—decided that we would not tolerate our nanny being overtaxed and frustrated with any outside, additional responsibility. We also would not want our nanny watching other children while she was caring for our three—not without a prearranged time and date set, or without an agreement made previously with our nanny. Three children are enough to overload anyone, and we do not want to add to her workload. Because we had discussed our expectations and concerns, our nanny knew that she could say no with our support, or she could say yes, but clearly set the exact time and day she would be available to help.

We can do this because we have set a comprehensive work arrangement and have built a relationship that enables mutual trust and open communication.

We always recognize our nanny for her accomplishments and encourage her. We try to help her in any way possible, and we often provide examples of alternative ways to handle various day-to-day situations. Diane and I communicate continuously and openly with our household help—not only to set initial standards and boundaries, but also to maintain and build on the employer-employee relationship.

All household employers should strive for open communication. With nannies, you have added a new member to your parenting team, and all of you need to be on the same page when handling the children. At my home, we have a ten-minute huddle when the nanny arrives in the morning and when she is just about to leave in the evening. (We do the same with our housekeeper.) We inform one another of the day's or night's events—for example, Elise was running a fever, Jeffrey didn't complete his homework, or Michael stayed up late last night watching a movie and is sluggish this morning. Also, we discuss what needs to be done during the day and any activity that is on the schedule. This provides the nanny with the information she needs to be successful, and in turn, she provides us the details we need to be effective parents and feel secure about our children while at work.

The ten-minute morning huddle also allows us to compliment and support our nanny on her work, particularly with the children. If there is a problem to discuss, we talk about it candidly and make sure we all agree on any decisions made. Open communication means that both the employer and employee are up front with one another, are in agreement, and can move forward as a united team.

We were not always so proficient in working with our help. In fact, like many families, we employed several nannies before refining our household management skills. It is interesting to note that while the nanny we first hired for our firstborn was terrific at the time, she would not have worked successfully with our middle child. A nanny who works wonderfully with a newborn may not be the nanny to employ for an older child. It is all part of the learning process, and this can be helped by being alert to the employment situation and relationships, as well as your family's needs.

—*Guy Maddalone*

Types of Household Help

Itt is not easy to define a household employer or household employee, because the terms are used in so many different ways—almost as many ways as there are household help professions. The U.S. Internal Revenue Service (IRS) defines a *household employer* as any person who employs housekeepers, maids, gardeners, and others who work in and around an individual's private residence. A nanny is an example of such an employee. That is, a nanny is a household employee, stationed within the home, tasked with tending to a child's care.

In the United States, we tend to think of a nanny as a benevolent woman endowed with magical powers or as a young woman spending time working as a nanny until something "better" comes along. In fact, a nanny is very different, and those of us with images of Mary Poppins or Nanny McPhee in our heads need to understand the reality of a nanny's job. A nanny is a professional worker who has, over time, honed his or her talents and expertise in caring for children and in developing his or her chosen career.

Outside the United States, nannies do not suffer from a blurred definition. In countries such as England, Ireland, and Germany, nannies and other household employees have long been defined and, thus, treated as professionals. Although employing household help is very much a personal decision, we all need to see nannies, housekeepers, senior care workers, gardeners, maintenance workers, and other household employees as *real* people performing *real* jobs—professional jobs. The only difference is that these professionals perform their work in your home.

For whatever reason, in the United States, nannies and other household employees have often been viewed as temporary workers, a position taken by people who are deciding on other aspects of their life (such as those who are deciding whether to pursue higher education, what profession they "really" want to do, or where geographically they want to reside). This is changing rapidly, as more and more U.S. households are hiring employees to help achieve a manageable life-work balance.

Household Employers

Household employment is no longer only for the wealthy. As the number of U.S. household employers grows today, the spectrum of household employers increases to six basic types:

1. The wealthy

2. The established household: a comfortable dual-income family with parents who both want to maintain their careers

3. The young family: a dual-income family just getting by with parents who both need to work—even if one parent would prefer to stay home to care for the child

4. The single parent who is dependent on one income or a combination of incomes from different sources

5. The sandwich-generation family tasked with caring for aging parents, as well as young children

6. The mature family with grown-up children that is hiring care for one or more elderly parents

The following are some important characteristics involved with the different household employer types.

-   *The wealthy.* This group often has little difficulty providing a good household workplace for employees because, most often, the wealthy have grown up with household help around them. They are very in tune with this being a work relationship and often have few problems with an employee being in their home environment. This group may be more concerned with, and put more emphasis on, confidentiality than other groups. Wealthy families generally hire nannies, housekeepers, household managers, housemen, and cooks.

- *The established household.* These households may have two to three children. They are working to maintain a successful balance between work and life. Hiring a nanny or other household professional is a way for them to do just that. Many of these families are relatively new to household employment; they likely have employed help for about five years, have learned how to best manage household employees through trial and error, and often find themselves on their third nanny hire before basic employment elements are worked out and agreed on. These families may benefit considerably by following the work procedures offered throughout this book. Established households generally hire nannies or household managers, a housekeeper, and a handyman.

- *The young family.* This household may have one or two children, is balancing work and life, and has accessed household help to permit the parents to continue their careers while at the same time beginning and growing their family. The young family sees household help as a structured, professional situation that allows it control in managing its home life. So new is this group to household help that it will need to establish the home as a workplace, forge a satisfying employee-employer relationship, manage payroll and taxes, and so on. These families may not necessarily have considered employing household help but have found that they need and want in-home care to provide the best possible environment for their children and to help them maintain a rich quality of life. The young family generally hires a nanny.

- *The single parent.* This household usually has one to three children and may be dependent on one income or a combination of incomes from different sources, such as child support. The parent has to work and has opted to have in-home child care as the most convenient and flexible option for his or her work-life schedule. Pressured for time and workload, this family will benefit greatly from building a strong relationship with its household help and by treating him or her professionally so the nanny can help the parent out when the parent has out-of-home commitments. This family usually hires a nanny.

- *The sandwich-generation family.* This household is becoming increasingly common in the United States. With elderly parents living longer and families choosing to care for them in the home, as well as having a family of their own, the breadwinners are tasked with managing the care of their dependents around their careers. With so many different pressures on them, these families can save a lot of time and hassle by understanding the correct way to look after their household workers from the start. With more and more available senior care and child care options for the home environment, this family can hire a nanny and a senior caregiver to achieve a successful work-life balance that benefits everyone in the family.

- *The mature family.* With grown-up children living or working independently or at college, these families now have to care for one or more of their elderly parents who need care while still maintaining their own professional lives and giving support to their older children. Arranging senior care services is often difficult and emotionally and financially draining. Many families are opting to allow seniors to age in place (i.e., in a home environment—either in the senior's home or in the family home) to maintain stability and familiarity for the senior they love.

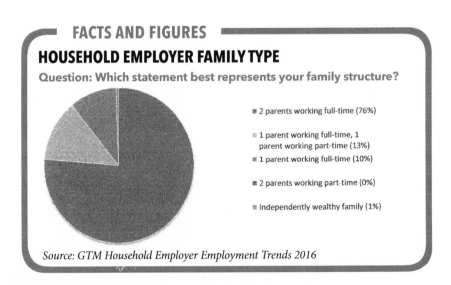

FACTS AND FIGURES

HOUSEHOLD EMPLOYER FAMILY TYPE

Question: Which statement best represents your family structure?

- 2 parents working full-time (76%)
- 1 parent working full-time, 1 parent working part-time (13%)
- 1 parent working full-time (10%)
- 2 parents working part-time (0%)
- Independently wealthy family (1%)

Source: GTM Household Employer Employment Trends 2016

Household Employees

As the needs of the American family have grown, the demand for different skills has expanded, and as a result, various household positions have developed. Popular household positions in the United States include:

For children
- Au pair
- After-school nanny
- Baby nurse
- Babysitter
- Doula
- Governess
- Mother's helper
- Nanny
- Special needs caregiver
- Summer nanny
- Tutor

For the home
- Cook
- Gardener
- Groundskeeper
- Housekeeper
- Household manager
- Maid or house cleaner
- Maintenance worker
- Pet sitter

For the senior
- Certified Nursing Assistant (CNA)
- Chore worker
- Companion
- Geriatric care manager
- Home health aide
- Homemaker
- Licensed Practical Nurse (LPN)
- Nutritionist
- Occupational Therapist (OT)

- Physical Therapist (PT)
- Registered Nurse (RN)
- Senior care provider
- Social worker
- Speech therapist

For the household employer
- Driver or chauffeur
- Personal assistant

There is a household position for any of the multiple operations that keep a home running. How to go about hiring and maintaining your household help is discussed in future chapters. However, it is critical that prospective household employers begin with a clear definition of what they want in a household employee. First, understand what your objectives are in bringing an employee into your household. Many people have taken that nerve-racking first step. For you, it does not have to be a step into the unknown. The experiences detailed throughout this book will help you bypass some of the pitfalls and smooth out some of the complexities associated with employing staff.

Q & A

Q. What is the difference between an au pair and a nanny?

A. An au pair is a foreign national living in the United States with a host family who receives a small stipend in exchange for babysitting and help with housework. Legally authorized to live and work (only as an au pair with the host family) in the United States for up to one year to experience American life, an au pair may or may not have previous child care experience. An au pair is usually provided with a weekly stipend that is calculated as the federal minimum wage, less an allowance for room and board.

In contrast, a nanny works in the household, where he or she may or may not live, undertaking all tasks related to the care of the children. Duties are generally restricted to child care and the domestic tasks related to child care, such as preparing a child's meals and doing a child's laundry. Although a nanny may or may not have had formal training, she or he often has a good deal of actual experience, and often has been educated in child development. A nanny's workweek usually ranges from 40-60 hours, and a nanny typically works unsupervised.

Deciding What Works for You

Viewing a situation from another person's perspective is always a good barometer for how something will work out. When it comes to employing household help, ask yourself the following questions.

- What do I want to accomplish in the short- and long-term?
- What problem am I trying to solve?
- Who does this benefit?

Most household employers want to balance their personal life with their work life. They want to know that their child, parent, or home is being cared for so that they may focus on their careers. By employing staff to tend to concerns at home, they are then able to devote time and energy to their careers. Hiring household staff is often the best solution to cultivating a lifestyle of convenience, peace of mind, and freedom.

You may be surprised to discover that more than just the people living in your household are stakeholders in some way or another to your household employment. Other than your spouse, children, and you, a household employee could affect and benefit extended family members, neighbors, friends, and co-workers, among others.

In any household employment, the biggest mistake any one of us can make is not planning on being successful. Many people do not take the time necessary to be a proactive employer or manager. They do not plan for, or practice to be, a household employer. Without a well-designed ground plan, your nanny, your family, and you may be unprepared for the day-to-day issues that arise. These issues often result in wasted effort and time, often pulling the employer away from his or her professional duties to attend to a household matter that could likely be handled individually by the nanny or housekeeper if plans had been established from the start.

No matter whether you are hiring a nanny to care for your child, a senior care provider to care for your parent, or a houseman to care for your property, you need to make a real effort to learn about, plan for, and practice being a manager of a household employee. Naturally, you will need to manage your way through some bumps in the road, but once everyone is engaged, you will be positioned to build and maintain a successful employment relationship. No matter who is working in your home, keep in mind the reality of the situation. You are making difficult decisions that affect your household and your family. Household employment is very much a personal endeavor. You do it to manage your life, provide optimal care for your children or ailing parents, and maintain a smooth and peaceful household. It is not easy, and there is no other hire as important. No matter what the type of household employee, the process is the same—learn, prepare, plan, communicate, gather feedback, and revise (if necessary). By preparing, planning, and practicing as a household employer, you are on your way to engaging a critical member of your household team, one that will help you with your goal of achieving work-life balance.

Hiring Your Nanny or Other Household Help

Household employment is increasing for Americans who continually strive for a manageable balance between life and work. For many, the solution to managing pressures and obligations in personal and professional worlds is hiring staff to work in the home. Whether an employer hires a household manager to maintain an estate, a senior care provider to tend to a disabled parent, or a nanny to care for young children, he or she is working to ensure that his or her home is happy, secure, and comfortable. Maintaining committed and satisfied household help keeps employers and their families content. A happy employee equals a happy employer, which ultimately yields a happy family.

Employing household help is not just any personnel decision. As a household employer, you are entrusting to your employee what you hold most precious. This is one of the most important employment decisions you will ever make. Your loved ones, your property, and your privacy are all dependent on the household employee's skill and professionalism.

The Citizen and Noncitizen Employee

Household employers should hire only those people who are legally authorized to work in the United States. These people include U.S. citizens; legal permanent residents; and other aliens authorized to work, such as refugees, asylees, and persons in Temporary Protected Status. Many household employers in the United States who hire noncitizens should be aware of the specific hiring laws relevant to hiring a foreign worker. For more information about hiring a noncitizen employee, see Chapter 3.

The 1986 *Immigration Reform and Control Act* (IRCA) makes *all* U.S. employers responsible for verifying, through a specific process, the identity and work authorization or eligibility of all individuals, whether U.S. citizens or not. All employers are required to complete Employment Eligibility Verification Form I-9 for all employees. (See Chapter 3 for more details.) This can be completed by filling out the I-9 form (see Appendix E) or by using the USCIS' I-9 Central website for employers and employees with access to resources, tips, and guidance (www.uscis.gov/i-9central).

Employee vs. Independent Contractor

Household employers need to recognize the difference between an employee and an independent contractor. The employer's tax requirements are contingent on whether the professional is working for the employer or is actually working for him- or herself. It is therefore paramount that an employer knows the difference between the two for tax purposes, so that both parties' tax returns are filed properly. An employer can be penalized with having to pay 100 percent of associated payroll taxes of any payments made for services if the worker status is determined incorrectly. Additional fines, penalties, and interest may apply, and the effect on the family-nanny relationship could be devastating if it is determined the worker owes years of unpaid taxes.

Under the U.S. *Fair Labor Standards Act* (FLSA), household employers need to determine whether they have control or direction over the worker. For more information on FLSA, go to www.dol.gov.

The IRS uses three main categories to determine worker status: behavioral, financial, and type of relationship.

1. **Behavioral**: Does the employer control or have the right to control what the worker does and how the worker does his or her job? The more control an employer has, the more apt the worker is to be considered an employee. Whose equipment and facilities is the worker using to perform the job? If the worker attends to job requirements on-site at the employer's home or facility, and uses

the employer's equipment and tools to do so, then she or he is probably deemed an employee.

2. **Financial**: Are the business aspects of the worker's job controlled by the employer? (These include things like how the worker is paid, whether expenses are reimbursed, who provides tools and supplies?) Then the worker would be considered an employee. Are the worker's contributions integral to the business? Will the business suffer if the worker was not contributing to its operations and success? If so, employee status is likely. On the other hand, if the worker faces an economic risk in doing the job, he or she would more likely be identified as an independent contractor.

3. **Type of Relationship**: Are there written contracts or employee type benefits (e.g., pension plan, insurance, vacation pay, etc.)? Will the relationship continue and is the work performed a key aspect of the business? Is the working relationship permanent? A permanent working relationship is likely an employer-employee relationship.

The vast majority of nannies are *employees*, not independent contractors and that is how the IRS classifies them. They should have taxes properly withheld and receive a W-2 at the end of the year. For assistance in determining status, the IRS offers *Form SS-8* (*Determination of Worker Status for Purposes of Federal Employment Taxes and Income Tax Withholding*), which can be downloaded from www.gtm.com or www.irs.gov or found in Appendix E. You can file this with the IRS if you are unclear about the status of your worker; the IRS will then review and officially determine the worker's status for you.

The IRS also uses a handy list of 20 factors when determining the status of an employee or independent contractor. Many of the IRS factors follow the FLSA considerations, and both can be used to determine a worker's status. According to the IRS factors, an employee relationship exists when a worker:

1. must comply with the employer's instructions about when, where, and how to do the job

2. receives training from or at the direction of the employer

3. lacks a significant investment in facilities used to perform services

4. receives payments for business and/or traveling expenses

5. does not offer services to the general public

6. receives payment of regular amounts at set intervals

7. cannot make a profit or suffer a loss from services

8. can be terminated by the employer

9. can quit work at any time without incurring liability

10. has a continuing working relationship with the employer

11. provides services that are integrated into the business

12. must provide services personally

13. hires, supervises, and pays assistants on an employer's behalf or pays assistants for the worker

14. must work in a sequence set by the employer

15. must submit regular reports to the employer

16. relies on the employer to furnish tools and materials

17. works for only one employer at a time

18. follows set work hours

19. works full-time for the employer

20. does work on the employer's premises or on a route or at a location designated by the employer

(For more information, go to www.irs.gov.)

Employee	Independent Contractor
An employee is one who is directed by the employer.	An independent contractor works for self-profit or loss and chooses his or her own hours.
An employer will have direction and control over the work and hours of the employee.	Independent contractors furnish their own tools and supplies necessary to complete the job.
An employer will also furnish a workplace and supply the tools necessary to do a specified job.	Independent contractors may work at an employer's workplace, or deliver completed goods to the employer.

Employers hiring independent contractors are not required to withhold income tax or make employer contributions to the worker's Social Security fund. If an employer pays an independent contractor $600 or more per year, then he or she must report it to the IRS using Form 1099-Misc. On hiring the contractor, an employer should request the contractor complete a Form W-9, which provides his or her Social Security number or employer identification number (EIN).

When hiring any employee, be sure all employment documents have been completed and verified prior to the start of work. An independent contractor should also be asked to verify insurance for the work required, if necessary.

FACTS AND FIGURES
MISCLASSIFICATION IS "STILL A VERY BIG ISSUE"

According to the U.S. Treasury Department (in its 2013 report, "Employers Do Not Always Follow Internal Revenue Service Worker Determination Rulings"), the IRS estimates that employers misclassify millions of workers as independent contractors instead of employees, thus avoiding the payment of employment taxes. "The determination of whether a worker is an employee or an independent contractor has significant tax implications for the worker, employer and IRS…", stated the report. "Misclassification of employees as independent contractors is a nationwide problem affecting millions of workers—and which continues to grow…"

According to Department of Labor (DOL) Wage and Hour Division (WHD) Media Liaison, Michael Kravitz, misclassification is "still a very big issue." Kravitz added that the IRS has a different test from DOL to determine whether a worker is an employee or a contractor. He also noted that while DOL does not ignore the individual household employer, strategic enforcement efforts are more focused on ensuring compliance at the industry level. In addition, Kravitz noted there are many exemptions to the minimum wage and overtime laws when applied to household help, which exempts companions from overtime protections.

"The WHD is not just about enforcement," said Kravitz, "but will help employers confidentially determine whether they employ an employee or independent contractor." He explained that help is available at the more than 200 DOL offices throughout the nation, via toll free at 1-866-4USWAGE (879243) and its website at www. dol.gov/whd.

The Hiring Process

There are many concerns to consider when you are involved in hiring an employee, as well as many legalities to abide by to ensure equitable and fair employment opportunities. By taking the hiring process one step at a time, you can proceed with well-planned and well-researched employment offers.

Live-in or Live-out Nannies

There are many considerations to attend to if you choose to have a nanny, or other household help, live in your home. There are financial implications, such as the extra cost of food and heating; practical issues like providing a room for the live-in nanny and access to a bathroom; emotional implications, such as giving her privacy and downtime, especially from your children; and also just getting used to having, at first, a stranger in your family home. Live-in nannies are not as popular as they used to be, but sometimes having child care help right in the home is invaluable to certain family setups. An employer needs to be aware of his or her state's laws on what a full-time workweek is for a live-in nanny and any other specific working conditions required for live-in employees, such as work schedule, labor hours, days off, and housing issues. (See Chapter 8, for information on full-time hours).

Developing the Job Description

First and foremost, a thorough, comprehensive, and well-developed job description will help any employer immensely in the hiring process. Really think about what the job will entail; cover all aspects of household duties, tasks, responsibilities, work hours, and requirements—and put it into words that everyone will understand. The best job description will clearly set out what the position needs to accomplish; what essential and nonessential tasks and duties are needed; and what skills, abilities, and talents are best used to adequately complete the job. This job description not only helps start the job search, it also helps tremendously in developing the work agreement with the hired employee.

A job description should include the following elements.

- *Title*—The official title of the position for which you are hiring.

- *Type of work*—Whether the work is full-time or part-time, live-in or live-out, and so on.

- *Summary*—A one- to two-sentence summary that states the primary function of the position.

- *Dependents*—If the role requires the care of dependents, list the ages and names of each one.

- *Essential functions*—A list of the primary responsibilities of the position. These are the functions that are necessary and must be performed on a regular basis.

- *Nonessential functions*—A separate list of responsibilities that account for only a small part of the job.

- *Knowledge, skills, and abilities*—A list of topics that an employee should have knowledge of and at what level (i.e., basic, intermediate, or expert), and an outline of specific skills (e.g., reading and writing) and abilities (e.g., lifting heavy objects or children, climbing stairs) that the position requires.

- *Supervisory responsibilities*—If managing other employees, list the job titles of those employees.

- *Working conditions*—Guidelines on the working conditions and a description of your home or estate and its layout, provisions for food, any pets in the house, whether or not a vehicle will be provided while working, if work performed will be at any other additional residences, and so on.

- *Minimum qualifications*—A list of criteria to be met, such as educational background, license requirements, years of experience required, and so on.

- *Success factors*—A list of qualities or personality traits that would make someone successful in this position.

Both the employer and the employee should have a copy of the final job description.

See Appendix D for job description samples for a nanny, senior care provider, and maintenance worker. Also, see Chapter 6, for more on the *Work Agreement*.

Countdown to Hiring

Develop job description
- Position title
- Summary of functions
- Desirable experience and skills
- Working conditions
- Minimum qualifications
- Success factors

Conduct the interview
- Know employment laws
- Be professional
- Ask open-ended questions
- Plan for a two-hour interview to be thorough

Perform background screening
- Get a signed release from applicant (see Appendix D)
- Consider background checks, employment and personal references, and drug testing

Make the offer
- Verbal and in writing
- Create work agreement
- Meet with applicant to review the job offer
- Agree on hire date, work hours, and other key information

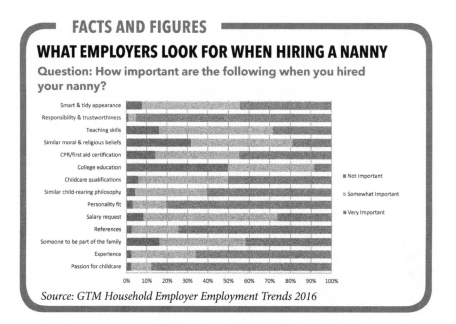

FACTS AND FIGURES

WHAT EMPLOYERS LOOK FOR WHEN HIRING A NANNY

Question: How important are the following when you hired your nanny?

Source: *GTM Household Employer Employment Trends 2016*

CASE STUDY

• •

JIM CHANEY
HOUSEHOLD EMPLOYER
ATLANTA, GA

The trials and tribulations of raising a child were not new to Jim Chaney, father of two older children, and who began a second family with his wife, Carla Chaney, upon the birth of their son, Brandon. The trials and tribulations of human resources (HR) were also not new to either the Chaneys, as both are HR executives with Georgia-Pacific (GP), in Atlanta, GA. When the Chaneys decided to hire a live-out nanny, they went to an Atlanta agency for help.

"This is not like any other employment," said Jim Chaney, HR vice president for GP's building products division. "It is much more meaningful. I hire people [at GP] with whom I don't spend nearly as much time talking with as I did with our nanny. I had to think, 'Do I really, really want this person in my house alone with my baby?' This is the most important hire you'll ever make. Make sure you do it well."

The Chaneys both work demanding and time-consuming jobs. (Carla Chaney is HR director for GP's consumer products division.) While GP offers a company day care center that Jim Chaney said is "attractive and wonderful" and had a space available, the Chaneys decided to hire a live-out nanny for the first year after Brandon was born. They believed that the nanny solution would save their son from disrupted sleep and schedules, protect him from germs and sickness, and ensure that their son had someone to immediately respond to his cries.

The Chaneys required child care from 7:00 a.m. to 6:30 p.m., flexibility to travel with them, and the ability to stay later into the evening when provided with enough notice. "It was hard to find someone to commit to that," Jim Chaney noted. Luckily, the couple found a nanny, who had two school-age children of her own, to fill the job in under five weeks' time.

"You can press right through," Jim Chaney said. "It took three weeks to contract with the agency and go through the applicants. The agency checked references and did background checks. Then, interviewing took about two weeks. I use agencies all the time [for GP]. That's what I pay them for. You can do it [all] yourself, but you're going to spend a lot of time. It can be overwhelming."

Despite a wealth of experience in HR and previous experience hiring household employees for senior care, Jim Chaney admitted that he was surprised by several household employment issues that arose during the hiring process. Some such issues follow.

- Costs. "Quite frankly, it's pretty shocking when first finding out the prices of nanny services," he said, adding that there are "hidden and below-surface" costs that may present a challenge. "The margins of whether a person can afford a nanny become somewhat of an issue, but the trade-offs are well worth it."

- Gross vs. net. "You need to understand when negotiating with nannies that they clearly understand what their pay will be," he emphasized. "If a nanny says she needs to be paid $500, you need to be clear if that $500 is $500 less taxes [net]. So, the amount she takes home and the amount stated on her check may not say $500. Or, if she says $500, that $500 will be the full amount she takes home. That was a big thing."

- Auto insurance. According to Jim Chaney, he required his nanny to be a licensed driver with a safe driving record. The nanny uses the Chaneys' car when she is on duty, and the Chaneys ensure that she is covered under their auto insurance.

- Holidays. "Typically, a nanny expects holidays off," Jim said, which he admitted was a surprise. The senior care workers with whom he worked in the past were ingrained to 24-hour care, holiday or not. Much of this was worked out through the agency and the nanny prior to hire. Following a format offered by the agency, the Chaneys and their nanny pored over a work agreement for more than an hour to clarify expectations. "To [the nanny's] credit, she asked for the work agreement," Jim Chaney said, "and we went over it together."

"It's wonderful having a nanny," he added. "She's got a lot of freedom, and we've built a lot of trust."

One of the biggest challenges facing the new household employer is creating the job description and becoming a manager of an employee while ensuring that all is within budget. The household employer must simultaneously:

- manage hiring agreements, job requirements, and salary negotiations

- communicate effectively

- assess who is the best choice to become the household employee

To access a handy tool to negotiate and communicate gross to net salary, visit GTM's online salary calculator at www.gtm.com.

—Guy

CASE STUDY

• •

LIZ
NANNY
STAMFORD, CT

Liz, a professional nanny for 16 years, came to Connecticut for work by way of Saudi Arabia, Germany, England, and Scotland. Born and raised in Ayr, Scotland, Liz said she heeded her mother's advice to be a nanny because of her love of children and because it is a good career choice in the United Kingdom. First, she worked for a single father in Scotland, and then she moved on to work for military families in Germany and England. Next she served as nanny for the Saudi royal family, and finally she journeyed to the United States—first to New Orleans and then settling in Stamford, Connecticut.

"To be a nanny, you have to be very adaptable," said Liz, who did not want her full name disclosed. "You have to be flexible to family dynamics, the way the family operates. You bring a lot of yourself to the job—your knowledge and experience."

According to Liz, she prefers to work as part of a team with the parents. "You're ultimately responsible for that child and what takes place on a daily basis," she said. "Nannies and families can outgrow each other and, over time, families can take nannies for granted—especially in the United States, where nannies need to be recognized as professionals. In the United Kingdom, being a nanny is a career choice."

The disparity between how America and the United Kingdom view household staff propelled Liz to become a political activist. With her knowledge and experience, Liz worked with her congressman and the U.S. Department of Labor (DOL) to gain federal acknowledgment of nannies and other household workers as skilled professionals. To win recognition of the problem and support for a resolution, she spent much of her own time and money to travel to Washington, D.C., for meetings; to make important telephone calls every day; and to send faxes to more than one hundred political offices. She said that the DOL has opened the door to defining nannies and household workers as skilled professionals.

One of the problems in the United States, said Liz, is that many people seek household employment while still deciding which profession they really want to pursue. This results in the attitude that being a nanny is not a true profession but a stepping-stone to something else.

"We take our jobs very, very seriously," said Liz. "That child is a very high priority."

According to Liz, a nanny needs the respect and trust of the family to do the job. She recommends that families pay fairly and above board so both the family and nanny are protected, and that they offer benefits. "A happy nanny is a good nanny," said Liz, "so treat her well."

It is important for household employers to determine how employees view their positions. Perceptions and actuality can often be very different. The employer's realization of how employees feel within the household organization and how employees feel about their jobs could cause an employer to adopt different management and employment practices.

—Guy

Advertising a Job Position

With a comprehensive job description prepared, a job advertisement can be written and placed in various media or provided to an agency. Be as specific as possible in the job ad. List your requirements, such as previous experience, education, a current and valid driver's license, fluency in English (or other languages), clean background check, and the work schedule. (See Chapter 4, for elements of a job advertisement.)

Interviewing by Phone or Online

The initial interview, or screening of a candidate, can be done in a variety of ways. If using an agency, the agency will perform the phone interviews for the employer, as part of the agency fee. This saves a lot of time and hassle. However, if the employer is hiring independently, it falls to the employer to conduct the initial interviews to select the best candidates from the pool of applicants. Many household employers do an initial phone interview to select the most appropriate candidates. Increasingly common is the use of online technology to perform web interviews, such as Skype or FaceTime. This can be particularly useful if the candidate is applying from out of state or internationally. Whichever method, the general recommendations for interviewing a candidate remain the same and are outlined in detail below.

Interviewing in Person

It is good practice to open an interview by reviewing the job requirements (provide a written copy to the applicant) and confirming at the start of the discussion that the applicant can meet them. Prepare a list of questions before the interview so that you can find out certain information, such as what prior experience the interviewee has, what kind of household he or she has worked in, when he or she is able to start work, and so on. (See Appendix B, for sample interview questions.) Having a prepared list helps to keep the interview on track and helps ensure that all questions are asked and all topics discussed. This is also helpful when multiple candidates are interviewed, thus allowing the employer to make comparisons and considerations by examining different answers to the same questions.

Employers interview to learn about the candidate, so allow the candidate to do the majority of the talking. You need to hear about the candidate's experiences and how he or she handled various situations. Employers need not dominate the discussion. They can, however, direct it by asking open-ended questions, which require the candidate to do more than answer yes or no. This will generate more knowledge about the candidate and force the interviewee to respond more fully. Open-ended questions usually begin with the words *how*, *why*, *when*, *who*, *what*, and *where*. For instance, when interviewing a candidate for a gardener position, ask, "What is it about gardening that you like?" instead of "Do you like gardening?" The same phrasing can be used when interviewing another candidate. For example, ask a nanny candidate, "Why do you want to work with children?" not "Do you like children?"

Another useful interviewing technique is to begin with softer questions, thus allowing the interviewer to build a rapport with the candidate. This can help keep him or her talking openly once more difficult or uncomfortable questions or topics are broached.

When hiring a nanny or other employee who will be working in your home with your family, take the time you need during the interviews to fully cover all the information. For face-to-face interviews for your top candidates, you should plan two hours for one nanny interview. Remember, an interview is instrumental in helping you gauge:

- whether this person would be a good addition to your household
- how his or her temperament would fit with family members
- whether he or she has the know-how needed for the job
- what his or her career or employment priorities are
- how responsible and reliable he or she will be with your children and other family members
- how he or she interacts with your children and whether there is a good personality fit between the candidate and those he or she will care for

The interview is also your opportunity to evaluate your perception of the person and to listen to your instinct. Go with your intuition on whether the candidate will work well for you.

Many interviewers rate a candidate on his or her job ability, experience, presentation, communication skills, interaction with others, and attitude, as well as on how he or she will fit in with the household. In addition, use the interview to help determine your household's needs for both today and tomorrow. Think about the future and ask yourself (and maybe even ask your interviewee) if the person you are hiring can do the job now and in six months, or even a year from now. Many household employers are so focused on getting someone into the position as soon as possible that they barely think about the future of the household and the employee. You should think about the longevity of the job and ask candidates if they see themselves in the same position for the desired time period that you are looking for help. For example, will he or she want to work with you until the kids are in school?

It is also possible to ask the candidate you like most whether he or she can work some trial days after the interview and before the offer of employment, which you will reimburse them for. This is an excellent way to determine whether you have found the right person for your household's needs.

All of this should be considered before offering the candidate a position. It is easy to be swept up in an interviewee's excitement or to focus on a common interest and neglect an important consideration. With just a little preparation before the interview and review of the *General Application for Employment* (see Appendix D), an employer helps ensure that he or she gathers all the necessary information from the individual candidates.

A household employer should be prepared to answer questions, too. This exchange enables the candidate to have a clear understanding of the position and workplace, and it lays the groundwork for the work agreement to be developed.

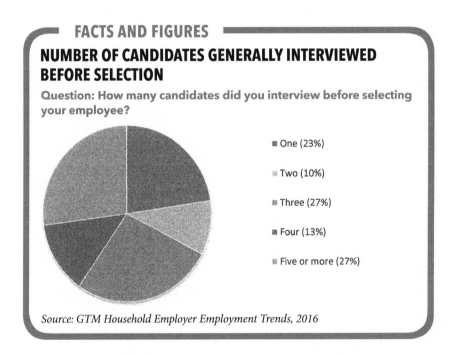

■ FACTS AND FIGURES ■
NUMBER OF CANDIDATES GENERALLY INTERVIEWED BEFORE SELECTION

Question: How many candidates did you interview before selecting your employee?

- One (23%)
- Two (10%)
- Three (27%)
- Four (13%)
- Five or more (27%)

Source: GTM Household Employer Employment Trends, 2016

Interview Questions: Legal vs. Illegal

United States law—in particular, the Equal Employment Opportunity Commission (EEOC) (see Chapter 12)—protects against employment discrimination by prohibiting employers from asking the applicant certain questions. The "Facts and Figures" section that follows lists some examples of legal and illegal questions to ask an applicant.

FACTS AND FIGURES

LEGAL VS. ILLEGAL APPLICANT QUESTIONS

Legal:	Illegal
Your (applicant's) full name?	Your (applicant's) maiden name?
Have you ever been convicted of a crime?	
Is there a felony charge pending against you?	Have you ever been arrested?
Are you 18 years or older?	
What is your date of birth?	What is your age?
How long have you been a resident of this state?	Where were you born?
Are you a U.S. citizen?	In what country are you a citizen?
Name and address of person to be notified in case of emergency?	Name and address of nearest relative in case of emergency?

Source: U.S. Department of Labor

FACTS AND FIGURES

ACCEPTABLE AND UNACCEPTABLE INQUIRIES FOR INTERVIEWS AND/OR APPLICATIONS

Topic	Acceptable	Unacceptable	If Unacceptable, What Is the Reason?
Age	If age is a legal requirement, can ask "If hired, can you furnish proof of age?" or a statement that hire is subject to age verification	What is your date of birth?	Could be viewed as age discrimination
Attendance/ reliability	What hours and days can you work?	How many children do you have?	Could be viewed as discriminatory toward females

Attendance/ reliability	Are there specific times that you cannot work?	What religion are you?	Could be viewed as religious discrimination
Attendance/ reliability	Do you have responsibilities other than work that will interfere with specific job requirements such as traveling?	What are your child care arrangements?	Could be viewed as discriminatory toward females
Attendance/ reliability	Do you have a reliable method of getting to work?	Do you own a car?	Could be considered racial discrimination
Citizenship/ national origin	Are you legally eligible for employment in the United States?	What is your national origin? Where are your parents from?	Could be considered national origin discrimination
Citizenship/ national origin	Have you ever worked under a different name?	What is your maiden name?	Could be considered national origin discrimination
National origin	None	What is your father's surname? What are the names of your relatives?	Not only are these irrelevant, but they could be considered national origin discrimination
Arrest and conviction	Have you ever been convicted of a felony? * Please see note below for additional guidance	Have you ever been arrested?	Could be considered racial discrimination
Disabilities	Can you perform the duties of the job you are applying for?	Do you have any disabilities?	Could be considered discrimination against people with disabilities
Disabilities	None	Have you ever filed a workers' compensation claim?	Could be considered discrimination against people with disabilities
Disabilities	None	Have you ever been injured on the job?	Could be considered discrimination against people with disabilities

Emergency contact information	What is the name and address of the person to be notified in case of an emergency? (Request only after the individual has been employed.)	What is the name and address of a relative to be notified in case of an emergency?	Could be considered national origin discrimination and could possibly violate state antidiscrimination laws relative to sexual orientation
Credit record	None	Do you own your own home?	Irrelevant and could be considered racial discrimination
Credit record	Credit references may be used if in compliance with the Fair Credit Reporting Act of 1970 and the Consumer Credit Reporting Reform Act of 1996	Have your wages ever been garnished?	Irrelevant and could be considered racial discrimination
Credit record	None	Have you ever declared bankruptcy?	Irrelevant and could be considered racial discrimination
Military record	What type of education, training and work experience relevant to the job did you receive while in the military?	What type of discharge did you receive?	Irrelevant and could be considered racial discrimination
Language	What languages do you speak and write fluently? (if the job requires additional languages)	What is your native language? How did you learn to read, write or speak a foreign language?	Could be considered national origin discrimination
Organizations	Inquiry into an applicant's membership in organizations that the applicant considers relevant to his or her ability to perform the job	List all clubs, societies and lodges to which you belong	Could be considered racial or national origin discrimination

Race or color	None	Complexion or color of skin	Could be considered racial or national origin discrimination
Weight, height, eye color	Only if there is a bona fide occupational qualification		Could be considered racial or national origin discrimination
Religion	Only if there is a bona fide occupational qualification	What is your religious denomination, religious affiliations, church, parish, pastor? What religious holidays do you observe?	Could be considered religious discrimination
Gender	Only if there is a bona fide occupational qualification	Do you wish to be addressed as Mr.?, Mrs.?, Miss? or Ms.?	Could be considered gender discrimination
Previous and current addresses	What was your previous address? How long did you reside there? How long have you lived at your current address?	Do you own your own home?	Could be considered racial or national origin discrimination
Education	Do you have a high school diploma or equivalent? Do you have a university or college degree? (if relevant to job performance)	What year did you graduate from high school or college?	Could be considered age discrimination

*Note on arrest records: Using arrest or conviction records as an absolute bar to employment dispro-portionately excludes certain racial groups. Therefore, such records should not be used in this manner unless there is a business need for their use. Thus, an exclusion based on an arrest record is justified only if the conduct is job-related and relatively recent and also if the applicant or employee actually engaged in the conduct for which he or she was arrested. According to the EEOC, whether there is a business need to exclude persons with conviction records from particular jobs depends on the nature of the job, the nature and seriousness of the offense, and the length of time since the conviction or incarceration. In addition, some states bar the use of arrest records in employment decisions.

Source: Society for Human Resource Management article Guidelines on Interview and Employment Application, 2015.

Expert Advice

"The biggest part of hiring our nanny was the actual interviewing process. I've been in the retail business for years and am very experienced with interviewing. I've always learned more by asking my own questions other than the rote questions that candidates have formulated an answer to ahead of time. I find out about their families and what they like to do in their free time. Their answers show what they are really like. My advice is to ask a lot of questions—it makes so much sense than anything else. We wanted (our daughter) Grace to be there for the face-to-face interview because her feedback was very helpful. When all is said and done, go with your gut—it tells you the right thing to do."

>—Gretchen Weisman
>Household Employer
>Minneapolis, MN

Investigating Backgrounds and Checking References

As with any job application, checking background and references is one of the best ways to learn about a candidate. By speaking with references, employers can learn crucial information about the candidate's abilities, personality, strengths, and weaknesses. You can tell a lot about what a reference really thought of the candidate in question from the tone of voice he or she uses. Now that more hires are done online, and not through an experienced agency, it is even more important that employers carefully check the reference sources that a candidate supplies. Even if you are using an agency, you should ideally perform your own reference checks—sometimes a previous employer will open up more to a family than to agency personnel. Employers should also be aware of fake references provided by a candidate's family or friends. Although most references are honest, it is not always the case.

Checking references is particularly important in household employment, according to the owner of a Texas-based nanny agency: "Nannies are people with special talents and personalities that you can't really test for, so this is where references come into play."

A good practice is for an employer to obtain a signed release from the candidate to check employment and personal references. (See Appendix D, *General Application for Employment.*) Provide a copy of the reference release to the candidate. (The original should be filed with the applicant's completed job application and should remain in the employee personnel file if he or she is hired.) Employers need to be cautious not to violate an applicant's right to privacy when performing background checks. Many employers check financial backgrounds to help judge a candidate's responsibility, maturity, and honesty. According to the U.S. *Fair Credit Reporting Act,* if an employer uses credit reporting as part of the background investigation, then he or she must provide an applicant with a copy and summary of his or her credit report if he or she is rejected for employment.

A Midwestern agency owner said that, although her firm checks references, clients are strongly encouraged to perform their own reference checks: "Sometimes a mom talking with another mom will provide more information."

Placement agency owners agree that the Zoe Baird Nannygate incident instigated standard background checks on prospective household employees. "In the 1980s, background checks were rarely done," said a Texas-based agency owner. "Since then, the household employment world has changed significantly." She added that she only interviews potential nannies who have legally lived in the United States for at least three years. Why? "It's just too hard to check credentials in some foreign countries," she said, adding that available foreign information is often suspect, because many records are not updated.

Spending an average of two hours with each prospect prior to accepting him or her as a nanny candidate, the Texas-based agency owner cautiously checks backgrounds, only accepts references from the United States, questions the nanny on why he or she wants to be in the profession, and studies a nanny's social interaction. The agency also recommends its clients do the same.

"Now you can't be too careful," said the agency owner, noting that today, parents' fear extends beyond the U.S. Immigration Service to include kidnapping and child abuse. "You have to become a detective yourself."

When speaking with references, some good questions employers need to ask include the following.

- Would you hire him or her again, and why or why not?
- What do you believe are his or her strengths and weaknesses?
- Why did he or she leave your employment?
- What were the dates of employment?
- Was he or she punctual?
- Were all aspects of the job completed?

FACTS AND FIGURES
EMPLOYERS: CHECK APPLICANTS' RÉSUMÉS

In a tight job market and in the age of internet-based "diploma mills," résumé fraud is an increasing concern among employers. In contrast, with today's web-enabled easy and cost-effective access to information, employers can easily verify résumé facts with a few clicks of the mouse.

It is bewildering that candidates continue to misrepresent facts on résumés, knowing that employers will check and that any misrepresentation, lie, or fraud on an application or résumé is grounds for immediate dismissal—no matter how long an employee has been with an employer or how far up the organizational chart the employee has climbed. The following examples show how seriously résumé fraud is taken.

David J. Edmondson, Radio Shack CEO, resigned under pressure after it was learned that nearly a decade earlier, he had claimed on his résumé that he held two degrees from a Bible college. The company learned that the school had no record of Edmondson graduating.

Notre Dame football coach George O'Leary was forced to resign just five days after stepping into the coach position after it was revealed that he lied about his academic and athletic achievements.

George Deutsch, NASA's press liaison, resigned after it was found that he falsely claimed he graduated from Texas A&M University.

Employers report a growing concern of résumé fraud. A Monster.com 2016 article stated that HireRight.com, an international employment background screening firm, found that 34 percent of job applicants lie on résumés—most commonly regarding education, employment dates, job titles, and technical skills. According to a 2014 CareerBuilder.com survey, 58 percent of hiring managers reported they identified a lie on a résumé. Of those employers, 33 percent say they have seen an increase in "résumé embellishments" post-recession. In addition 51 percent of employers said they would automatically dismiss a candidate if he or she lied on his résumé, while 41 percent said dismissal would depend on what the lie was about. Only 7 percent said they would overlook a résumé lie.

Résumé lies may not only cause the employee to be fired but he/she may also face civil penalties and criminal charges. According to Shake Simply Legal, in 2016 résumé fraud in New Jersey may incur a civil penalty of $1,000 for each offense. Texas and Kentucky treat résumé fraud as misdemeanors. The Texas penal code states it is illegal to falsely claim to have received a degree from an actual, accredited university or list a degree from a diploma mill, an unaccredited institution offering a "degree" for a flat fee. This is a Texas Class B misdemeanor with a civil penalty of up to $2,000 and six months in jail. In Kentucky, lying job candidates face one year in prison.

Today's social media, in particular LinkedIn and Facebook, make it much easier for employers to detect résumé lies, said Monster.com. A 2016 CareerBuilder.com survey of 3,000+ employers showed that 60 percent use social networking sites to research candidates (up from 52 percent reported in 2015). Of the employers surveyed, one-third said social network screening caused them to hire a candidate: 44 percent of those employers reported background information supported job qualifications; 44 percent said the candidate conveyed a professional image; 43 percent said the candidate's personality appeared to be a good fit with the company culture; 40 percent inferred from the candidate's postings that he or she was well-rounded and had a wide range of interests; and, 36 percent said the candidate's social presence showed "great communication skills." In addition, hiring was not the only time employers accessed social networks to view employees' postings. According to the 2016 CareerBuilder.com survey, 41 percent of employers said they researched current employees—nearly 26 percent of those employers reported accessing content that caused an employee to be reprimanded or fired.

Expert Advice

"The key to finding the right nanny for a family is honesty: honesty in job description, honesty in duties and responsibilities, hours, expectations, living arrangements (if a live-in job), etc. Parents that sugarcoat the difficulties of the job are simply going to find themselves hiring the wrong nanny for the job. The net result is that the family will end up in a revolving-door situation. If more families recognize this simple fact, there would be a lot less problems making proper matches."

> —Bob Mark
> Retired agency owner
> America's Nannies
> Paramus, NJ

Suggested Background Checks and What They Can Tell You

Many first-time household employers are surprised at what can be determined by performing standard checks into an applicant's background. These are necessary—and common—procedures for hiring any employee, and household employers should do thorough background checks.

- *Driving record*—A Department of Motor Vehicles (DMV) check is very important for any applicant seeking a position that requires driving. A DMV check reveals driving history of the applicant and any alcohol- or drug-related incidents.

- *Social Security*—Checking that the applicant's Social Security number is that person's ensures that the applicant is not fraudulently using another person's number. In addition, a potential employer may verify the applicant's current or prior addresses via the Social Security Administration.

- *Credit history*—Checking an applicant's credit history is becoming more and more common during the application process. Credit history demonstrates an applicant's financial performance and allows a potential employer to judge an applicant's responsibility.

- *Criminal conviction* (county, state, and federal)—Shows an applicant's criminal activity and prevents negligent hiring.

- *Drug testing*—Presents any drug use by the applicant.

- *Personality testing*—Guides employers in hiring decisions, often allowing employers to gauge whether an applicant will mesh with others in the workplace.

- *Sex offender and child abuse registry*—Lists any person charged with any crimes involving children.

- *Professional licensing*—When a professional designation is necessary for the job, determining whether the applicant possesses the designation or certification also helps determine whether he or she is qualified to do the job.

- *Higher education verification*—Checks the accuracy of the information submitted by the applicant and, depending on course of study, demonstrates to a degree whether he or she is qualified for the job.

- *TrustLine* (for California)—Ensures the applicant has been cleared of background checks and fingerprinting by the FBI and California Department of Justice.

- *Fingerprinting*—Verifies whether the applicant has a criminal history.

- *Character references*—Verifies authenticity from the applicant and allows the employer to determine characteristics of an applicant (e.g., hard worker, caring person, loves children, strongly believes in education).

- *Employment references*—Verifies past employment and dates, as well as the accuracy of the information the applicant submitted.

- *Other screening*:
  - U.S. Department of Commerce Denied Persons List
  - U.S. Department of Commerce Entity List
  - U.S. Department of Treasury Specially Designated Nationals and Blocked Persons List
  - U.S. Department of State Proliferation List
  - U.S. Department of State Debarment List

There are also newer screening methods that allow an employer to check out a candidate, which more and more employers are using to narrow down the search for a new employee. For example, by accessing social media networking sites to check a candidate's digital footprint, such as Facebook, LinkedIn, and Twitter. According to a 2015 Harris Poll of hiring and HR managers conducted for CareerBuilder, 52 percent of employers use social networking sites to research candidates (a trend that has increased from 2014 and 2013) and 51 percent of them use search engines to do the same. Googling candidates may provide a wealth of information about what job applicants might have done or said or achieved in the past.

According to the same survey, some things employers are attempting to investigate via social media and search engine research are:

- 60 percent are looking for information that supports their job qualifications
- 56 percent want to see if the candidate has a professional online persona
- 37 percent want to see what other people are posting about the candidate
- 21 percent admit they are looking for reasons not to hire the candidate

The survey revealed that employers use online research of a candidate's digital footprint both to persuade them to hire a candidate (such as supporting background information that qualifies them for the job, an online personality that is a good company fit, a professional image, good communication skills, and creativity); and to support them rejecting a candidate (such as provocative or inappropriate photographs, evidence of drinking/drug use, bad-mouthing previous employers, poor communication skills, and discriminatory comments related to race, religion, gender, etc.).

However, a word of caution: an employer must be very careful not to discriminate against a candidate according to the law. (See Chapter 12 for more details.) The problem with researching the candidate online is that the employer can inadvertently allow prejudice and bias to influence the decision. It is also worth remembering that a candidate has a professional and a personal life, and therefore an online persona might not truly represent the candidate's character strengths and weaknesses. Before doing any background check, it is advisable to obtain prior written consent with a signed release from the job candidate (see Appendix D, *General Application for Employment*).

Expert Advice

"We wanted the kids to be on their own schedule, not on our [work schedule]."

—Denise Shade
Household employer
New York, NY

Expert Advice

"A good household employee has dignity, nobility, great discretion, and not an ounce of judgment. Judgment is often the death curse for a domestic employment relationship."

—Leann Brambach
Experienced agency owner and operator
Seattle, WA

Maintain Professionalism

Mind your business and stay on track with questioning as it relates to the job and how the applicant will perform the job duties.

In the corporate world, quite a lot of effort, time, and expense is taken to perform background checks on every new hire. The corporate process may include personal and professional reference checking, criminal background checks, drug screening, a DMV check, personality testing, and even checking someone's credit history for a look into his or her responsibility and fiscal management. All this is done for a corporate job. How much more important is it when you are hiring an employee to come into your home? Your children and loved ones are so much more valuable—and more vulnerable.

Keep them safe by going the extra mile or two with your background checking. Most importantly, follow your instincts.

This will be well worth the effort in hiring an employee who makes everyone in your household feel comfortable and safe and happy. You are hiring a nanny to help you *not* worry about what is going on at home. Take time to check out the person you are bringing into your home and who you are entrusting with your loved ones, your property, and your memories.

Family Interaction Test

When you have finally decided who are the best candidates, make sure you let them meet the family members they will be looking after. For nannies, you can tell a lot from how they interact with your child. You should be there to watch and to facilitate the interaction, but you should also move to another room and listen in on the conversation and actions of the nanny and the child. You want there to be warmth between the caregiver and the child; you want both to have fun; you want the candidate to be polite, caring, and professional. The child should feel safe and happy in the person's care. If you are comfortable with the idea, you can also arrange another interview time to give a trial run of the nanny and then gently ask the child for his or her opinion and whether the child enjoyed being with the nanny and liked him or her. You could choose not to pay for this as part of the interview process, but you need to make sure the nanny is aware that this is unpaid interview time before you make arrangements. Or you could choose to pay the nanny for this time as a goodwill gesture to keep the candidate interested and to set up an employment relationship of trust from the beginning.

Expert Advice

"I want the nanny to be nurturing and warm. My main concern was whether my children would be loved and played with. There was warmth with our nanny from the beginning. When I interview I like to talk about the position first and not talk about salary right away. With our nanny we had a long conversation about the children, what she was looking for and what I was looking for. She had the right prior experience, a real interest in being a nanny, and was willing to please."

—Maria Ascenzo
Household employer
Scotia, NY

FACTS AND FIGURES

AT-WILL EMPLOYMENT

All household employees are employed at will. This employment is at the discretion of the employer and the employee. Employment may terminate with or without notice or cause. Employees are also free to end employment at any time, for any reason, with or without notice. (See Chapter 7, for an example of an at-will statement.)

Making an Offer

An offer should always be made verbally and in writing. Offer letters can also be emailed to candidates with the job offer and job description as an attachment.

When offering employment to an applicant, take care to avoid any appearance of a promise of long-term employment. Send a job offer letter that states the position, whether it is full time or part time, the start date, the schedule, the starting salary, and any available benefits. Remember to state if he or she is an at-will employee. (See Appendix D, for an example of an offer letter for household employment.) Ask that the letter be signed, dated, and returned to the employer for the offer to be accepted. It is okay for the employer to request that the letter be signed and completed by a certain date. That way, the employer may contact other candidates until the job is filled.

Stephanie Oana, a lawyer in Oakland, California, and a GTM payroll and tax service client, employs a nanny to care for her two young children. According to Oana, she writes extensive offer letters that include all of the terms of employment. The offer letters, she notes, serve as the work agreement. "The candidates really prefer it, because with it they know what the employer wants," she states.

Oana prefers using the offer letter because in the business world, a countersigned offer letter often acts as the work agreement. Oana includes all pertinent and relevant information in the offer letter, including benefits, vacation, insurance, use of car, use of telephone, hours, when overtime applies, and so on.

Rejecting a Candidate

While not mandated by law, it is common HR practice to inform rejected candidates that another person has been hired. Many rejection letters (see Appendix D, *Rejection Letter to Candidate*) simply state that another candidate deemed more appropriate for the job has been hired.

The letter should be filed with the application and other information regarding that particular candidate. Rejecting candidates is often an awkward and unpleasant task. The benefit of working with an agency is that the agency handles candidate rejection, not the household employer (see Chapter 5). These days, many rejection letters can be accomplished easily by email, especially if you have conducted the hiring process through an online site. This makes the task quick and easy to perform; however, you should be aware that you do not want to enter into a discussion about why the candidate was not employed. You may want to carefully consider if you wish to use email and whether a personal email address is a good idea. It may be safer and easier to set up a temporary email address for contacting candidates throughout the hiring process, which you can terminate once the job has been filled.

Hiring Laws

Employers must be aware of several federal, state, and local laws when hiring an employee. Key federal laws that all employers must follow are discussed in this section. There are, of course, specific hiring laws relating to hiring a noncitizen which are discussed in Chapter 3.

Verifying Employment Eligibility (Form I-9)

According to IRS Publication 926, it is mandatory that all employers ask their employee to fill out the I-9 form *before* the hire date to determine whether the employee is eligible to work in the United States. Particularly in the household employment industry, there are many illegal hires of undocumented illegal workers, and Form I-9 aims to reduce this occurrence and also protect the employer from penalties associated with hiring workers who are not allowed to legally work in the United States. Care must be taken when filling out this form and reviewing the documents used to establish validity of work. For more information, see Chapter 3 and Form M-274, *Handbook for Employers*. Employers are strongly advised to complete the I-9 process for their employees. If an employer hires an alien not authorized to work in the United States, he or she may be fined up to $3,000 per employee and even face a prison sentence for criminal violation of I-9. They may also incur civil violation fines of up to $16,000 per worker (third offense).

ADA

When hiring employees, employers with 15 or more employees must comply with the *Americans with Disabilities Act* (ADA) and Title VII, which prohibits discrimination, and the *Americans with Disabilities Act Amendments Act* (ADAAA) (see Chapter 12). Even though many household employment situations do not have 15 or more employees, it is advisable to be aware of the laws and, when possible, to try to comply with ADA and ADAAA requirements.

EEOC and Affirmative Action

Federal and state *Equal Employment Opportunity Commission* (EEOC) regulations protect people from discrimination regardless of race, color, gender, age, national origin, religion, disability, sexual orientation, marital status, citizenship status, genetic predisposition, or veteran status. *Affirmative action* is how an organization or an employer addresses protected classes—such as minorities, women, people with disabilities, and veterans—from problem areas, which may include under-representation in the workforce or some action that may adversely affect that group (or employee). Employers need to be sure that their commitment to the EEOC guidelines and affirmative action is included in hiring, training, compensation, benefits, retention, and promotions.

Employee Polygraph Protection Act

The *Employee Polygraph Protection Act* bars private employers from using any type of lie detector test for either pre-employment screening or for testing current employees.

Q & A

Q. How can I legally ask an employee candidate if she or he smokes?

A. An employer can ask a candidate whether he or she smokes while working on the job. It is important to keep it in context of the job to be performed.

CASE STUDY

● ●

STEPHANIE OANA
HOUSEHOLD EMPLOYER
OAKLAND, CA

After Stephanie Oana watched friends maneuver through their own nanny searches, she and her husband, Joe Osha, elected to use an agency. She said doing so saved her time and helped ensure she was hiring for the role she wanted. With both parents busily juggling demanding schedules, frequent business travel, and unpredictable work hours, they have over several years hired three nannies: one who lived outside their home in New York City and two live-in nannies in the San Francisco Bay area.

Oana, a lawyer, said she worked with a number of agencies simultaneously each time she searched for a nanny. "You have to be very clear with the agency about what you want," she said. "Agencies are very helpful with identifying and screening applicants, but the matchmaking is up to the employer and the candidate."

"Families need to think clearly and be up front and fair to the people interviewing," said Oana, "and give a realistic view of the situation." Oana addressed her unpredictable work schedule during the interview process to ensure that the nanny would be flexible. "It is a lot easier to balance a schedule with weird hours with a live-in nanny," Oana added. "It can be very hard to balance certain responsibilities if a nanny has her own children or obligations she needs to get home to."

According to Oana, as the job evolves, communication is very important. "I talk every day with my nanny about the kids," she said. "At least every couple of months, we speak about the job and issues."

Oana cited an incident in which a nanny wanted a raise. Because open communication was fostered, Oana and the nanny were able to talk about the circumstances and strike a balance. "It was a very beneficial conversation," noted Oana.

The Oanas sought in-home child care because they believe very young children need a lot of individual attention. "My kids have gotten the kind of attention they would receive from a stay-at-home parent," Oana stated. "I was not interested in being a stay-at-home parent, but I could hire a nanny to provide high-quality, in-home care."

> Stephanie Oana's practice of clear communication and presenting a realistic view of the job makes for an effective working relationship—and no surprises for either Oana or her nanny. Plus, Oana's use of an extensive employment offer letter as a work agreement contributes to an accurate view of the household's situation. In short, she is ensuring that the candidate fully understands the job requirements prior to accepting the position. Employers who do this are crossing their *t*'s and dotting their *i*'s before employment begins. As a result, they are preventing problems from arising.
>
> —Guy

Where You Live Determines the Law

Every household employer is subject to federal, state, and local laws. Jurisdiction is generally based on the physical location of the household. Examples from several states and localities follow.

Domestic Workers' Bill of Rights

In November 2010, New York State took an unprecedented step and passed the New York State Domestic Workers' Bill of Rights (better known as "the nanny law", according to *The New York Times*). The first of its kind in the nation, the law grants new rights and protections to domestic workers, who are housekeepers, nannies, and any other person employed in the home or residence for any domestic purpose. Excluded from the law are those who work on a casual basis, such as part-time babysitters, those who provide companionship services, those who are employed by an agency, and those who are relatives of the employer.

Furthermore, the law protects an employee from harassment by the employer based on gender, race, religion, or national origin. Domestic workers are also protected from retaliation by their employers for complaining of such harassment. The Domestic Workers' Bill of Rights, like all labor and tax laws, applies to all workers, regardless of their immigration status or eligibility for employment status.

The law amends New York Labor Law to entitle domestic workers to receive the following rights.

- Pay frequency: all domestic workers are classified as manual workers and therefore must be paid on a weekly basis, within seven calendar days of the end of the workweek.

- Pay at least the minimum wage. Credit toward minimum wage may be applied if meals and/or lodging are provided.

- Overtime compensation: overtime pay of one and a half times the regular rate of pay is required for an employee working more than 40 hours per week, which amounts to 44 hours per week for all live-in employees.

- Time off:

  - For paid time off: one day of rest is required in each calendar week. If employees choose to work on their day of rest, they must be paid at one and a half times the hourly rate of pay.

  - After one year of work with the same employer, employees are entitled to at least three days off each calendar year, paid at their regular rate of compensation.

- Insurance: Workers' Compensation insurance is also mandatory for workers who work 40 or more hours per week.

- Employee notice:

  - All new employees must be notified in writing at the time of hire: their hours of work, their rate of pay, their overtime rate, their regular payday, the employee's policy on sick, vacation and personal time, and the policy on holiday leave.

- All employees must receive a pay statement showing the number of hours worked, gross wages, deductions, and net wages.

- Record keeping: all employers must maintain accurate records, showing hours worked, rate of pay, and deductions taken.

- Unlawful discrimination: it is an unlawful discriminatory practice for any domestic employer to engage in unwelcome sexual advances, request for sexual favors, or other verbal or physical contact of a sexual nature to any domestic worker.

- Notification to employees: employers are required to post notice of this law in a visible place in their home where employees can see it.

New York enacted the new law to protect the rights of the state's hundreds of thousands of domestic workers *and* their employers. For more information, go to www.labor.ny.gov or call 1-888-52-LABOR.

Other states have also enacted laws to protect domestic workers' rights. Following New York State, Hawaii (2013), California (2013), Massachusetts (2014), Oregon (2015), and Connecticut (2015) enacted domestic worker protections. Illinois' Governor signed a similar bill in August 2016, which made Illinois the seventh state to have a Domestic Workers' Bill of Rights when it took effect in January 2017. While the California Domestic Workers' Bill of Rights was enacted in 2013—entitling domestic workers to overtime pay, eased eligibility requirements for workers' compensation and provided meal and rest breaks—one year later (2014) it was updated with new mandated standards of employer regulations and worker protections for the household employment industry. In 2016, the California law made the overtime requirements permanent. Illinois' 2016 Domestic Workers' Bill of Rights Act amends four state laws to provide domestic workers labor law and human rights protections.

FACTS AND FIGURES

THE LATEST DOMESTIC WORKERS' BILL OF RIGHTS: ILLINOIS

Signed into law in mid-2016 and effective January 1, 2017, the Illinois Domestic Workers' Bill of Rights amends four Illinois laws to include domestic workers—household workers who are employed in the home with a one-on-one agreement (work agreement), hired by an agency and/or live-in. The Domestic Workers' Bill of Rights entitles domestic workers to state minimum wage ($8.25/hour) and basic labor protections, such as the One Day Rest in Seven Act that requires employees get at least 24 hours of rest in each calendar week and a 20-minute meal break for every seven and a half hours worked. In addition, Illinois domestic workers will be covered by the Illinois Human Rights Act, protecting against sexual harassment, and Wages of Women and Minors Act, prohibiting "oppressive and unreasonable" wages.

California Fair Employment & Housing Act

The *California Fair Employment & Housing Act* (FEHA) requires that any person employing five or more employees does not harass or discriminate on the basis of race, color, religion, sex, gender, gender identity, gender expression, sexual orientation, age, national origin, ancestry, marital status, mental and physical disability, medical condition, pregnancy or military veteran status. In 2016, the law was extended to include: unpaid interns and volunteers; updated definitions and updated obligations for pregnant disability leave; antibullying training for employers with 50 or more employees; and, mandated employer distribution of written policies in English and other languages spoken by at least 10 percent of the workforce.

Massachusetts Labor Law

The Massachusetts Department of Labor requires all placement agencies to inform clients about labor laws that apply to them. Each agency has to provide a copy of the Department of Labor's leaflet, which discusses the Massachusetts *Minimum Fair Wage Law* (including information on who is covered, payment of wages, overtime, child labor, service, deductions, meal breaks, minimum daily hours, and so forth) to every family and every employee who applies to the agency.

New York City Local Law No. 33

The City of New York Local Law No. 33 (Standards and Conduct of Employment Agencies) mandates that every licensed employment agency under the jurisdiction of the commissioner and engaged in the job placement of household employees must provide to each applicant for a household employment job, and to his or her prospective employer, the Department of Consumer Affairs (DCA)'s "Domestic or Household Employees: Statement of Employee Rights and Employer Responsibilities." This is a written statement indicating the rights afforded to household and domestic employees under the law, as well as employer obligations under the law ("the law" is that of New York City, New York State, and the United States), such as obligations regarding minimum wage, overtime, hours of work, record keeping, workers' compensation, Social Security payments, and unemployment and disability insurance coverage. It can be downloaded at www1.nyc.gov/assets/dca/downloads/pdf/businesses/Domestic-Household-Employee-Rights.pdf.

Licensed employment agencies must also use DCA's Job Description Form (Statement of Job Conditions), that fully and accurately describes the nature and terms of employment, including the name and address of the person to whom the applicant is to apply for such employment, the name and address of the person authorizing the hiring for such position, wages, hours of work, the kind of services to be performed, and the agency fee. The agency must give this completed Job Description Form to every job applicant the agency refers to a position as a domestic or household employee. One can be downloaded here: www1.nyc.gov/assets/dca/downloads/pdf/businesses/Domestic-Household-Employee-Job-Description-Form.pdf.

At present, this is the only such local law in the nation, but it may be replicated in other localities.

CASE STUDY

● ●

JOHN ROBERTSON
INTERNATIONAL HOUSEHOLD TRAINER, COACH, CONSULTANT
LONDON, ENGLAND

A leading trainer and coach for all aspects of the personal service industry—in particular, household services—John Robertson said that after working in the personal service industry and in the corporate world, he much prefers personal service.

Robertson began his career in his early twenties as a household manager and butler in North America and then spent many years in the Fortune 500 business world. Robertson has also operated his own international training company for employees and employers in the personal service industry, and has taught at the International Guild of Professional Butlers' International Butler Academy in the Netherlands. Traveling throughout the world, he works one-on-one with household employers and employees, as well as with private associations and service-centered businesses, such as luxury hotels and golf clubs.

In addition, private service employers contract with Robertson to assist them in hiring service employees. Robertson conducts telephone interviews to narrow the field of candidates. One of the first questions he asks candidates is what good service means to them; by identifying the experience that made someone feel like a million dollars, he can readily equate that episode with what the employee will be doing daily for his or her employer.

"The most important thing to understand in household employment is where you are and what you are doing," he said. "High energy, motivated people do well…Being in service does not mean being servile…The job is not to set the table; it's to support a lifestyle, to provide service…I can teach pigeons to set a table!"

Every household employee must know his or her employer's mission of the home, said Robertson. The key focus of the home may be on the family, the children's education, recreation, charitable fund-raising, or political endeavors. Everything the employee does furthers that mission, he said.

"It is a true honor to be allowed to work with someone in his or her home," said Robertson. There is "tremendous...trust and responsibility—even if the job is dusting baseboards with a toothbrush."

Laughing, Robertson said he "was born a butler. I thought it was the neatest job...It is a job for someone who takes control, organizes, and strives for perfection...It must be perfect; that's what we do."

According to Robertson, general awareness of the private service market has grown, particularly within the United States. Stressing that personal service employees must be in the field for the right reasons, Robertson noted that, while the industry offers no job security and no unions, there is a job for everyone—those who want to work weekends, those who do not, and so on—and that if someone loves what he or she does for a living, then the money will follow, and overall employee benefits and perks can be tremendous.

> When interviewing, a household employer should try to determine the candidate's attitude toward personal service and the potential effect it may have on the household. Ask yourself, "Is this applicant's outlook appropriate in order to meet the household's service goals?"
>
> —Guy

Hiring Checklist

- Know and abide by federal, state, and local employment and labor laws.

- Determine whether the job requires an employee or an independent contractor and know how this implicates tax filing.

- Be thorough and clear in writing job descriptions and work agreements or contracts. To help you keep focused on your objectives, refer to the job description often—in interviews, in offer letters, and so on.

- Be professional—household employees are pursuing their careers in "real jobs."

- Confirm household employees' employment eligibility status by completing Form I-9.

- Interview, check references, send offer letters, and provide new hires with an employee handbook.

- Obtain and file a signed release from the job applicant to complete the background checks, and follow the suggested background checks.

- If working with an agency, contact the agency to determine whether any additional action needs to be done prior to making your hiring decision.

- Before making your final decision, review the applicant's references and make calls to the applicant's prior employers and co-workers.

- When contacting the applicant to offer the job, have your offer letter prepared, as well as any other pertinent information, such as a work agreement or contract.

- Finally, schedule another meeting with the applicant. Review the job description, offer (as written in your prepared letter), work agreement, and so on. Use this meeting to address any outstanding issues at this point and to finalize the hiring process (e.g., start date, work hours, etc.).

- Be aware of any state or local laws that govern employment for household help.

- Most importantly, when hiring a nanny or other person to work within your home, always hire the best, and never compromise.

3

Employing a Noncitizen

Household employers should hire only those people who are legally authorized to work in the United States. These people include U.S. citizens; legal permanent residents; and other aliens authorized to work, such as refugees, asylees, and persons in Temporary Protected Status.

Many household employers in the United States hire noncitizens, largely for financial reasons, and many hire people not legally authorized to work in the country. There are many reasons you should not hire illegal workers, most of all because you can face harsh penalties if you do so and because there is the risk that the worker may have to be deported back to his or her country of origin. It is also much harder to perform background checks and gain verifiable references when contacting international sources.

According to Pew Research Center's 2015 report, "Unauthorized immigrant population stable for half a decade", in 2014 there were 11.1 million unauthorized immigrants in the United States, based on the last U.S. Bureau of Labor Statistics' Current Population Survey. According to Pew, this population remained stable for the past five years after 20 years of change due to little fluctuation in recent years because the number of new immigrants is about the same as the number of those deported, those who converted to legal status and those who left the United States on their own. The new unauthorized immigrant total includes those who crossed a border illegally or those who remained in the United States after their visas expired.

Employers hiring noncitizens must comply with filings and proce-dures stipulated under U.S. immigration law. Compliance is particularly important in light of the U.S. Homeland Security programs. All employers in the United States must complete a Form I-9 for every employee hired. Form I-9 attempts to ensure that only people legally able to work in the United States are hired. Therefore, employers use Form I-9 to verify the identity and employment eligibility of employees.

FACTS AND FIGURES

ESTIMATES OF THE U.S. UNAUTHORIZED IMMIGRANT POPULATION, 1990-2014 (MILLIONS)

Estimated unauthorized immigrant population in the U.S. rises, falls, then stabilizes

In millions

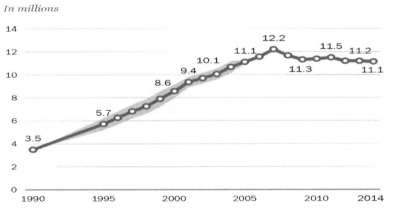

Note: Shading surrounding line indicates low and high points of the estimated 90% confidence interval. The 2009-2014 change is not statistically significant at 90% confidence interval. Data labels are for 1990, 1995, 2000, 2001, 2003, 2005, 2007, 2009, 2011, 2013 and 2014.
Source: Pew Research Center estimates for 2005-2014 based on augmented American Community Survey data (IPUMS); for 1995-2004 based on March Supplements of the Current Population Survey. Estimates for 1990 from Warren and Warren (2013). "Overall Number of U.S. Unauthorized Immigrants Holds Steady Since 2009"

PEW RESEARCH CENTER

Source: "Unauthorized immigrant population stable for half a decade" Pew Research Center, Washington DC (July 2015) http://www.pewresearch.org/ fact-tank/2016/09/21/unauthorized-immigrant-population-stable-for-half-a-decade/

FACTS AND FIGURES
LIVE-IN DOMESTIC WORKERS: THE HISTORY

For decades, undocumented immigrants from non-English-speaking countries have sought employment as domestics in American households, where they could have a place to live and work at the same time. The advantage for the household was often that the immigrants would accept a lower wage than American citizens looking for similar employment. This has left a legacy of household employees being underpaid, paid illegally, and hired illegally that still tarnishes the industry today, even though the occurrence of this is far less. Most employers are aware of the potential liabilities of hiring illegal workers in the home, and some celebrities and high-profile employers have been exposed publicly for doing so. There is also a decreasing trend overall of household employees wanting to live with a family, especially with immigration laws being far more stringent and the documentation of illegal workers being far more greatly enforced. Unfortunately, adhering to the law with regard to live-in employees, especially when they are illegally working in the country, is harder to comply. An employer who wishes to hire a live-in usually does so because personal or career commitments require household help for longer hours. Most live-ins are considered "on call" for household work, even when their workday is over, and many rarely get paid overtime or have the legal amount of free time that they should have. If an employer is interested in live-in help, particularly with regard to noncitizens, then the employer should take great care to adhere to all labor laws and ensure a professional legal working environment for the employee.

Immigration Reform and Control Act of 1986

The Immigration Reform and Control Act of 1986 (IRCA) requires employers to ensure that employees hired are legally authorized to work within the United States by verifying the identity and employment eligibility of all new employees. At the same time, the law prohibits employers from committing document abuse or discrimination on the basis of citizenship status (see citizenship discrimination below). Households with three or fewer employees are not subject to the IRCA's provisions on antidiscrimination. However, IRCA does require that Form I-9 is completed by *all* employees when beginning a new job, and it is the responsibility of all household employers to request this at the start of a new hire. (See IRS Publication 926 and the U.S. Citizenship and Immigration Services' *Handbook for Employers* M-274.)

The I-9 Process

You have probably filled out several I-9 forms over the course of your employment, and the I-9 form probably looks very familiar to you. You may remember when starting work at a new company or organization that some time during the first three days of your employment you submitted to human resources, or to your new supervisor, certain documents—such as your driver's license, passport, birth certificate, or Social Security card—that verified your identity and your ability to legally work in the United States. According to IRS Publication 926, it is mandatory that employees fill out this form before they start work.

Since November 2016 the Form I-9 has been revised so that it is easier for employers to fill out—it now includes online fill-in fields to aid completion. This 'smart' Form I-9 can be accessed and filled out on USCIS's website and includes a number of new features, including drop-down menus, hover text, and real-time error messages. Using the new, smart Form I-9 is not required—employers can still opt to simply print out the form and complete by hand.

The fifth page of *Form I-9* (Appendix E) provides lists of acceptable documents for verifying an employee's eligibility to work in the United States. These lists are there to help you, as an employer, determine what the U.S. government considers valid documents to establish identification and employment eligibility. An employer needs to examine these documents carefully.

Such documents can include the following:

- a U.S. passport, an alien registration receipt card, or a permanent resident card (Form I-551)

- an unexpired foreign passport containing an I-551 stamp

- an unexpired employment authorization document issued by the USCIS that contains a photograph (Form I-766)

The employee must produce proof of employment eligibility and identity within three business days after she or he begins work.

However, employers must use some caution when reviewing and accepting an employee's Form I-9 and documentation. The best place to access resources, tips, and guidance to properly complete Form I-9 and better understand the I-9 process is at the USCIS' I-9 Central website (www.uscis.gov/i-9central). Form M-274, *Handbook for Employers*, is another tool that employers can access to help them ensure the validity of documents presented with Form I-9. Form M-274 offers illustrations of various documents and information on such things as which types of green cards or Social Security numbers were issued and when. Employers may refer to M-274 when a questionable document is presented to them or when they are uncertain whether a particular form of a document is still valid. Sometimes unauthorized workers modify older documents with newer photos. For example, if a 40-year-old uses a picture of a 20-year-old on official documents such as a green card.

Employers are strongly advised to complete the I-9 process for their employees. If an employer hires an alien not authorized to work within the United States, he or she may be fined up to $3,000 per employee and even face a prison sentence. It is wise to fill out Form I-9 correctly, because doing so protects an employer from any liability, even if the employee turns out to actually not be authorized to work. Form I-9 must be kept by the employer for three years after the date of hire, or one year after the termination of employment date, whichever is later.

Citizenship Discrimination

Title VII of the *Civil Rights Act* of 1964, the *Immigration Reform and Control Act* of 1986 (IRCA), and other antidiscrimination laws prohibit citizenship discrimination against individuals employed in the United States. Employers of more than three employees are covered by the IRCA antidiscrimination rules (as opposed to the 15 or more employees required by Title VII of the *Civil Rights Act*). Therefore, although these laws may not apply to some household employment situations with only one to three employees, it is wise to adhere to best practice and not discriminate against any person lawfully admitted and authorized to work in the United States. Further details are outlined in Chapter 12. It should be noted that an employer should not ask the candidate's country of origin or native language or treat employees differently based on their last name, skin color, or accent.

Illegal Immigrants and Immigration Reform

The United States has always relied on immigration to provide employment. According to the Pew Research Center's 2015 report "More Mexicans Leaving than Coming to the U.S.", the United States began regulating immigration soon after winning independence, and today, by a large margin, the United States has more immigrants than any other country in the world, with the U.S.-Mexico immigration corridor being the world's largest. (According to 2015 United Nations data, some 12 million people living in the United States were born in Mexico.)

There has been an abundance of state legislative action relating to immigration policy since 2005, especially as federal immigration reform has had a complicated history. Federal attempts to enact legislation to give illegal immigrants a path to citizenship and provide a guest worker program have been continually blocked. In the absence of federal legislation, the movement for new immigration laws has occurred at the state level—many with harsh consequences for illegal immigrants, particularly those that are seeking employment. According to FindLaw, an online legal information provider for law and business firms, state laws are typically related to employment, education, licensing, and state benefits.

Arizona enacted in 2010 one of the nation's toughest state immigration laws, much of which was struck down by the U.S. Supreme Court just two years later because the state "crossed the constitutional line". Struck down was the controversial requirement that made it a misdemeanor for immigrants to not carry registration documents at all times.

California has a number of immigration laws that set it apart. California does not require law officials to check immigration status during traffic stops or similar circumstances and is debating whether to "opt out" of the federal fingerprint requirement that checks immigration status. It prohibits employers from using E-Verify to check the status of existing employees or employees who have not received an offer, unless doing so is required by federal law or as a condition of receiving federal funds; allows access to public benefit programs, particularly health care, no matter what the immigration status; and allows students who are undocumented immigrants to pay the same public university tuition that in-state legal residents do through its DREAM Act. Related legislation will allow these same students to apply for and receive financial aid benefits.

In February 2011, a Texas bill made employers who "intentionally, knowingly, or recklessly" hire an unauthorized immigrant face up to two years in jail and a fine of up to $10,000. However, there is an exemption for those hiring domestic workers. Surprisingly, the state's exemption for maids, landscapers, and other domestic help within a one-family home will most likely proliferate the hiring of undocumented workers for domestic work, despite the stringent penalties associated with the hire of illegal immigrants in other state workplaces. (Source: CNN, "Texas Immigration Bill Has Big Exception," March 2, 2011).

In 2011, Georgia and Alabama enacted tough enforcement laws authorizing police officers to check the immigration status of certain suspects and to detain them if they are in the country illegally.

Immigration laws continue to burgeon. The National Conference on State Legislatures found that enacted legislation dealing with immigration increased by 26 percent in 2015, with 216 laws enacted compared to 171 laws in 2014. (Texas was the most active state in 2015 with 84 resolutions and 15 laws followed by California with 66 laws and two resolutions.) With the increased attention on legal hiring practices and legal payroll and tax payments, it is critical that household employers follow the laws and requirements established in their states and municipalities, even if the employee is not authorized to work in the United States. (For more on managing payroll and taxes, see Chapter 10.)

FACTS AND FIGURES

STATES WITH LARGEST UNAUTHORIZED IMMIGRANT POPULATIONS, 2012 (THOUSANDS)

TABLE 1.1

States with Largest Unauthorized Immigrant Populations, 2012

In thousands

	Estimate	Range (+ or -)
California	2,450	45
Texas	1,650	40
Florida	925	25
New York	750	20
New Jersey	525	25
Illinois	475	25
Georgia	400	15
North Carolina	350	15
Arizona	300	15
Virginia	275	15
Maryland	250	15
Washington	230	15
Nevada	210	10
Colorado	180	10
Pennsylvania	170	15

Note: All numbers are rounded independently and are not adjusted to sum to the total U.S. figure or other totals. Differences between consecutive ranks may not be statistically significant. See Methodology for rounding rules. Range based on 90% confidence interval.

Source: Table A1, derived from Pew Research Center estimates based on augmented 2012 American Community Survey data from Integrated Public Use Microdata Series (IPUMS).

PEW RESEARCH CENTER

Source: "Unauthorized Immigrant Totals Rise in 7 States, Fall in 14" Pew Research Center, Washington, DC (November, 2014) http://www.pewhispanic. org/2014/11/18/unauthorized-immigrant-totals-rise-in-7-states-fall-in-14/

Hiring a Foreign Worker

According to the U.S. Department of Labor Employment and Training Administration (DOLETA), qualifying criteria for hiring a foreign worker include the following.

- The foreign worker must be hired as a full-time employee.

- The employer must have a bona fide job opening.

- Job requirements cannot be tailored to the foreign worker's qualifications, but must follow what is customarily required for the job in the United States.

- The employer must pay at least the prevailing wage for the job in the location of the anticipated job.

Q & A

Q. How do I hire or sponsor someone who is not legally authorized to work in the United States?

A. The DOLETA website at www.doleta.gov provides information on hiring foreign workers, as well as access to the necessary forms. According to DOLETA, hiring foreign workers for employment in the United States normally requires approval from several governmental agencies. A labor certification filed with the Department of Labor is often the first step. The employer needs to complete Form 9089 (Application for Permanent Employment Certification) or Form 9142 (Application for Temporary Employment Certification), as appropriate. The Department of Labor works with the local State Workforce Agency to process the form. Then, an employer must petition the U.S. Citizenship and Immigration Services for a visa by submitting Form I-140 (Immigrant Petition for Alien Worker). With a visa number issued by the State Department, the foreign worker gains entry to the United States. Also, an applicant must prove that she or he is admissible to the United States under the Immigration and Nationality Act. For more information, see www.foreignlaborcert.doleta.gov/perm.cfm.

Immigration Hiring Information

Just as it is difficult to define household employment and positions in the household employment industry, employers new to hiring foreign nationals, immigrants, nonimmigrant aliens, and so on, may quickly find themselves confused and uncertain. Just reading about the types of immigrant employees is enough to intimidate most of us. There are so many different definitions, each with its own specific hiring requirements and legal issues, that it is a courageous household employer who takes on the extra worry and paperwork when he or she hires a noncitizen.

Yet since nearly one-quarter of the household industry's employees are noncitizens, immigration is a very real and very important consideration for hiring household help.

What Employers Need to Know about Hiring Foreign Workers

While hundreds of pages could be spent on this area alone, this section is a nutshell guide for dealing with immigration issues and hiring.

Employment-based immigration is a complex process that involves a number of government agencies—the U.S. Departments of Labor, State, and Homeland Security. The *Immigration and Nationality Act* (INA) regulates the admission of foreign workers into the United States, with the Departments of Justice, State, and Homeland Security all serving as administrators of its mandates.

As a U.S. employer, you need to be aware of the 'aliens' who are authorized to work within the United States, and whether such employment is restricted in any way. There is no such thing as a general *work permit* under U.S. law. Work authorization for aliens is always connected to the visa status that they hold in the United States. The following three classes of aliens are allowed to work in the United States:

- aliens authorized to work per their immigration status, such as green card holders
- aliens permitted to work for a specific employer per their immigration and/or visa status (this is the case for almost all nonimmigrants that seek to work in the United States)

- aliens who must first apply for and obtain permission from the U.S. Citizen and Immigration Services to accept employment within the United States (this is the case with aliens who are enrolled in U.S. universities and who are authorized to work in certain circumstances as part of their education)

Legal permanent U.S. residents (green card holders or immigrants) are legally entitled to work for any U.S. employer with no further paperwork, just as a U.S. citizen could. All other nonimmigrant aliens must either hold a visa authorizing them to work (e.g., students with work authorization) or be sponsored by a U.S. employer for one of the visa categories authorizing them to work for that employer.

Immigrant Status (Permanent Resident or Green Card Holder)

An *immigrant* is a foreign-born person who has been sponsored by a qualifying family member or employer, and who has approval to reside permanently in the United States as a lawful permanent resident. This person holds a Resident Alien Card, known often as a *green card*.

Nonimmigrant

A *nonimmigrant* is an alien who seeks entry into the United States or who has already been admitted for a specific purpose for a temporary period of time. These temporary periods can range from a few days to many years. Nonimmigrants come to the United States for many different purposes, including temporary work, longer-term work, study, travel, training, or to participate in athletic, cultural, or performance events.

For a nonimmigrant alien to travel to the United States and to apply for admission at a U.S. port of entry, he or she must usually have an entry visa, issued to him or her abroad by a U.S. consulate for the category of activity in which the nonimmigrant wishes to engage. This entry visa allows the individual to travel to a U.S. port of entry and apply for admission, within the dates stated on the entry visa. According to the U.S. Citizenship and Immigration Services (USCIS), possession of a current, valid visa does not guarantee admission into the United States. At the port of entry, USCIS will inspect the visa and question the alien to determine whether he or she shall be admitted to the United States and for how long. Note that the Form I-94 and Form I-94W are no longer issued to an individual on admittance to the United States. Customs Border Protection (CBP) uses an automatic electronic system to gather travel records for air and sea travelers (only land travelers need a paper form I-94). A CBP officer will stamp travel documents upon arrival in the United States for each arriving non-immigrant traveler. Those who need to prove their legal-visitor status—to employers, schools/universities, or government agencies—can access their CBP arrival/departure record information online. While an entry visa is necessary to travel to and apply for admission into the United States within the time period authorized by the visa, the entry visa alone does not provide any immigration status or employment authorization. It also does not control the period of time the alien is authorized to remain in the United States. It is the CBP officer who controls the duration of the alien's stay in the United States and lists the classification under which the alien is admitted (all stamped on the travel document at the point of entry into the U.S.). The electronic arrival/departure record can be obtained at www.cbp.gov/I94 if at any time the nonimmigrant requires a paper version.

Once within the United States, many nonimmigrant aliens can extend their nonimmigrant stay under the same classification or change to a different nonimmigrant status (apart from those on the Visa Waiver Program, as discussed later). However, an alien can change or extend status only if he or she is currently in valid nonimmigrant status. If the alien violates his or her admission terms—such as by overstaying his or her visa before applying for an extension—the application for extension or change will be denied. Form I-797, Notice of Action, provides the alien approval to extend his or her stay and, if applicable, to change status.

Visa Waiver Program

Some visitors to the United States are exempt from the entry visa requirement for a short period of time. Aliens from certain countries with low overstay rates may travel to the United States for business or pleasure trips for *up to 90 days* without a visa stamp. This *Visa Waiver Program* (VWP) currently applies to aliens from Andorra, Australia, Austria, Belgium, Brunei, Chili, Czech Republic,

Denmark, Estonia, Finland, France, Germany, Greece, Hungary, Iceland, Ireland, Italy, Japan, Korea (Republic of), Latvia, Liechtenstein, Lithuania, Luxembourg, Malta, Monaco, Netherlands, New Zealand, Norway, Portugal, San Marino, Singapore, Slovakia, Slovenia, Spain, Sweden, Switzerland, Taiwan, and the United Kingdom. As of 2009, valid Electronic System for Travel Authorization (ESTA) approval is required for all VWP travel to the United States. This is an automated system used to determine the eligibility of visitors to travel to the United States under the VWP but does not guarantee whether a traveler will be admitted to the United States upon arrival. It collects biographic information and answers VWP eligibility questions. Also, ESTA applications may be submitted at any time prior to travel and are generally valid for up to two years. A small fee applies. It should be noted that as of April 1, 2016, each traveler must have an e-Passport (enhanced secure passport with an embedded electronic chip inside) to use the VWP.

However, there are restrictions on the type of employment-related activities allowed. Meetings and conferences in relation to the alien's profession, line of business, or employer in his or her home country are generally acceptable, but gainful employment is not. Therefore, this program is not suitable for international household employees hoping to work in the United States.

Many foreigners on the VWP wish to extend their stay or change status. This cannot be done. A person entering the United States under the VWP cannot request an extension of the original allowed period of stay (although this practice is allowed to those holding regular visas). Additionally, a person who entered the United States under the VWP may not request a change of immigration status while in the country (e.g., one is unable to change status from tourist to student, or from tourist to worker).

Employment Authorization Document

An Employment Authorization Document (EAD, and sometimes called a work permit) allows an employee, regardless of citizenship or national origin, to be allowed to work in the United States. This is different from a green card (permanent resident or immigrant), and the employee needs to apply for it to work officially in the United States. An employee does not need the EAD if he or she is a U.S citizen or a green card holder (otherwise known as a permanent resident). The EAD is proof that an employee is allowed to work in the United States and is generally only valid for one year.

USCIS gives, renews, and replaces these permits to particular categories of nonimmigrants, including asylees and asylum seekers, refugees, some students, applicants adjusting to permanent residents, those applying for temporary protected status, fiancées of American citizens, and dependents of foreign government officials. See USCIS Form 1-765 (Application for Employment Authorization) available at www.uscis.gov/files/form/i-765.pdf.

The authorization can be renewed annually, although there is no guarantee that it will always be renewed.

It is very important to check the date on the document, especially if it is due for renewal. If this is the case, the employee should be able to furnish a letter from the USCIS saying that the renewal has been approved and a new card will be issued. An employee with an EAD may not be able to leave the United States unless he or she is willing to risk losing employment eligibility.

FACTS AND FIGURES

SOME EXAMPLES OF NONIMMIGRANT VISA TYPES

J – Au pair (exchange visitor)

B-1 – Business visitor

B-1 – Domestic employee or nanny—must be accompanying a foreign national employer

J – Exchange visitor

Q – International cultural exchange visitor

H-1B – Specialty occupations in fields requiring highly specialized knowledge

F, M – Student: academic, vocational

H-2A – Temporary agricultural worker

H-2B – Temporary worker performing other services or labor of a temporary or seasonal nature

B-2 – Tourism, vacation, pleasure visitor

H-3 – Training in a program not primarily for employment

V – Nonimmigrant visa for spouse and children of a Lawful Permanent Resident (LPR)

K – Nonimmigrant visa for U.S. citizen fiancé(e) and spouse for immigration related purposes.

Note: *By statute, citizens of Canada are exempt from the entry visa requirement into the United States for tourist and non-paid business events. If they want to enter on a work or other nonimmigrant status, they may do so. Citizens of Mexico may obtain border-crossing cards instead of visitor visas. Mexicans seeking entry in other than visitor status must obtain visa stamps at a U.S. consulate in Mexico.*

Q & A

Q. I have a nanny candidate who is foreign and here on a H-4 visa. Is she eligible to work in the United States?

A. Maybe. As of May 26, 2015, the Department of Homeland Security (DHS) extended eligibility for employment authorization to certain H-4 dependent spouses of H-1B nonimmigrants who are seeking employment-based lawful permanent resident (LPR) status. DHS amended the regulations to allow these H-4 dependent spouses to accept employment in the United States. Not all H-4 visa holders may be eligible, so be sure to check if your particular nanny candidate meets requirements and has filed a Form I-765, Application for Employment Authorization.

Sponsoring Foreign Workers for Temporary Employment

There are very few nonimmigrant visa categories that allow nonimmigrants to engage in household employment, and these visa categories are very restrictive. The most common categories are A-3, B-1, G-5, H-2B, and J-1.

A-3, B-1 and G-5—Personal Employees to Foreign Diplomats, Government Officials, and Temporary Business Visitors

Personal or domestic servants who are accompanying or following an employer to the United States may be eligible for B-1 visas. This category of domestic employees includes, but is not limited to, cooks, butlers, chauffeurs, housemaids, valets, footmen, nannies, au pairs, mothers' helpers, gardeners, and paid companions.

Those accompanying or following to join an employer who is a foreign diplomat or government official may be eligible for an A-3 or G-5 visa, depending on the employer's visa status. Generally, G visas are given to individuals employed directly by an international organization, or representing a foreign government to international organizations. A visas are given to diplomats representing a foreign government traveling to the United States on official activities for that government.

Personal employees, attendants, domestic workers, or servants of individuals who hold a valid G-1 through G-4, or NATO-1 through NATO-6 visa, may be issued a G-5 or a NATO-7 visa, if they meet the requirements and have a valid employment contract that they keep with them, along with their passport. This type of visa is specific to staff sponsored by the World Bank, IMF, United Nations, and other nongovernmental organizations. There are a variety of suitable domestic positions for a G-5 holder, including cook, butler, valet, maid, housekeeper, governess, janitor, launderer, caretaker, handyman, gardener, groom, chauffeur, babysitter, or companion to the aged or infirm.

An applicant is required to be interviewed at the embassy or consulate prior to receiving the visa. Proof that the applicant will receive a fair wage, sufficient to financially support him- or herself, comparable to that being offered in the area of employment in the United States is required. In addition, the applicant needs to demonstrate that he or she will perform the contracted employment duties as set out in a signed employment contract from the employer. Domestic employees should understand that their contracts provide working arrangements that the employer is expected to respect according to law. Employers and employees should review the Nonimmigrant Rights, Protections and Resources pamphlet provided by the U.S. Department of State. (See www.travel.state.gov/content/visas/en/general/rights-protections-temporary-workers.html)

The employer must pay the domestic's initial travel expenses to the United States, and subsequently, upon termination, travel back to the employee's country of normal residence. In addition, the employer must demonstrate that he or she will have sufficient funds to provide a fair wage and working conditions, as reflected in the contract.

The G-5 holder can generally stay in the United States for a period of up to three years. After that he or she has to apply for an extension of stay with an increment of two years.

H-2B—Nonagricultural Temporary Worker

The H-2B category allows a foreigner to work for a period of up to one year in a temporary job. *Temporary* means a job that is seasonal, a one-time occurrence, peak load or intermittent need employment. The job will expire by its own terms within a year. The job itself must be temporary—it cannot be a permanent job that is temporarily vacant. An employer seeking an H-2B worker must advertise the position in accordance with Department of Labor requirements to ensure that there are no qualified U.S. workers for the position.

The H-2B visa is issued for a year or less. If an alien seeks to continue the same position without interruption, the visa can in theory be extended for up to three years, but the employer must prove each year that the position continues to be temporary. This is a heavy burden. The H-2B visa is often used for seasonal employment, such as landscape workers, summer restaurant help, or summer nannies. The H-2B visa can also be used for child care, where the child care requirement will terminate when the child goes to school. Some families have also sponsored senior care assistance, seeking to keep their elderly parents at home a little longer before a nursing home is unavoidable.

Only 66,000 H-2B visas can be issued each year to new H-2B work-ers—33,000 issued in each half of the government's fiscal year, and employ-ers frequently find themselves unable to bring in workers on a timely basis because of cap issues. Returning workers—that is, seasonal workers who have held H-2B visas within the previous three years, but who have returned home at the end of their temporary employment—are not subject to the cap.

J-1—Exchange Visitor

The J-1 visa is for cultural and educational exchange visitors and covers a vari-ety of different visa types intended to create exchange opportunities for for-eigners, like the au pair program. The J programs are administered by entities approved by the U.S. Department of State and include several different visa types interesting to household employers. For example, there is a program that permits families to bring a foreign au pair to the United States for up to one year (with the option to extend to up to two years) to help with child care. There are rules in place on how many hours the au pair can work each day, and other conditions of employment. For more information, see www.j1visa. state.gov/programs/au-pair.

There are also summer work-travel programs for foreign college stu-dents. This program and the program used for training and or internship cannot be used for child care or eldercare work. On entering the United States, J-1 visa holders should apply for their own Social Security num-ber, and employers must report all tax withholdings using that number. Household employers interested in such visas should contact one of the State Department-designated sponsors authorized by the Department of State to administer such programs.

FACTS AND FIGURES
THE LOWDOWN ON AU PAIRS

An au pair is a young foreign person (usually between ages 18–26) who lives with an American family for a full year. The au pair needs to commit to the position for one year but may extend for another year if necessary. The au pair requires a J-1 visa to come into the United

States and is not to work more than ten hours a day or 45 hours per week. Families wishing to hire an au pair must work with a designated au pair agency, which can be found on the Department of State's website at www.j1visa.state.gov. Au pair agencies (many of which are online) match an au pair to the family; organize the visa and flights; screen the au pair; and even may provide au pair orientation, CPR courses, health and travel insurance, and driving training. The cost of hiring an au pair depends on many factors: where the au pair is flying from, how much experience he or she has, the duties the au pair will perform, his or her qualifications, and so on. Just like any other hire, you need to determine the right wage and take into consideration the cost of the au pair living with you.

Bear in mind that au pairs are considered to be household employees. Au pairs are generally exempt from Social Security and Medicare taxes because of their status as a J-1 nonimmigrant and as a nonresident alien, but their income is considered wages and could have an income tax liability and they are therefore required to file U.S individual income tax forms.

A payroll and tax company, like GTM Payroll Services Inc., can help provide relevant information for families who hire an au pair to help them file their employment taxes accurately.

There are very specific employer requirements for hosting an au pair in your home for host families:

- pay up to $500 toward the cost of the au pair's required academic course work
- provide an appropriate suitable private room and three meals a day for the au pair
- be U.S. citizens or legal permanent residents fluent in spoken English
- pay a weekly minimum stipend based on the program option selected
- give the au pair one complete weekend off each month (Friday evening to Monday morning)

- facilitate the care provider's requirement to enroll in and attend an accredited post-secondary institution to fulfill her/his Educational Component requirement

- provide a minimum of two weeks paid vacation for each 12 month exchange term (prorated for extension periods of six or nine months), in addition to regular weekly/monthly time off

- include the au pair whenever possible in family meals, outings, holidays, and other events

- host families and au pairs must sign an agreement detailing the au pair's obligation to provide child care prior to the au pair's placement in the host family's home

Source: http://j1visa.state.gov/programs/au-pair#hostsemployers

FACTS AND FIGURES

TEMPORARY NONIMMIGRANT WORKERS' RIGHTS

1. To be paid fairly.

   - To be paid for all work done.

   - To be paid at or above the federal legal minimum wage or applicable state minimum wage—whichever is higher, in the same manner as a U.S. worker.

   - To be entitled to overtime pay (usually one and a half times the amount of their hourly wage for any hours worked over 40 hours per week).

   - Deductions must be clearly identified on the paycheck and may not reduce compensation below the legally required wage rate.

2. To be free from discrimination.

3. To be free from sexual harassment and sexual exploitation.

4. To have a healthy and safe workplace.

5. To request help from union, immigrant, and labor rights groups.

6. To leave an abusive employment situation.

Amended from Source: Know Your Rights Pamphlet, 2016, U.S. Department of State, Bureau of Consular Affairs. Note: this pamphlet should be provided to anyone on an A-3, G-5, H, J, NATO-7, or B-1 domestic worker nonimmigrant visa at their visa interview from a consular officer. Source: https://travel.state.gov/content/dam/visas/LegalRightsandProtections/Wilberforce%20Pamphlet_June2016.pdf

Sponsoring Foreign Workers for Permanent Employment

Under Sections 203 and 204 of the INA, employers may petition the federal government for approval to hire a foreign worker to work permanently in the United States. However, this is very difficult to do. The employer must engage in a defined recruitment process to establish that there are no qualified U.S. workers to take the position. Most categories require an employer to get a labor certification and then file a Form I-140, *Immigrant Petition for Alien Worker*, which is a very complex process. The best advice is to consult an experienced immigration lawyer to see if there is a chance that this process would be successful in a particular situation. The petition, filed with the USCIS, seeks to have the foreign worker approved for a visa in one of the categories for which an immigrant visa (green card) can be issued. This can take from nine months to two years, depending on USCIS backlogs at any point in time.

The final step is an application by the foreign worker to have the green card actually issued to him or her. At this point, the process breaks down. There are usually more applicants for green cards than there are green cards available, and long waiting lists can exist, particularly for the visa categories with lower education and experience requirements. U.S. immigration policy limits the yearly amount of green cards granted to citizens of a specific country. Some countries like India, China, Mexico, and the Philippines have high-volume immigration and so citizens of those countries will most likely endure the worst waiting periods for green cards. Waiting periods for professional and skilled workers can be years, and waiting periods for unskilled workers are the longest. This is not currently a realistic option for most household employers.

Consequences of Hiring an Unauthorized Alien

Under the *Immigration Reform and Control Act of 1986* (IRCA), employers may hire only persons who may legally work in the United States—U.S. citizens, legal permanent residents, asylees, refugees, and other aliens authorized to work in the United States. Employers who knowingly employ an unauthorized alien in the United States can be ordered to cease and desist, and they can be fined a civil penalty for failing to comply with Form I-9. Employers who commit a *first* offense of hiring a single employee or two, knowing that the person is not authorized to work in the United States, can face a fine of up to $3,200 per worker.

The U.S. Citizenship and Immigration Services' goal is compliance, not penalization of unknowing employers. Employers who engage in a *pattern and practice of employing unauthorized aliens* can also incur criminal violations, as issued by the U.S. Department of Homeland Security, that can result in full penalties and additional fines of up to $3,000 per unauthorized employee and potential jail time of up to six months. Subsequent offenses can receive a fine of up to $16,000 for each unauthorized alien.

Employers must verify the identity and employment eligibility of anyone to be hired through completion of Form I-9 (*Employment Eligibility Verification*). Each completed Form I-9 must be kept on file for at least three years, or one year after employment ends, whichever is longer. Employers who fail to properly complete, retain, and present Form I-9 for inspection (as required by federal law) may incur civil penalties of up to $1,100 per form.

Employees who knowingly use fraudulent documents, identity documents issued to other people, or other false materials to meet the employment eligibility verification requirements in Form I-9 may also face fines and potential imprisonment.

Hiring a Noncitizen Checklist

- Never hire an unauthorized alien to work within the home.

- Confirm household employee's employment eligibility status by completing Form I-9 and checking work authorization documents.

- Verify Social Security number and its validity for employment.

- Verify valid driver's license.

- Know and abide by federal, state, and local employment and labor laws.

- Know thoroughly the noncitizen's visa or green card status and all the conditions related to it.

- Be sure that employees meet the USCIS's requirements for their status.

- Consult with an immigration attorney if there are any specific issues that need to be attended to.

- Be aware of discrimination issues related to nationality and immigration status.

- Thoroughly check references and work and education history with foreign contacts.

- Treat the noncitizen authorized for U.S. employment professionally, and as you would a U.S. citizen.

- Ensure that the hire is the best you can find, and use the tips and checklist in Chapter 2 to help you.

4

Finding Help on Your Own

Hiring household employees is not easy. There is much to know and much to do. Personal contacts, professional recommendations, newspaper advertisements, social media networks, and the internet are all available sources that help families find their nanny or other type of household help on their own. But first, before taking any steps to hire someone to work in your home and care for your loved ones, be prepared. Know what you are getting into and budget your time and money accordingly.

Using Your Personal Network to Find Household Help

Just as with any new endeavor, many people rely on their personal contacts—friends and professionals—to learn the best ways to go about hiring household help. As in the corporate world, some quality hires result from personal recommendations and word of mouth. Reaching out to your personal network of contacts is natural—you know and trust the people in your network, and you can rely on their input. Along with family, friends, and neighbors, you may wish to access your professional contacts as well. When looking for a nanny, you may ask your nearby day care provider or fellow parent in the parent-teacher association for a recommendation; when looking for a senior care provider, your doctor or other medical professional may be a key contact; and when hiring a gardener, your local nursery staff may advise. An additional resource often overlooked is a local religious official who knows his or her locality in depth and may be of great assistance.

In recent years, the network of contacts recommended by word of mouth has grown to include an online community of help. This is increasingly important for any business (many professionals maintain their business contacts all around the world via social networking sites such as LinkedIn, Facebook, etc.) and it is no different in household employment. For instance, a nanny in Arlington, Massachusetts, was hired for her present household via an online chat room. Her previous employer was losing her position as her company downsized and mentioned on an online mothers' support group that her nanny would need to seek other work. The nanny was soon hired by a fellow group member.

As more and more social networks develop online, families are finding child care and household help from online neighborhood groups, community networks, school parent pages, and other sources. Bear in mind that a nanny that works well for one family might not fit your needs as perfectly; and therefore this chapter has many useful recommendations to help you find the right help.

Hiring household help is so important that you will want to investigate every available avenue. Personal contacts and their experiences will probably unveil candidates with the best recommendations. A family's trust in its own network of friends and family brings added value and helps begin a good working relationship with the employee by having something in common with him or her from the start.

Posting a Job Advertisement

For those who want to hire on their own, the first step is, of course, posting a job ad in the newspaper classifieds, on the community bulletin board, or on various job websites. This begins with writing out all your needs and wants for your nanny or other household help to form a comprehensive job description (see Chapter 2). Be as specific as possible and really think about what the job will entail. List your requirements: previous experience, education, a current and valid driver's license, fluency in English (or other languages), work schedule, and live-in or live-out help. As noted in this handbook, the job description not only starts the job search; it also helps tremendously in developing the work agreement (see Chapter 6). With a comprehensive job description prepared, a job advertisement can easily be created for posting in different media and/or provided to an agency. In addition, a specific job ad will help you manage your time by culling out the candidates who do not meet or cannot perform the listed requirements, and attracting the type of candidates you are ultimately seeking.

Job Ad Elements:

- job title

- job location

- work hours, including start and end times (if nonstandard hours will be required at times, include the need for flexibility in the ad)

- expected length of position (e.g., three months, one year, two years)

- specific job duties (e.g., if you want your nanny to prepare meals for the children while providing child care, you need to make that clear; if you need your nanny to wash the child's clothing, list it)—the candidate should know by reading the job ad the general scope of his or her daily job activities

- desired experience (e.g., three years as a nanny, years as a day care professional)

- desired education and/or training (e.g., associate's degree in early childhood development, etc.)

- mandatory skills (must-haves)

- additional talents that may be helpful but not required

- salary range and benefits offered

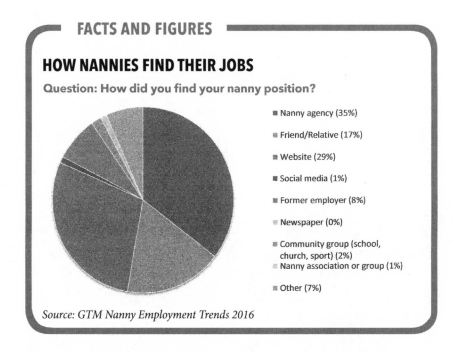

FACTS AND FIGURES

HOW NANNIES FIND THEIR JOBS

Question: How did you find your nanny position?

- Nanny agency (35%)
- Friend/Relative (17%)
- Website (29%)
- Social media (1%)
- Former employer (8%)
- Newspaper (0%)
- Community group (school, church, sport) (2%)
- Nanny association or group (1%)
- Other (7%)

Source: GTM Nanny Employment Trends 2016

Using the Internet to Find Household Help

The internet has changed our lives in so many ways—even with hiring someone to help in our home. Using the internet to help hire a nanny or other type of household help may make sense to many families looking for in-home child care. The handy, do-it-yourself attitude and the assumption that using the internet will save money are the main reasons people try to hire online.

Despite its convenience and low-cost fees, hiring on the internet comes with risks. There are stories in the press of dangerous hires from the internet and neglected children. However, if done diligently, with thorough research, and using a reputable site, many families can find good help this way. The best policy is to proceed with caution, not hire in a hurry, and do your homework as an employer. This handbook can guide you.

Trade-offs

No doubt, many families like the feeling of being in charge that using the internet for their nanny search provides—as well as automatic matching any time of day and night, instant results with no intermediary, and no wait to find a nanny match. Using a website rather than an agency comes with trade-offs, though. Without an agency, a family may experience a more streamlined process, but one that also forgoes experienced agency staff and bypasses the agency's screening and qualification of its candidates, as well as its firsthand and in-depth knowledge of the hiring process.

It should be noted that there is a broad range of quality among sites that advertise that they hire household help. Online hiring sites run the gamut of extremely sophisticated, well-known sites with robust technology, many satisfied users, and support materials to help and educate the employer in how to be successful; to the other extreme, where the site is little more than an online bulletin board where anyone can sign up and post information with no verification or qualification. By their nature, many websites are often basic and hold unverified information on candidates; therefore, they leave the bulk of work of hiring to the employer. The employer must be prepared to invest more time and money on his or her end when hiring—he or she must prepare the job description, the work agreement, do the interviewing, check backgrounds, and vet the candidates. This can take up more time than a family has budgeted for and should be considered carefully before embarking on an online search for candidates. Plus, with internet hires, the list of candidates can seem endless, with hundreds of candidates to choose from. The employer must spend a lot of time selecting the best from a large candidate pool. So, although an online match may be easy—in fact, just a few clicks on the computer keyboard—finding the perfect match will require quite a bit of extra effort. The following worksheet is aimed to help you figure out just how much time you may need to invest if you hire a nanny on your own and what the value of your time to do so might be.

FIGURING OUT THE REAL COST OF HIRING HOUSEHOLD HELP ON YOUR OWN WORKSHEET

Do-It-Yourself Hiring Task	COLUMN A: Hours it would take (suggested hours)	COLUMN B: Value of your time, per hour	Total cost of your time, multiplied by number of hours to complete task (column A × column B)
Time invested in preparing job description and advertisement.	_____ hours (e.g., 3 hours)	$_____ per hour	$_____
Time taken to perform background checks.	_____ hours (e.g., 10 hours)	$_____ per hour	$_____
Time to select 10 candidates for phone interview.	_____ hours (e.g., 2 hours)	$_____ per hour	$_____
Time to prepare interview questions.	_____ hours (e.g., 2 hours)	$_____ per hour	$_____
Time to schedule and phone interview best candidates.	_____ hours (e.g. 5–10 hours)	$_____ per hour	$_____
Time to arrange and conduct home interviews of 3 most desirable candidates.	_____ hours (e.g., 5–10 hours)	$_____ per hour	$_____

Time to schedule and phone previous employment and educational references.	_____ hours (e.g., 3 hours)	$_____ per hour	$_____
Time taken to make job offer and prepare rejection letters for unsuccessful candidates.	_____ hours (e.g. 1 hour)	$_____ per hour	$_____
Time to prepare your work agreement.	_____ hours (e.g. 5 hours)	$_____ per hour	$_____
Time to research salary, tax, insurance compliance information.	_____ hours (e.g. 5 hours)	$_____ per hour	$_____
Time to research employment laws relevant to location and type of work.	_____ hours (e.g. 3 hours)	$_____ per hour	$_____
Time to investigate human resources information and personnel policies.	_____ hours (e.g. 2 hours)	$_____ per hour	$_____
Time to research all necessary legal, tax, insurance, and payroll forms for hire.	_____ hours (e.g. 5 hours)	$_____ per hour	$_____
TOTAL	_____ hours (e.g. 61 hours)	$_____ per hour	$_____

Note: To calculate the value of a stay-at-home spouse when using this worksheet, Salary. com estimates that a stay-at-home parent with two preschool children has a national median salary of $143,102 per year in 2016 (calculated from $48,509 base salary assuming 40 hours per week and $94,593 overtime assuming an extra 52 hours per week). Divided by 52 weeks, divided by 40 hours per week, this is approximately an average of $69 per hour. (See www.salary.com/2016-mothers-day-infographics/)

FACTS AND FIGURES

HOW EMPLOYERS FIND THEIR NANNIES

Question: How did you find your current nanny?

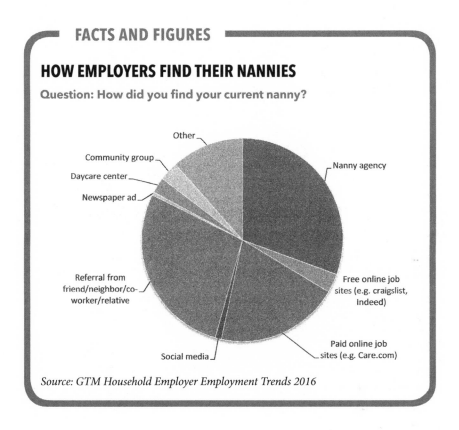

Source: GTM Household Employer Employment Trends 2016

Risky Business

The *Wall Street Journal* (2008) reported that the IRS saw a 10 percent drop in household employment tax filing with the increase in internet hiring. Now hiring a nanny or other home help online is even more popular that it was then. According to the U.S. Labor Department, the blame for a reduction in household employment tax filing is because of the internet—household employers using hiring websites to save on hiring costs seem to want to extend their savings by illegally avoiding mandatory employment taxes. Furthermore, IRS estimates that employers misclassify millions of workers as independent contractors instead of employees. The misclassifications allow employers to avoid paying significant amounts in employment taxes.

This is risky business. Misclassifying workers subjects employers to severe penalties and interest—and the federal and state governments are aggressively targeting employers to uncover misclassification. Employers may be held personally liable for all income and FICA taxes that the employer willingly either failed to withhold from employee wages or failed to pay to the IRS and state tax agencies. Even if an employer avoids the 100 percent penalty because it was not willingly done, the employer may still face smaller penalties for misclassifying employees.

If you decide to hire independently, you need to be extremely careful to remain legal and tax compliant. Whether you hire a nanny on the internet, through your personal contacts, from a newspaper, or via an employment agency does not matter—what is important is that the employee is paid legally (see Chapter 10). Some websites contain good information on tax compliance and other human resources for household employees. Some do not. It is best to thoroughly research these issues before you hire your nanny. This handbook aims to help with all these matters.

Researching Options and Finding the Right Site

It is wise to do your homework on online sites that match families and nannies and learn the different options offered before registering with any website. Today, there are many websites and apps that use custom-made online databases that instantly match families with available nannies, as well as nannies looking for families. But before using any website or app, ask friends, relatives, day care centers, other nannies, neighbors, and other families about their recommendations and where it is best to begin your search. Once you have made a list of potential sites, check out reviews from articles or business bureaus about them. Even though you cannot see the people behind the website or app, you want to gain some trust in it. Look for favorable testimonials, reviews, and posts of good experiences—preferably those not on the sites themselves, but from news articles and reputable parent blogs or networks.

What to Look for in an Online Hiring Site or App

- Good reviews from the press—the site or app should be well-known.
- Favorable testimonials from customers.
- Experience—has been in business for more than five years.

- User base—how many families and nannies are registered (overall since it started and in the current year).

- Sophisticated technology—if you don't get a good result through a quick search on your ZIP code, abandon the site.

- User-friendly site—is the website easy to use and is it simple to find what you are looking for?

- Number of available screenings, and whether screenings are free or paid for.

- Fees—are these comparable to other sites? Do they suit your budget? Are there any hidden extras?

- Free background and/or reference check and what this entails.

- Free advice—interview questions, nanny fees, sample contracts, information on nanny taxes.

- Contact—is it easy to contact a "real person" via the customer support email or phone line?

- Good guarantee—What does it provide if the hire doesn't work out? Will the site give you another month's membership for free? Will it refund?

- Human resources advice—tips on working with your nanny, employment benefits, and so on.

- Secure technology that protects online payment.

After researching several popular sites, select which one(s) you think will be best to work with. But, even then, some more work must be done. First, see if you can preview a sample pool of candidates or perhaps join via a trial membership for a limited time.

Many sites allow you to search candidates for free just by entering your ZIP code, which allows an employer to determine the quantity of the database entries and how well it matches a family with a candidate. You can learn about the availability of nannies in your area and about the candidates through their profiles. Plus, many sites offer refined searches once you register with them. This is valuable for those looking to match specific requirements, such as a special needs nanny, a newborn nanny, a nanny who can speak a foreign language, a nanny who has experience with multiples, etc.

CASE STUDY

● ●

REX HABERMAN, MD
HOUSEHOLD EMPLOYER
ST. PAUL, MN

Dr. Rex Haberman and his wife, a physician's assistant, hired a nanny through an agency in the past, and now with four children (two of whom need a nanny) looked to the internet to hire their present nanny. "At first we used an agency to find a nanny. She went on to graduate school. We thought that the agency charged quite a bit, so we looked online for alternatives," Haberman said. "You're spending a lot of money for that service…So, I googled nannies and Nannies4hire came up."

Through the website, Haberman was able to search by ZIP code to locate potential nannies in his area of St. Paul, Minnesota, and then carefully read through the candidates' bios to decide who he wanted to interview for the new nanny position. The bios included information on the candidates' education, which was an important consideration for him. In addition, the website allowed him to post a job ad describing what the family was seeking. Of the nearly 30 online profiles he selected as potential nannies, he narrowed his selection down to ten people and then performed phone interviews. He further narrowed his selections, interviewing five candidates in his home with his children present to ensure that they liked the candidate. "Your kids know [who will be good]," he added. He then conducted background checks, unless the reference checks were so stellar that he felt comfortable proceeding without one.

To get a feel for how the nanny works, he included in the interview several scenarios and asked how the nanny will perform in them, such as the following: "You are changing the baby on the changing table and note that the diaper box is empty but there is a new box five feet away. What do you do? You are bathing the baby and the doorbell rings, what do you do?"

Despite the selection process, Haberman said his family went through three nannies to find the right one: the first had a transportation problem and the second missed several workdays. The third actually contacted the family through the ad Haberman placed on the website. She has now been with the Haberman household for nearly three years.

"The nanny we hired had a college degree in early childhood education, interviewed professionally and presented herself well, answered questions with well thought out responses, and had good references including from a college day care," said Haberman. "So, we hired her in a second...We went with what we felt was right...Now she is a part of the family."

According to Haberman, household employers must keep looking until they find the right person. "The child care provider is an extension of the parent...You have two parents and then an assistant parent...," he said. "She is in your home eight to fourteen hours a day. You had better like her...If you don't like her, don't keep her."

Another key component to hiring, Haberman said, is to visit unannounced during the first workday and see how all is going. "With our present nanny, I stopped home and she was conducting a reading class. It was the cutest thing I've ever seen."

Since the Haberman household is an exceptionally busy one, along with a full-time nanny, the family employed a part-time nanny, also hired through Nannies4hire. Now that the Haberman children are older, the part-time nanny is needed as a backup.

Haberman and his wife work hard to ensure that the employment works for the family, as well as the nanny. First, the Habermans pay a good wage, and since both Habermans have very busy work schedules and are occasionally away on business, the nanny is paid time and a half for every hour she puts in over her standard 40-hour workweek.

In addition, the Habermans assist her with college loans. "She's struggling [with college costs]," he noted. "Her goal is to own a preschool. So, we offered to help her with her loans." The Habermans also offer both nannies health insurance, which covers 80 percent of each nanny's medical costs.

"Our offering help with student loans and health insurance is much more valuable for a nanny than for us paying an agency to employ her," noted Haberman. Altogether, Haberman estimated that he and his wife spend $50,000 per year for child care, but noted that others offering fewer benefits could probably manage it for $30,000 per year.

According to Haberman, there is always a bit of uneasiness when the nanny first enters the home, but it is quickly erased once the nanny has been in the household for a while. "It's all a matter of communication and being comfortable with each other," he said. "As a new parent and new household employer, you have a lot of fear…Your child is the most precious thing ever…and you want to do it right."

> Dr. Haberman and his family do a fantastic job of making their nanny as comfortable in her job as possible—even providing assistance with college costs, a set 40-hour workweek, time and a half for overtime, and also providing health insurance. Dr. Haberman's interviewing method of stating scenarios and hearing how the nanny would respond is a good way to judge how she works and whether her responses agree with the Habermans's child-rearing philosophy. Also, stopping home for a surprise visit during the first few workdays is a good way to ensure that the nanny is performing as expected.
>
> —Guy

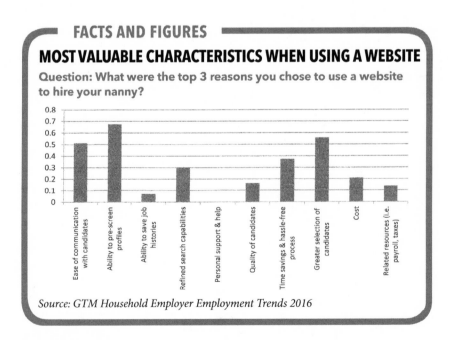

FACTS AND FIGURES

MOST VALUABLE CHARACTERISTICS WHEN USING A WEBSITE

Question: What were the top 3 reasons you chose to use a website to hire your nanny?

Source: GTM Household Employer Employment Trends 2016

Online Classified Ads

Many people are familiar with online classified ad sites, such as Craigslist. These are low cost, easy to use, and work much like posting an ad on a college bulletin board or in the local newspaper. These sites also advertise local nannies and families looking for nannies—and while these sites may be good resources for many things, there are two main drawbacks pertaining to nannies and other household help: time and safety.

Families looking for nannies or other household help via classified ads can expect to find it to be very time consuming. Just as with a newspaper classified ad, the burden is fully on the seeker to do all the work—all the contacting, interviewing, checking and vetting, and so on.

Safety is another key issue. Those advertising on these sites have paid to place an ad. There is no other criteria—and they could be anyone. In addition, when using internet classified ads, anyone can view these ads and access your information. It is never wise to give out personal data (e.g., name, telephone number, address, email address) in a public area. These ad sites are not protected by passwords and are unsupervised for the most part. In contrast, traditional nanny-hiring agencies and most reputable online hiring sites do not allow the general public to see your information. It is always better to use an experienced and reliable website with a good reputation than a listing or online classified ad site—especially if you are hiring for the first time.

There have been many news articles on the safety issues of hiring someone using a site like Craigslist. Although the site, and many articles, warn users of criminal misuse and instead encourage those who find jobs on the site to meet in a public place, many users do not heed the warning. There have been cases where criminals have posed as babysitters. Obviously, care should be used if posting an online classified ad, just as you would be vigilant about the candidates who contacted you about a newspaper ad or from a bulletin board. With your family's care, no amount of precaution can be considered too much.

The Online Hiring Process

The process involved in using an online site is easy and simple.

1. You use an initial (often free) locator tool that matches your ZIP code to the online database. Usually the closest candidate is at the top of the list.

2. You may also sometimes register for free and do a slightly more advanced search on the candidates. (Most sites ask you to join for advanced and refined searches.)

3. You can then join (paying a membership fee—usually for one month, three months, six months, or a year) and post a job description online under your name, whereby potential interested candidates registered with the site can contact you. You will need to describe your requirements, such as experience, expected salary, education, live-in or live-out nanny, hours, and job duties. The average fee for a three-month or 90-day membership is between $40–$120, depending on what services are bundled with the search tool (background checks are extra on some sites and included on others).

4. There should be at least five to ten good candidates local to you on the search list. Normally the search produces much more (in excess of 20, and sometimes more than a 100). The candidates will be displayed according to their profiles: includes a photo, basic particulars like age and location and citizenship, experience, background and skills, employment history, education, and availability. If you have joined the site, there is often an advanced search feature that allows you to further narrow your search to include candidates who, for example, have CPR training or experience with special needs children or multiples.

5. You may then sort your top picks into favorites.

6. If you have joined the site as a member, the caregiver candidates' contact details will be available to you to contact for an initial interview by the site's own internal messaging system, email, or phone.

7. You will usually be offered to background check your candidates. This is absolutely essential and different sites have different options, ranging from free initial checks to full-on hiring of private investigators. (See the next section for more details.)

8. You will end up with a list of a few key candidates who meet your requirements and who you have background and reference checked. These are the ones you will phone interview or meet in person. Usually, you email them directly from the website to arrange a time to call.

FACTS AND FIGURES

TIPS FOR CONTACTING A CANDIDATE ONLINE

- Always email using the website contact email first.
- Be specific in the subject line of the email to show why you are contacting and to stand out from other messages and spam.
- Be professional and format the email as you would a letter (using "Dear" and "Yours sincerely").
- Include which website you found the nanny on (many nannies are registered with a few at the same time).
- Keep the email clear and concise—be professional.
- Outline a specific time you can call, but give only one other alternative time.
- Make sure they know the phone interview could take up to 30 minutes and they should allow time for that.
- Thank them for their time.

Expert Advice

"No matter how you find your nanny—online or via more traditional means like a newspaper ad or local bulletin board—the bottom line is that you, the parent, still have the ultimate hiring decision. If you opt not to use an agency, you must perform due diligence by checking the references, history, and background of the candidate…and it's a lot of work. Online, it is very easy for people to misrepresent themselves. You must know who is going to be caring for your kids. We live in a fast-food type of society where we want instant gratification, but when using the internet people forget they are [still] dealing with human nature. You really do get what you pay for: that is why I recommend paying the professionals who know what they are doing. But, regardless of how you hire your nanny, it is important to screen thoroughly and correctly."

—Michelle LaRowe
Parenting author, and nanny expert
Cape Cod, MA

FACTS AND FIGURES

IMPORTANT WEBSITE FEATURES FOR HOUSEHOLD EMPLOYERS

Question: How important were the following when deciding to use a website to find your nanny?

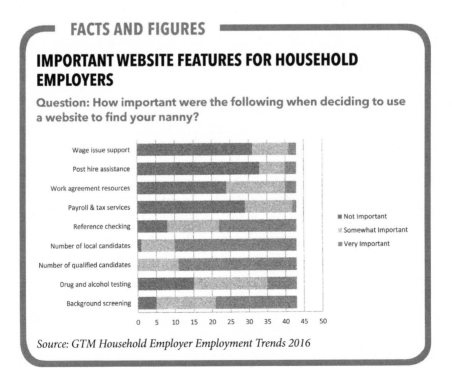

Source: GTM Household Employer Employment Trends 2016

Background Checking and References

The main issue most employers have with using online sites is the issue of screening and background checks. Many people want someone else to do this for them. And this is the issue that most families looking for domestic help worry about, because they will be inviting a stranger to come into their home and care for their family. They want the hire to be safe, and they want their family and home to be safe. Safety is being directly addressed by some websites that match nannies with families, but it is still a very sticky issue.

Online sites usually have two options for background checking.

1. The first is the basic background check. Many sites often advertise this as free because it is little more than a statewide criminal history check. It is wise to be wary of these basic checks, especially as some online companies use computer databases to generate the searches and, therefore, they can be inaccurate. They must assume that the databases are updated and fully comprehensive. In comparison, many traditional agencies are much more thorough with background checks. (They often use a company that actually sends a person to the courthouse to check for current records.)

2. The second option is usually cited as an "advanced background check" and usually consists of a multistate criminal history check, sex offender check, driving record check, and Social Security number check. Some also offer drug testing and past employment and education verification. The more the merrier when it comes to checking, so look for the site that offers you the most comprehensive screening methods for the best price.

Some of the better-known online hiring sites include a criminal background check for an additional fee or included in the basic membership fee. However, most sites actually do not do a comprehensive check. The goal of many sites is solely to matchmake. Once they have your membership and provided you with candidates, they can be hands off. Carefully read the site's policy on background checks before assuming that the site does thorough and comprehensive checks. Note that the potential employee should authorize all background checks. Most professional agencies ask candidates to sign a release, as do corporate employers. Not all online hiring sites do so. Therefore, ask the site whether this is done. A reputable site will do so and confirm that it asks all its candidates for authorization before completing any checks. Usually, when using websites, the families are also left to perform the most crucial aspect of the safety check on their own: the interview and the background research. Many have little experience to do this effectively. Of course, if you are hiring independently, the best method to investigate anyone's personal background and credibility is to hire a private detective. To be safe, some families do this. For more information on suggested background checks, see Chapter 2.

FACTS AND FIGURES
NEW INDUSTRY: NANNY SPIES!

During the past several years or so, a cottage industry has developed to investigate household help. Called nanny spies, the new trade arose to alleviate parents' fears for their children's and home's safety and welfare. Nanny spying includes performing extensive background checks, investigations, and surveillance of nannies at work via detective teams and/or nannycams.

According to the NY Post (2015) and NBC News (2016), nanny spies:

- uncovered falsified references, sexual misconduct charges, and prior fraud and grand larceny arrests

- witnessed a nanny drinking on the job and taking her charge with her to a liquor store, a nanny napping in the park as a child played, a nanny leaving a child alone outside while she went shopping, and another nanny waiting to respond to a crying child for more than 40 minutes

- exposed a nanny who stole and then sold a family's prescription medications

FACTS AND FIGURES
THE DANGERS OF HIRING WITHOUT BACKGROUND CHECKS

The media is rife with stories on the dangers faced when a household employee is hired without first performing a background check. Even more stories are bandied about the household help community by word of mouth. The dangers of hiring household help without performing background checks range from theft to physical harm. All of which may be avoided by thoroughly checking an employment candidate's background.

In early 2013, a nanny from Ireland was accused of killing the one-year-old Cambridge, MA, girl in her care from physical trauma much like shaken baby syndrome. A simple background check would have showed orders of protection against her and a violent past. (While the nanny spent two years in jail, the Massachusetts state medical officer in 2016 reversed the medical decision in this case as well as two others dealing with shaken baby syndrome, resulting in the nanny being immediately deported to Ireland. The case remains in the news as 1,800 medical pediatricians petitioned the Massachusetts governor in 2016 to review the state medical officer's controversial decision.) (The Boston Globe, WCRB)

A mother, who wrote a 2015 parenting.com article, details why a background check could have saved her family from a dangerous situation. The mom admitted she did not perform a background check when she hired her nanny via Craigslist. "Had we done a simple search," she wrote, "we would have uncovered her [the nanny's] history of passing bad checks and a string of arrests from her early 20s. But we didn't, and we got burned—bad." The nanny also worked as a restaurant hostess, a job the nanny did not disclose to her household employer, and also created a website featuring poses in various states of undress. The nanny stole credit card information from restaurant patrons and ended up in jail.

Household employers must be sure to be thorough in their checks. Employers who relied on a national agency to perform background checks are finding its checks were insufficient—and have paid dearly. In 2014, A California nanny who had been hired online physically abused the twins she was charged with caring. In

2013, a greater Boston area nanny—a notorious thief with dozens of larceny and fraud charges and who served jail time—stole some $280,000 from her employer's checking account. And, in Chicago in 2013, a three-year-old child died from a fractured skull while in the care of a nanny with previous legal run-ins and a 2010 DUI conviction.

The importance of background checks—and the increase of parents asking for background checks on their nannies—markedly increased after a nanny stabbed two New York City children to death and then tried to kill herself. This horrific 2012 Upper West Side murder opened parents' eyes to the dangers of ignoring background checks.

FACTS AND FIGURES
EMPLOYERS' TOP CONCERNS WHEN HIRING ONLINE

Question: What did you like least about using a website to hire your nanny?

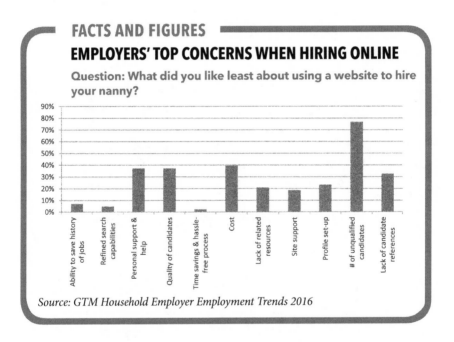

Source: GTM Household Employer Employment Trends 2016

Checking a Candidate's Online Profile

With social networking sites such as Facebook and Twitter, it is easy to check at least the basics of a candidate's online presence. Social networks may hold material about candidates' personal activities: the types of friends they have; the blogs they might have written; their likes and dislikes, which can be informative—and entertaining—reading. However, remember that this is their personal life (that they have decided to make public) and that casting judgment too harshly may inhibit good candidates from getting the job. It is always advisable to obtain prior written consent in the form of a signed release from the potential employee before looking at his or her online history or performing a Google search.

CASE STUDY

● ●

APRIL MUSSON
HOUSEHOLD EMPLOYER
COLONIE, NY

April Musson and her husband didn't think that they could afford a nanny for their two daughters, age 18 months and age four, but after talking with friends they soon discovered that hiring a nanny wasn't quite as expensive as they first thought—especially if they hired the nanny using an internet hiring service. Almost all their friends had hired nannies online and been successful.

Unfortunately for the Mussons, although using an online site saved them money, the cost was high in a lot of unnecessary emotional turmoil. The Mussons hired two nannies through one of the most popular online nanny sites, and "both were bad experiences," said Musson.

Musson and her husband had never hired a nanny before. The website they used was recommended by friends and the "membership was affordable. We thought it was the easiest way," said Musson. They joined and searched easily through a lot of local candidates' profiles.

When Musson interviewed a few candidates in her home, she soon realized that many of the pictures displayed on the website were misleading. "Only one looked like the person that actually came to the door," she noted. "My husband was always saying, 'She doesn't look like her picture online!'" This misinformation also resurfaced during the interview questioning. Musson was only interested in nonsmoker candidates and checked their profiles to ensure that all interviewees didn't smoke. When one candidate turned up, Musson said, "You could smell it on her clothing." When asked, the candidate said she wouldn't get an interview at all if she ticked the smoker box on the website.

As Musson stated, "It doesn't change the fact that she lied." Lying on an online profile makes all the other included information appear potentially misleading (like experience and education) and is a standard cause for firing within the corporate world. "They do not have to be completely honest, and they can write anything on their profile as it isn't checked," added Musson. Hence, the background check is paramount to any household help hires, especially for nannies.

The first nanny the Mussons hired online turned up dressed inappropriately and on the second day arrived late without an explanation. "I fired her on the spot," she said. "She even tried calling my husband [at work] to try and get her job back, but we had specified that punctuality was an important component [of the job]."

The second nanny appeared to be perfect at the start: she had all the right experience and education and a good résumé. She went "above and beyond the job description," said Musson. Only it became evident after about a month and a half that she had some personal issues and this was spilling over into the workplace: the Musson's home.

What Musson noticed at first was that the older daughter started acting out and appeared to be bored: "coloring on the furniture and doing stuff she didn't normally do," said Musson. It also became evident that the nanny had taken the children to places without asking the parents' permission. (The agreement established that the nanny must inform the parents if she was taking the children out to child-friendly venues, such as the library or the park, and phone one of the parents when they returned home). "At this point, she was already on strike two," stated Musson.

Then, one Monday, said Musson, "We got a call from her estranged husband saying she was ill and wouldn't be in until Thursday. I left a message on her phone to say that we hoped she was feeling better and when would she be back at work. She didn't get back to us. I even got to the point of calling area hospitals to see if she was there because I was worried something had happened to her. I looked up her profile on [the website] and her profile city had changed to one in Florida! She had just took off, never returned, and took our car seats with her. That was that."

The nanny has never been heard of since. And, even after the nanny left, other issues came to light. Musson reported, "My daughter said that one day the nanny had spilled her coffee and they had to go out and get a new one, but she did so when the baby was upstairs sleeping. So [the nanny] left the baby on her own in the house while she and our elder daughter went to Dunkin' Donuts to get a new coffee!"

From her experience, Musson offered the following advice to other families trying to hire a nanny:

- use general caution
- realize that an online profile is not necessarily the truth
- do a thorough interview so you and the nanny are in sync
- trust your instincts
- do a background check
- check references with a previous employer

The Mussons regard their "biggest mistake" as not taking the time to do thorough background checks and look into references. "It would have been nice to have spoken to a former employer," said Musson. While Musson noted that on many online sites you could request a background check with the profile, but these were very basic. There was, however, an option on the website she did use, which listed references, but the majority of nannies didn't populate this area; and, if they did, the references were usually not former employers. "We didn't check references because we were so desperate for care," admitted Musson.

The Mussons' story demonstrates how critical background checks are—and not something to skip no matter how you may initially feel about the candidate. It is easy to let your guard down, especially when you are busy, but never lower your guard when hiring child care. Online hiring is truly a gamble if you hire without performing background checks—and no one wants to gamble with their family or their home. So, invest time in checking the candidate out, and if you don't have time, hire a professional to do it. Without verifying history, checking references, etc., you just do not know who you are allowing to enter your home and what the consequences could be.

—Guy

Fees and Payment

Often online hiring sites have fees that are based on the level of access a family needs. It usually relates to how many days employers wish to post their job position on the site for a nanny to find, and how many days they think they will need to look through local candidates' profiles (including contacting, interviewing, and setting up a hire date with potential employees). Most websites that help you search for household employees offer services for one, three, six, or twelve months. Depending on the site, these fees can include additional services such as background and reference checking. As with all payment online, the safety tips for secure payment should be adhered to rigidly to avoid fraudulent scams and identity theft.

- Make sure you read the site's secure payment notices and any small print on hidden fees.
- Always use a reputable, well-known, trustworthy site.
- Always type in the address in the URL bar, do not access the site from an email link or embedded website page link.
- Always check for the closed padlock in your browser when you are transferring credit card details and other information.
- Beware of spoof versions of the official site that may look very similar to the domain of the legitimate website (known as cybersquatting and typosquatting).
- Look for https:// in the URL address bar that signifies a secure site.
- Pay close attention to your bank statements, and check that the correct amount was debited at the right time.
- Don't use a debit card online—if your debit card is compromised, that affects the money in your bank account immediately. Credit cards have more protection and less liability.

- Secure your PC—update your critical security patches and antivirus software and only shop from a secured internet connection.

Using Caution and Common Sense

As with any hire, it is wise to treat every source for finding a nanny or other household help with caution and use common sense throughout the process. Each hire should not involve any short cuts. The methods and advice offered in this book are essential to the entire process, from making sure your interview questions do not discriminate against particular candidates to paying the right taxes for your employee. Similarly, the tendency to trust your instincts with a hire should be acknowledged—and with hiring on your own more so than ever: always proceed with caution and do as much checking as possible on the candidate. The old adage, better to be safe than sorry, cannot be more true when it comes to using sources to hire an employee for your home.

Finding Household Help on Your Own Checklist

If employers choose to search and hire a candidate on their own, from their personal network, an advertisement, or through a website, then there are certain tips which may help make the process go smoothly and avoid risks.

- Always be aware of the legal implications and tax and insurance requirements for hiring a nanny.

- Always conduct thorough background checks.

- Do reference checks yourself.

- Hire only someone legally authorized to work in the United States and make sure the employee completes Form I-9 before hire (see Chapter 3).

- Read IRS Publication 926 for household employers, to know all the issues relating to employing help in the home.

- Meet the candidates for the first time in a public place, or ensure that you have another adult in your house if meeting at home.
- Be thorough with your interview questions and research the best methods for effective interviews if you have not had much interviewing experience.
- Remove your job advertisement from wherever it is posted once you are sure that the hire has been successful.

In particular, in addition to the above, for online hiring, the following applies.

- Always do thorough research on the site and get recommendations from those who have already used it.
- Look at a variety of sites before choosing the one you want to use.
- Check out what is on offer for the price and look into the specific details of what is included—for example, find out how comprehensive the background check is.
- Work with a reputable site that has been in the business for a while and has experience in the industry (e.g., created by a former nanny agency, expert in the field, or household employer or nanny).
- Read the guarantees and confidentiality clauses in your membership registration carefully.
- Use common sense and caution when hiring online with regards to online payment methods and providing personal information over email.
- Be wary of out-of-date information on a website—you want the site to be as recent and up to date as possible.
- Never hire someone online without performing background screening and reference checking.
- Keep your guard up when exchanging information about you and your family online (personal details like your address, telephone number, and number and ages of children).
- Remove your job advertisement from the site or cancel your membership once you are sure that the hire has been successful.

5

Using a Professional Agency to Hire Help

Retaining a good agency is still a convenient and efficient option for many families. A good agency is a helpful resource in finding an employee. After all, household employers hire staff to make life more convenient, easier, and fun—enabling the employer to direct his or her energies toward enjoying his or her family or home. An agency will take applications; screen candidates; help match candidates with employers; conduct interviews; and offer advice on household employment, job descriptions, work agreements, and employment practices. Household employers may want to work with a licensed agency, leveraging the wealth of knowledge and experience to save time and do it right the first time—and learn along the way. After working with a reputable agency and gaining the knowledge and insight that really only comes with experience, a household employer may feel secure and comfortable when taking on the next household hire. Remember, you want to do this right the first time. It remains up to you to determine whether the nanny candidate will work best within your home. While your agency partners will be invested in getting this hire right for you, they will not be living it every day, every hour, every minute—you will.

In the household employment industry today, there are well over 300 agencies in the United States. The quality of agencies can be as different as night and day. Each offers its own experience level and candidate selection process. A consumer needs to know what to look for when selecting an agency. The following information should help.

There are many benefits to using an agency to hire household help. One benefit is saving time. An agency saves you significant time and effort by prescreening applicants for you. This involves phone screening, face-to-face interviews, personality testing, drug testing, education verification, and extensive reference and background checking. For example, an agency can identify any fake résumés by thoroughly verifying education records and can verify applicant's references, confirm employment dates, and check into any gaps in employment. All in all, this is a very time-consuming process, and most potential employers are unable to take the time out of busy schedules to conduct the in-depth screening needed for hiring a household employee.

A second benefit is that when you are hiring someone to work in your home, experience in finding applicants is a must. An agency is equipped with experienced personnel who are focused on finding the right help for you and your family. Some will also assist with the hiring process, such as helping you develop the job offer, job description, compensation package, and other considerations. An agency can also offer you resources, such as tax and payroll services, training for the new employee, and ongoing support for the household employee. While working with you, an agency should be an advocate before, during, and even after your nanny is hired. Experienced agencies consult with the family, counsel and advise the employer and the employee on the right match for each other, and vet candidates on the employer's behalf. These are the real values of using a good agency. Many agencies offer ongoing assistance after the placement has been made, which can be invaluable in resolving issues, asking questions, or even when considering new positions to add to the household.

VALUE OF WORKING WITH AN AGENCY

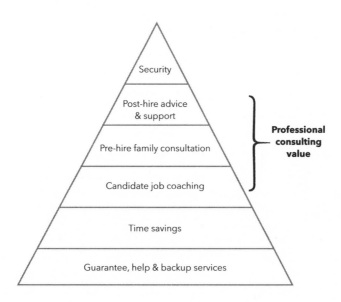

Expert Advice

"The expense of going through an agency is worth it—even during hard economic times. The decision to hire your child's caregiver should not be based on what you can afford but on what the nanny offers your child, such as experience and education. I am a nanny for a reason. I have more than 14 years of child care experience and an associate's degree in early childhood education. I am also involved in the International Nanny Association (INA) and many support groups. I am not just a babysitter who is there for the summer."

> —Stephanie Doyle
> Live-out nanny specializing in infants and toddlers
> Arlington, MA

How to Find a Reputable Agency

The best way to find a reputable agency is to talk to other people who have already hired a household employee through an agency. Personal recommendations give an honest story and will provide much-needed details. Also, employers may investigate agencies online and in the Yellow Pages. See if the agency is a member of an industry association. For example, a nanny placement agency may be a member of the Association of Premier Nanny Agencies (www.theapna.org) or the International Nanny Association (www.nanny.org). Also, when contacting an agency, always ask if it is licensed (if required by its state department of labor), insured, and bonded (which amounts to better protection for the client). It is also advisable to check the local Better Business Bureau to see whether there are any outstanding complaints against the agency and how these may have been dealt with.

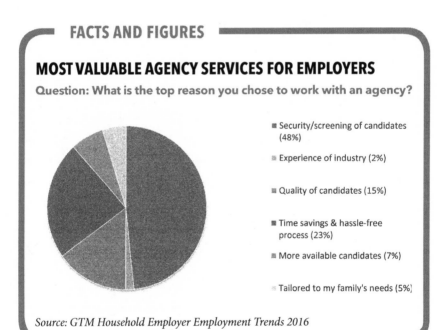

FACTS AND FIGURES

MOST VALUABLE AGENCY SERVICES FOR EMPLOYERS

Question: What is the top reason you chose to work with an agency?

- Security/screening of candidates (48%)
- Experience of industry (2%)
- Quality of candidates (15%)
- Time savings & hassle-free process (23%)
- More available candidates (7%)
- Tailored to my family's needs (5%)

Source: GTM Household Employer Employment Trends 2016

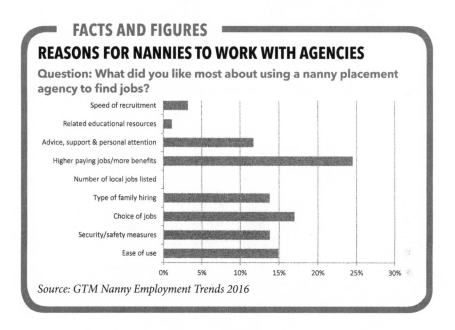

FACTS AND FIGURES

REASONS FOR NANNIES TO WORK WITH AGENCIES

Question: What did you like most about using a nanny placement agency to find jobs?

Source: GTM Nanny Employment Trends 2016

Expert Advice

"There are several nanny-sharing scenarios, including having one nanny watch children from several families simultaneously or having one nanny work part time for two different families, spending a few days with each family. These options help reduce costs, while still providing the benefits of having a nanny."

—Candi Wingate
President
Nannies4hire.com

CASE STUDY

● ●

MARIA ASCENZO
HOUSEHOLD EMPLOYER
SCOTIA, NY

Maria Ascenzo had a very positive experience with her agency, A New England Nanny, based in upstate New York. She and her husband are full-time professionals and have needed help at home since their daughter, Ava, was born. With no family help in the area where they live, Ascenzo said, "We had reservations about having a nanny and wished I had my mom or a cousin nearby who could provide recommendations and references. The reason I used an agency was to have another person who could give me a reference. Deb [at the agency] knows my personality and what I'm interested in. Every family is different, and she knows what my family needs. She's my reference."

According to Ascenzo, they had a wonderful experience with their first nanny, but after four great years working with the Ascenzo family, she had to leave for medical reasons. When Ascenzo and her husband had three children, they hired another nanny to work three days a week.

Ascenzo cited time saving as a key benefit to using an agency. Ascenzo noted, "It was very easy for me [to hire a nanny by using an agency] and there was no going back and forth with lots of candidates. [The agency] knew my schedule and what I needed."

The agency selected its most appropriate candidates for Ascenzo to interview, first on the phone and then at home. "When I interview, I like to talk about the position first and not talk about salary right away. With [my current nanny], we had a long conversation about the children, what she was looking for and what I was looking for. She had the right prior experience, a real interest in being a nanny, and was willing to please," added Ascenzo.

Ascenzo emphasized that warmth is the most important thing she is looking for when she hires a nanny, "I want the nanny to be nurturing and warm," she said. "My main concern was whether my children would be loved and played with. I wanted someone to cuddle, play, and tickle them. I wasn't concerned with the housework."

Ascenzo said she thinks that her relationship with her nanny is so successful because of open communication and consistency about behavior and discipline. "Open communication is very important, especially with my son," she said. "Sometimes he can be challenging as he's getting into the terrible twos. I need a good communicator for him. She also follows through with everything. We would collectively talk and try and find out why he was screaming and find an approach that would work so we could both be consistent for him. I did some research and put it on the fridge for her to follow, and she did."

Before she hired her current nanny, Ascenzo said she looked at one of the biggest nanny placement websites in the country. "I did a search on where I live, and a bunch of people came up," she said. "I looked at their pictures, profiles, and descriptions about themselves. The candidate pool wasn't what I hoped for."

According to Ascenzo, the selection of candidates that the agency provided was much greater than what she found with her internet search, especially as many agency candidates had background training and experience in childhood education, child development, and nursing, which the website candidates did not. "I understand it is more costly [to use an agency]," she said. "But to me, it is the way to go."

> Finding a reputable agency where you are comfortable with the personnel is key. An experienced agency placement director will work with you and guide you through all the steps of the hiring process, from job description to best practice employment policies. Having a good rapport between agency staff and clients helps make the process an easy, efficient, and even enjoyable experience.
>
> —Guy

What to Ask an Agency

Be as specific as possible about your needs, so the agency can provide the best candidates to you for your position. The following paragraphs provide lists of questions to ask and some things to consider when first starting out with an agency.

The following are specific questions you should ask agencies you are considering.

- How long has the agency been actively placing household employees? What has been the agency's success rate (i.e., how many placements the agency has made, where were they, and how long did they generally last)?
- Does it have any accreditation or is it licensed by the state?

- Where are applicants recruited from?
- What experience and skills does the agency require from applicants?
- Does the agency provide training for employees (e.g., hold CPR classes for nannies or time management training for personnel assistants)?
- Does the agency have on-call hours for clients or candidates in case of emergencies?
- Can the agency supply a current family reference about its experience with the agency?
- Is the agency licensed, insured, and bonded?

Other information you will need to know when working with an agency include the following.

- The agency's placement practices (e.g., the agency provides the employer with a minimum of three candidates, and the agency will replace a worker if for some reason a placement does not work out during a set probation period).
- The agency's fees and what those fees cover (e.g., whether the agency fee covers a candidate's background checks, or whether that is a separate responsibility for the household employer).
- The kind of support the agency provides after a candidate has been hired.
- If the agency requires payment only when a nanny is placed, or if there are up-front fees that the household employer must pay.
- If there is a payment schedule.
- The agency's guarantee policy and what must occur to ensure that it is in effect (e.g., the employer and employee must fully complete and sign the work agreement and submit it to the agency within three weeks after hire).
- The agency's refund policy and replacement policy if the nanny hired does not work out.

- If the agency has candidates to fill the position immediately.

- The standard time frame to fill a position.

- How the agency screens applicants (e.g., whether all applicants are interviewed in person, and if so, how many staff members within the agency interview the applicant).

- Who pays for travel expenses when the household employer interviews candidates—the agency, the candidate, or the household employer.

- The number of references required for an applicant (also, what questions the agency asks, if the household employer can see the written references, and if the household employer may contact the applicant's references).

- Apart from background checks, whether the agency conducts other screening, such as personality profile, drug testing, or a medical exam.

- How information about the household is gathered (e.g., whether the agency visits the home or checks references of the family, and whether a written application is part of the placement process).

- The average candidate's profile (e.g., age, education, salary range).

- Whether the agency can advise on payroll taxes and required insurance, and if it recommends a service that does it for the employer.

Top Concerns

A household employer needs to discuss what he or she requires for the nanny to adequately fill the position with an agency. Thinking through these top concerns will help an employer target what candidate qualifications and skills are most important to the household. These top concerns include:

- relevant experience
- relevant qualifications
- personality type preferences
- references
- salary
- benefits (e.g., paid vacations, health insurance, car use, holidays, retirement plans, etc.)
- hours/schedule
- philosophy on service (i.e., a nanny's philosophy on child rearing)
- languages
- appearance and conduct
- responsibility
- communication skills
- team player
- reliability
- commitment

Q & A

Q. I recently found a candidate for our nanny opening online, on my own. She seems an ideal match for my family. But after reading an article, I am concerned that I need to do a thorough background check. I wonder if an agency can help and what other value an agency can offer me?

A. A local agency can help you screen a potential candidate, even if you have already selected the candidate on your own. Local agencies not only help you conduct thorough background and reference checks but also offer managerial advice for you as a household employer, provide job coaching support to the candidate, and help you with interim temporary babysitting services if your nanny is unavailable or sick after hiring, as well as many other educational materials and support for you and your nanny to help make the employment relationship successful.

THE DIFFERENCES: AGENCIES VS. ONLINE JOB SITES

	Traditional Agencies	Online Job Sites
Time Savings	All searches assisted by agency staff. Job postings managed by agency staff. Agency will generally offer a select few qualified candidates, helping employers to immediately target the best candidates.	Search on your own. Do the selection process yourself for your preferred candidates. Post jobs yourself. Develop job description and work agreement yourself (some sites offer templates or articles to help). Perform background checks on your own (unless included). *Note: There can be even more effort involved on your part, and therefore the process can take longer.*
Turn-around Time	Depending on the agency's current pool of candidates, this could be fast, or you may need to wait for a list of candidates which can cause a longer turnaround time.	Can help you find a number of prospective candidates in a matter of minutes, which may lead to your selection of candidates for interview.
Cost	Because you are engaging a consultant with staff, you will be paying a higher fee.	Membership to online sites tends to be less expensive; however, there can be additional fees in add-on services.
Screening	Prescreened applicants. Phone and face-to-face interviews conducted before family interviews. Reference and employment checks verified. Full background checks provided.	You may have to conduct all prescreening and interviews. You conduct your own reference and employment checks. You conduct background checks (unless included).
Expert Assistance	Assistance and guidance with job offer. Job description development. Compensation package. Experience based on agency selected.	No personal guidance. You are responsible for job offer. Limited resources for employment policies. Limited guidance on fair hiring and compensation.
Tax, Payroll, and Insurance Advice	Agency provides compliance education and materials. Referrals for detailed advice and free consultations.	You decipher compliance requirements. Some sites do refer to a tax and payroll service, such as GTM.com. Some sites do post articles on tax and payroll issues.

| Post-placement Support | Ongoing support after placement. Managerial advice and job coaching. Temporary babysitting services for vacations or unexpected absences of primary caregiver. | No managerial or personalized support after hire. |
| Guarantee | Usually an agency will guarantee a placement by providing a replacement or an extended membership so you can use its services again for free. | Limited or no guarantee. |

Expert Advice

"Good home care can have a beneficial effect on the children's development and on the family's home life. In-home child care [for instance] should not be perceived as a threat. It should be a welcome joy to a family."

—Ilo Milton
Experienced agency owner
Bedford, NY

What to Tell an Agency

Honesty is the very best policy. The agency needs a clear and accurate representation of the family, household, job requirements, and so on, to be able to place the best household employee for the position. Employers will need to apply their honesty in packaging themselves, their employment practices, the household's culture, and what they need and are seeking in the household employee. When speaking to an agency, employers need to specify details regarding:

- the hiring time frame
- the work schedule
- all individuals' needs within the household, including other household help; (e.g., information regarding the children, such as any special needs, special diets, allergies, medication, etc.)

- their expectations of the agency

- their expectations of the household employee

- compensation and benefits packages

- any and all special requirements, such as extensive travel with the family, holiday needs, and on-call hours

When first discussing your position, be sure to tell the agency:

- when you are looking to hire the employee

- how long of a commitment you are looking for from an employee

- what the job requirements will entail (e.g., strictly child care or any housework included)

- if there is a home office and if the parent/employer works from home (if so, also explain if the parent/employer will be on-site while the employee is working)

- what kind of surveillance you have installed or will install to covertly check on a nanny

- if travel will be required for this position

- if transportation is required for the position (reimbursement for gas or mileage)

Remember, open communication is the best policy when acquiring agency assistance. Anything but the truth will potentially delay the hire, misconstrue employment objectives; and create uncertainty, misunderstanding, and worse yet, hard feelings, mistrust, and anger.

CASE STUDY

• •

DENISE COLLINS
CEO
IN-HOUSE STAFFING AT AUNT ANN'S AGENCY
DALY CITY, CA

In-House Staffing at Aunt Ann's Agency, Inc., in operation for over 50 years, refers an equal number of nannies and other household help to clients in the

San Francisco Bay area. According to the agency's CEO, Denise Collins, clients are highly educated, highly salaried people who often have been raised with staff and are now hiring staff themselves. These employers offer benefit packages to their household help and recognize them as professionals.

"This has been our core clientele, and they take care of their household help very well," said Collins. "In the 1980s, we began to see two-income families looking to hire help, and we experienced huge growth in housekeeping placements and then child care. It is a quality-of-life decision, and along with that came a higher set of expectations that this person would be included in the family. New employers need to put in place all the tools to make the working relationship successful. They have to learn how to hire a person who will come into their home to work. The accountability of the working relationship is the family's—the employer's—not the agency's."

For these first-time employers, Collins said the agency needs to educate them on everything to do with employing household help. "Even people who handle HR issues at work need to be educated, because of differences in the workweek, payroll, taxes, and laws," she noted. "Plus, they must file different forms."

To help, the agency holds public education sessions on employing child care and senior care professionals in the home. "It's a buyer beware market," said Collins, who noted that some unethical agencies are a big issue in California. "There's no certification or regulation. It's pretty predatory, and the population most affected are the seniors."

An effective household employer conducts effective human resource management. This begins with deciding whether or not to outsource the recruiting and screening to an agency. The role of an agency is to make it a much easier, more convenient process while presenting the best candidates that match an employer's philosophy and position requirements. A good agency adds value by how well it advises an employer on the position, management techniques, and tools that help the employer be successful.

—Guy

Agency Fees

Agency fees—which will be *in addition* to the salary owed to the nanny or other household employee—generally depend on the following factors:

- where you live in the United States (some cities have more expensive agency fees than others)

- whether you need long- or short-term care (the difference between hiring a nanny for a year and temporary babysitting services)

- what the agency services provide (e.g., what kinds of prescreening methods, reference checking services, guarantees for placement, etc., are included)

Long-Term Care

Registration Fee

Most agencies charge families a onetime, nonrefundable registration fee for a long-term commitment (usually between $200 and $300). Sometimes this fee is credited toward the placement fee once the candidate has been hired. This fee is generally charged only after the agency has successfully placed an employee in the home. It covers the consultation, processing, and prescreening administration that the agency does on the employer's behalf. There is usually a guarantee that the agency will replace the employee within a specified period at no additional cost if it does not work out (generally between three and six months). This fee can also give the family access to other services from the agency, such as on-call temporary babysitting.

Placement Fee

Once the employee has been placed with the family, there is generally a placement fee that the agency requires associated with the hire. There are many different ways an agency can charge this fee.

- **The onetime fee as a percentage of salary:** calculating a percentage of the nanny's anticipated *annual* gross salary, and usually asking for a minimum amount. For example, for a full-time, live-out nanny, the agency asks for 10 percent–15 percent of anticipated annual gross salary with a minimum of $2,000–$3,000.

- **The ongoing fee:** calculating an ongoing fee for as long as the nanny is employed, per week (depending on whether it is a live-out or live-in placement). For example, for a full-time, live-out nanny, the agency charges $100 per week for as long as the nanny is employed with the family.

- **The onetime fee as a total amount:** a complete fee that covers everything, generally $2,000–$4,000 (depending on what kind of employment is required). Sometimes available as a split payment with an up-front cost when the employee is hired and then the remainder due within a set time after placement (say 30–60 days). Some agencies charge this as one month of gross salary (for example, if the employee earns $3,500 gross pay a month, then the agency's onetime fee would be the same).

Short-term Care

Registration Fee

One of the most cost-effective agency services is the short-term care program. Usually an initial fee is charged to access the agency's temporary, occasional, or babysitting services. This is generally around $100. This service usually lasts for about a year and then can be renewed every year from then on.

Placement Fees

- Daily fees (sometimes called on-call fees) once the babysitter or nanny is hired; there is generally a daily charge from the agency for every day the employee works. This is usually a fixed amount that is charged by the agency (usually $20–$40), and may be more for holidays, overnight, or weekends.

- If the placement becomes more permanent, the fees usually correspond with the placement fees for long-term care, as above.

Temporary to Hire Arrangements

Registration Fee

Like a traditional business-to-business employment agency, sometimes an agency offers a program whereby the agency initially screens and selects an employee for the family. Then the agency employs the caregiver for an initial time period (e.g., 600 hours), processing his or her payroll and covering insurance, taxes, and workers' compensation during that time. This gives the family the opportunity to try out the selected candidate before committing to being the employer. This also allows the family to utilize the agency's personalized services, screening, and supervision while paying the agency the fee as part of the caregiver's hourly wage without any additional placement fees. If the family is happy to continue to have this caregiver, it hires him or her as the employee after the duration of the time and takes on the employer responsibilities.

Ongoing Fees

There is no placement fee, but the price of the service is calculated as an hourly rate for the employee, ranging from $16–$30 an hour, depending on the candidate.

Employee's Wages

Even though the employee's wages are not charged by the agency, the employer should remember to factor in the cost of the care that is paid directly to the employee. Typical nanny salaries are discussed in Chapter 8. The amount charged per week by a household employee depends on whether he or she is live-in or live-out, full-time or part-time, weekday or evenings, weekends, and overnights, or in any nanny-share programs, or if he or she brings his or her own child to the job (usually 25 percent less). An employee's experience and job duties also factor in to the agreed salary.

The employer should take care to remember:

- the federal minimum wage is $7.25 per hour (2017)
- state minimum wages may be more (see Chapter 8)

- prevailing wage in certain metropolitan areas takes precedent over minimum wage
- employer should be aware of gross and/or net pay differences
- employer should be aware of tax requirements as an employer
- employer should negotiate the wages and payment method directly with the employee (but always inform the agency)

Using an Agency Checklist

- Find out as much as possible about the agency, including its placement procedures.
- Prepare a list of questions for the agency, including practices, fees, post-placement support, and background screening.
- Ask whether the agency belongs to any industry associations. If so, ask which ones.
- Ask for, and check, the agency's references.
- Go to an agency with a clear idea on the household employee required, and know what responsibilities, experience, and personality traits the household employee should have to best perform within the household.
- Be sure to ask the agency for a complete list of fees and what is covered. Pay attention to hidden costs, so you are not surprised down the road, when you are already entrenched with the agency in the hiring process.
- Ask for a copy of the signed contract with the agency.

6

The Work Agreement

Work agreements are essential with household employment, since household positions are so customized to the specific home in question. From the start, the work agreement establishes a clear understanding between the employer and employee regarding the employee's duties and responsibilities, and all that is expected from both the employer and employee. The most effective work agreement is in writing and covers all aspects of working in the household—including the employee's work schedule, required daily duties, compensation, benefits, termination, and a confidentiality clause. Lack of a work agreement can contribute to dissatisfaction and miscommunication in the workplace and a high employee turnover rate. Therefore, work agreements can be considered an important step in building a long-lasting relationship in which all parties clearly understand their responsibilities and expectations.

Job Description

A work agreement and job description go hand in hand. Often, they contain the same material, but a household employer needs to develop both, since a job description is written *before* an employee is hired, and a work agreement is written *after* the employee is hired and is developed *with* the employee before his or her first day on the job.

A job description is, essentially, all the work to be done by the nanny, housekeeper, houseman, and so on. It is really your first official document regarding your household employee hire. When developing it, in a way, you are detailing how you will accomplish your goal. Before you pick up your pen to write the job description, think about what it is you want to accomplish—what is the goal that has brought you to this need for hiring a household employee?

Thoroughly think through what the position needs to accomplish; which tasks and duties are required to achieve the position's goals; and what skills, abilities, and talents the employee must have to satisfactorily perform all that is required. Only then can a comprehensive job description be developed. (See Chapter 2, "Developing the Job Description".)

Consider, for example, the following questions.

- Will the household employee need a car and a valid driver's license? (Will the nanny be required to drive the child to a playdate or school? Will the cook need to drive to the grocery store for necessary ingredients? Will the gardener need to drive to a nursery or an equipment store?)

- Will a nanny be required to take the child to the park or playground on a schedule or from time to time?

- Will a nanny caring for two children be expected to prepare and feed the children breakfast and lunch?

- Will the nanny be required to clean lunch dishes after the children have eaten?

- Will all household employees be expected to answer the telephone and take messages?

- Will all household help be expected to sign for deliveries and packages?

- Will an employee need protective clothing or equipment? (Will the gardener need protective goggles when operating equipment? Will the driver need cover-ups and gloves for car maintenance tasks? Will the senior care employee need face masks, gowns, and protective gloves?)

There is a lot to think about and much to decide. If you are seeking a nanny, then you will want the nanny to focus fully on caring for the children—not to necessarily perform housekeeping chores. It may be that you need both a nanny and a housekeeper.

Each household's and each household employer's needs vary greatly with each situation. Job descriptions should list all of the necessary qualifications (skills, education, certification, or license), essential job functions, and functions that are desired but not mandatory. Comprehensive job descriptions begin the employment on solid ground. With the job description in hand, the hiring process can begin. (See Appendix D, for sample job descriptions.)

An owner of a Northwest placement agency said she can log as much as 150 hours on some accounts when placing a household employee, and she spends hours with clients, meeting in their homes.

"Every job is customized, so you can't have a cookie-cutter job description or profile," she said. "I spend a lot of time getting to know the family and know what they want. I walk them through the whole specifications of the job. This research ensures the right person for the job is placed."

This owner leans heavily on the job description and work agreement. Regarding nannies, the former nanny-turned-owner said, "Generally, people don't realize how tough of a job it really is—how much work and responsibility it is. It is a real job requiring superpower intuition and the ability to make executive decisions on behalf of someone else, sometimes without guidance or with little feedback."

FACTS AND FIGURES
A CRITICAL STEP IN BUILDING A SUCCESSFUL RELATIONSHIP

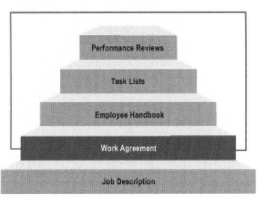

Performance Reviews. A means to communicate employer feedback to employees regarding how well they are meeting the objectives of the household, demonstrated by task-list activities and satisfaction of the employee's constituents, such as dependents, other staff, household manager, and homeowner.

Task Lists. The to-do lists to meet the job description's objectives. Could be daily, weekly, special projects, seasonal activities, and so on; and if a task has to be done with precision, it may call for a specific procedure.

Employee Handbook. Comprehensive set of policies addressing expectations for employment responsibilities and conduct. Includes use of property, time off, resignation, paydays, performance reviews, and so on.

Work Agreement. Detailed outline of the employment engagement with specific compensation, benefits, terms, and so on. Establishes a clear understanding between the employer and employee regarding the employee's duties and responsibilities, and all that is expected from both the employer and employee.

Job Description. A precisely written description of the responsibilities and requirements that specify employer objectives.

CASE STUDY

● ●

LIN TAYLOR-PLEIMAN
OWNER/PRESIDENT
AMERICAN DOMESTIC AGENCY, INC.
WHITEFORD AND GREENVILLE, DE

American Domestic Agency, Inc. offers domestic-related employment placements in Maryland, Delaware, and Pennsylvania.

Noting the delicacy of the household employment industry, Lin Taylor-Pleiman said a signed work agreement is proof that "the parties sat down, talked, and worked out issues so the employee and the employer are fully aware of each other's expectations."

The agency is so adamant about the written agreement that it requires clients to submit a copy of the agreement within seven days of an employee's start date. If a client fails to do so, the agency will not honor its replacement guarantee if the placement fails.

"We've learned it's a must," said Taylor-Pleiman. "It addresses a multitude of areas, even what happens when there's a snow day. Both parties must know the expectations of the other party in order to have a good relationship, in which the employee can focus on her duties and not worry about being treated unfairly."

Taylor-Pleiman speaks from experience. Her agency was begun after her daughter left a very dissatisfying experience as a nanny. "There are standard areas that need to be addressed, regardless of position," she noted. "The importance of communication is paramount. With this work agreement, most of the time problems can be rectified…Most employers want the employees to be an extension of the family, and for the most part, want a good, close relationship."

Stating that the work agreement is an advantage to both the employer and employee, Taylor-Pleiman said she believes the work agreement helps household employees gain recognition as professionals. "Employees are demanding taxes be paid and that they be legitimized. The work agreement is an instrumental step in that."

As a household employer, clear expectations are paramount. This is why the work agreement is so critical to the beginning of the employer-employee relationship, even for a relationship on the best of terms. Work agreements spell out the employment conditions, general tasks, and responsibilities of the employer and employee within that household. With them, both the employer and employee are reducing the likelihood that problems will occur.

—Guy

Work Agreement

The work agreement is an essential document for both the household employer and employee. A comprehensive work agreement—often written by both the employer and the employee—goes a long way in establishing a successful working relationship. Not only will it prevent problems from occurring, it will also set the tone of the working relationship with open and clear communication.

Expert Advice

"An in-home caregiver's primary responsibility is the care and the nurturing of young children, not folding the laundry or mopping the floor. Employers need to remember the nanny's priorities—first, provide a happy, safe, convenient child care atmosphere; then, if there's time, a nanny can fold the children's clothes."

> —Melissa Schoonmaker
> Agency director
> A New England Nanny
> Clifton Park, NY

Why the Work Agreement is Important

There are many reasons household employers enter into work agreements with their new household employee(s). The most popular reason is to help ensure clear and concise communication around terms and conditions of employment. As all relationships seem to have an initial honeymoon period, verbal agreements and commitments can sometimes be fuzzy and possibly forgotten, and as a result, can cause strain on the employment relationship. The work agreement outlines these commitments in a professional manner, creates the seriousness that the household position and employment require, and helps to reduce employment disputes.

Why Enter into a Work Agreement

The work agreement helps safeguard the cost of recruiting and obtaining a household employee. Turnover costs could run thousands of dollars, especially considering the cost of advertising; time spent to screen, interview, and check references; placement agency fees; training costs; and employer time lost from work or other activities.

A work agreement is legally enforceable. However, an employer may not want to enforce the terms of the agreement, as it would not serve the household to retain an uninterested or disgruntled employee. Yet an employer may very well want to enforce the *Confidentiality Agreement* (see Appendix E) to protect the family's personal affairs that an employee may have learned during the course of his or her employment. For the nanny or other household employee, a legally enforced work agreement serves to protect his or her compensation, benefits, and severance pay, as well as job description requirements.

Expert Advice

"People do treat the work relationship in a relaxed manner, as a friend rather than employer-employee. That's when issues come up."

—Sylvia Greenbaum
Co-owner
Boston Nanny Centre, Inc.
Boston, MA

CASE STUDY

• •

Crystal Hinman
Nanny
Albany, NY

Born to take care of children, Crystal Hinman has been babysitting and later nannying since she was 15 years old. Now a mother of three small children, she said she was lucky to find a "role model family" as her employer—smart, professional, kind parents who wanted to pay her on the books and treat her professionally. Noting that her employers actually found it difficult to find a nanny like Hinman who wanted to be paid on the books and above board, Hinman said she is paid on the upper end of the nanny salary scale. She reports that quite a few nannies did not want to work for the family because many did not want to be paid on the books. Many were double dipping (i.e., getting paid in two places at the same time).

Part of the problem, said Hinman, is that nannies are still not regarded professionally. According to Hinman, some people she has talked with considered her either a babysitter or an au pair. Although she gets a lot of respect from other moms because of the number of children she has cared for all at once—from teenagers to toddlers—other people are still confused by what she does. She must explain that nannies are very different from babysitters, she reports, as nannying requires learning the background of the family. She said she believes that a lot of people think "anyone can do child care" and that those that do don't need any background with children, qualifications, or experience, which is just not the case. "They think it's like a maid service—call and someone gets sent over," she said. "Personally, I've been lucky and have always been seen professionally by the family I work with."

But it is not all about being paid correctly and being treated professionally. One of the most important things for Hinman, and why she has stayed nannying with the same employer for nearly seven years, is their shared child-rearing philosophy. "I admire how they treat their kids and work together," noted Hinman of her employers. "They have a good balance between work and home, which is a very difficult thing to achieve. They listen to their children really well. When there are issues, they know how to resolve them. They are a nice and loving family to work with."

As a nanny, Hinman said her goal is to "make the family more efficient." Her advice to other nannies when beginning a job is "to observe: observe how parents already interact with their kids, observe what type of food the kids like for dinner, and so on. Your job is to make it easier for the family— learn how the house is run and how the family runs. For example, if the mom comes back to take one of the kids to a doctors' appointment, I would make sure I had that child ready with his shoes on and a packed snack. I'm always thinking, 'How can I help the family?' 'How can I help the kids?'"

Being a nanny means learning, said Hinman. The most important thing families can do, added Hinman, is to "recognize what behaviors they do and don't like in a child," so that the nanny can do her job and keep the same philosophy. It is best if families know what they want me to do so I can be the most effective I can be. Sometimes the parents have to think about it and set a course for what to do with a certain behavior. For example, they had an older infant who was biting but knew better not to. They thought about what they wanted to do and discussed it with me."

She advised other nannies to always respect the fact that the family is its own being. "As much control as I wished to exert—I always had to keep in mind the parents' ideas and wishes," she said. "I spent a lot of time in the first year asking them 'How would you handle this?' I didn't want to upset their strategies on parenting. I wanted to work with them."

Hinman credits her employers with teaching her many useful tips about parenting. "I use the same potty training methods they use," she stated. "I'm nursing, and I'm the only one in my family that nurses. I even used the same birthing methods!"

Hinman rated her nanny experience as "ten out of ten. It's been wonderful!" she exclaimed.

> Hinman and her employer have obviously been very fortunate in their nanny-family relationship and experience. It is an example of just how good working as a nanny and having a nanny in your family can be and how it can benefit everyone— most of all the children. Matching the child rearing philosophy with your employee is one of the key elements to building a successful relationship that will prosper.
>
> —Guy

Work Agreement Benefits

A work agreement is a win-win—it helps the employer and nanny clearly establish standards, rules, and procedures for the household and for the job. From listing the hours the nanny is expected to work and what his or her salary is, to explaining what a nanny must do if inclement weather prevents him or her from traveling to work, even to defining whether the nanny should be taking meals with the children—it is all specified within the work agreement. No matter is too small, because it all goes to one thing—the smooth operation of your household. This is how you set the stage for success in your employment.

There are many pertinent reasons why you should develop, maintain (i.e., update as needed), and enforce a work agreement.

- A written work agreement helps to ensure the employment of a particularly desirable employee. It protects an employer's confidential information. If a candidate does not want to join you in developing a work agreement, or does not wish to sign one that has been developed, red flags should appear immediately. You need to think, "Why does this nanny not want to enter into an agreement that details his or her job?" The actual existence of a work agreement acts as a tool for you to target the best candidates—and discount those who are disagreeable.

- The work agreement is a cooperative endeavor, ideally to be developed (and revised) together (employer with employee). It details:

  - the job, including establishing a term of employment (e.g., the nanny job may be for a one-year term, with a date to review the nanny's performance, the work agreement, and the possible extension of the employment to another year)

  - your expectations (spell out the nanny's duties—be specific and include important considerations to your household, such as protecting the confidential information contained within the home)

  - the employee's expectations

  - household procedures and instructions the employee will use daily in the job

  - the employee's compensation and benefits

- Written work agreements must meet the needs of all parties involved. It is even feasible to use a written work agreement to help determine whether an employee may be terminated without *good cause* and possibly on short notice (i.e., at-will employment). Use the agreement as a litmus test, checking whether the nanny did the tasks described in the work agreement, in the method described in the work agreement, and in the time frame specified in the work agreement.

- While compensation and benefits should be included in the work agreement, be mindful that the work agreement is an employment contract, and you, as the employer, must abide by it. Therefore, review the compensation and benefits wording to avoid any potential back pay liability.

- When developing a written work agreement, employers have many areas to consider. Be alert to the laws and standards involving employment. Employers must have a working knowledge of federal, state, and local laws, including the following.

  - Employers must abide by federal and state nondiscrimination laws. Many state laws go further than the federal law in barring discrimination based on marital status, arrest records, sexual orientation, pregnancy, and legal behaviors engaged in while off-duty (e.g., smoking). (See Chapter 12 for more details.)

  - Some states limit an employer's right to terminate an employment contract unless he or she can show good cause.

  - Be certain to consider the *Fair Labor Standards Act* (FLSA), the federal law governing compensation, minimum wage, and the hiring of minors, as well as the *Immigration Reform and Control Act* (IRCA), which requires employers to verify the eligibility of employees to work in the United States. Also, most states enforce some form of minimum wage law for those job categories not covered by the FLSA.

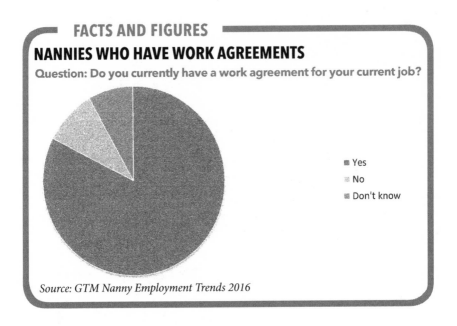

FACTS AND FIGURES

NANNIES WHO HAVE WORK AGREEMENTS

Question: Do you currently have a work agreement for your current job?

- Yes
- No
- Don't know

Source: GTM Nanny Employment Trends 2016

How to Create a Work Agreement

Ideally, consulting with an employment attorney is a best practice in developing a work agreement. However, some placement agencies may offer a work agreement template or provide samples obtained from its other clients. There are also many work agreements or sample contracts online that are offered for free when registering with an online hiring site. Employers may extrapolate ideas from template samples and obtain input from friends or colleagues who have developed their own work agreements for their own household help.

Key Elements of a Work Agreement

The following list of key elements provide an overview of the common components that are included in most work agreements. A sample agreement is also displayed in Appendix E.

Recitals—Employer is an individual and a household employer, resident of _____(state), and over the age of 18.

Employment—Employment under this agreement is to begin on _____ and continue unless sooner terminated as provided herein.

Compensation—Subject to the following provisions of this agreement, the Employer agrees to pay the Employee a gross compensation hourly rate of $_____. (An explanation of gross vs. net income is advisable.)

Benefits—Employee is entitled to _____ days of paid vacation annually. The vacation must be scheduled 30 days in advance and agreed to by the employer. Vacation is based upon normal payment for a 40-hour workweek.

Terms and conditions of employment—Employee may not drink alcohol, use illegal drugs, or smoke while on duty for the employer.

Termination of agreement—Employer may terminate employment for violation of the work agreement that holds that an employee may not drink alcohol, use illegal drugs, or smoke while on duty for the employer.

Modifications and interpretation—The job description may change by mutual consent. Therefore, the work agreement must be revised to reflect any changes.

Applicable laws—The provisions of this agreement shall be constructed in accordance with laws of the state of _____.

Signature and date line—Employer and employee should sign and date the original and each revision of the work agreement.

Work schedule (optional)—Additional detail of a daily schedule broken down by day and by hour.

FACTS AND FIGURES
REAL HOME ECONOMICS FOR DOMESTIC WORKERS

The 2012 National Domestic Workers Alliance report, "Home Economics: the Invisible and Unregulated World of Domestic Work", has details that provide useful background to some of the conditions that domestic workers face today. According to this report, low wages, limited employment options, and reliance on employer goodwill, together with historic exclusions from work-place laws, have plagued the industry and continue today. "If basic workplace protections actually covered this workforce—and they were enforced—it is indisputable that many workers would be found to have been subjected to gross violations of U.S. employment law," stated the report.

Low pay is a systemic problem in the domestic work industry, continued the report. Its 2012 survey of household workers found:

- 23 percent were paid below the state minimum wage with 70 percent paid less than $13 an hour. (67 percent of live-in workers were paid below the state minimum wage, with $6.15 as the median hourly wage)

- using a conservative measure of income adequacy, 48 percent were paid an hourly wage below the level needed to adequately support a family

Along with poor wages, household help rarely receive benefits. According to the Home Economics report:

- less than 2 percent receive retirement or pension benefits

- less than 9 percent work for employers who pay into Social Security

- 65 percent do not have health insurance, only 4 percent receive employer-provided insurance

According to the report, many household employees indicated that their most basic needs go unmet:

- 60 percent spent more than half of their income on rent or mortgage payments

- 37 percent paid their rent or mortgage late during 2012

- 20 percent reported that there were times during the previous month when they had no food to eat in their homes because they had no money to buy any

The report also highlighted illegal working conditions despite a formal contract in place:

- 35 percent reported they worked long hours without breaks during the prior 12 months

- 25 percent of live-in workers had responsibilities that prevented them from getting at least five hours of uninterrupted sleep at night during the week prior to being interviewed for the report

- 30 percent with a written contract or other agreement reported their employers disregarded at least one of the agreement's provisions during the prior 12 months

Other Home Economic findings reported that:

- among workers fired from domestic work, 23 percent were fired for complaining about working conditions and 18 percent for protesting contract/agreement violations
- workers risked long-term exposure to toxic chemicals and a range of workplace injuries, including (during the prior 12 months):

  - 38 percent suffered work-related wrist, shoulder, elbow, or hip pain
  - 31 percent suffered soreness and pain
  - 29 percent of housecleaners suffered skin irritation
  - 20 percent experienced trouble breathing
  - 36 percent of nannies contracted an illness while at work
  - 29 percent of caregivers suffered a back injury

The report added that 91 percent of workers surveyed did not complain of working conditions for fear of being fired.

CASE STUDY

● ●

SYLVIA GREENBAUM
CO-OWNER
BOSTON NANNY CENTRE, INC.
NEWTON, MA

According to Sylvia Greenbaum, co-owner of Boston Nanny Centre, Inc., the lack of clear job requirements is a top reason household positions do not work, particularly when a family wishes a nanny to perform other household work unrelated to child care.

Greenbaum cited an example in which a nanny placed through the agency was charged with caring for twins. A work agreement specified that the nanny tend to the twins, and it did not require that she do any household work. The nanny worked hard caring for the twins, and the family agreed that she was doing an excellent job. Yet, after some time, the family began leaving daily notes asking the nanny to perform household chores and tasks. She became nervous and upset about the daily notes and saw no end in sight to her compounding daily responsibilities, which were not stipulated in the work agreement. The family, first-time household employers, was upset with the nanny's attitude. Tension quickly and steadily increased. The parents then angrily confronted the nanny, who immediately resigned, believing that her employers did not value or appreciate the high-quality care she provided to their children. The family's anger increased when left without a nanny, and the family threatened to withhold payment for the five days the nanny had already worked that week. (The agency reminded the family that, as the employer, it was legally responsible to pay the nanny for days she had worked.) Both client and nanny felt angry and mistreated.

"Clearly, it would have been better had the family and nanny discussed what household responsibilities were needed and what the nanny felt comfortable doing," said Greenbaum. "If this had been written in the agreement, the nanny and family would not have each felt taken advantage of."

According to Greenbaum, mixing household chores with child care depends on the personalities involved. "Sometimes nannies will do other jobs [around the house] without being asked," she said. "It depends on the relationship. So many factors go into it."

Greenbaum's agency provides each client with a detailed work agreement and strongly encourages clients to complete it. However, many parents are new to parenthood, as well as to the employer role, and they do not yet realize all they wish their nannies to be and do. "They think that it's not totally unreasonable to say, 'Let's see how it is going,' or 'We're sure it'll work out,'" noted Greenbaum. "All nannies who care for children are doing other things, like preparing food, doing the children's laundry, cleaning, and organizing their toys. Yet when children are in school or napping, some will do some shopping, run errands, and put a load of the employer's laundry in the washer. Some say, 'I'll care for the child but not for the parents,' or some say, 'I like to keep busy.' It is so individual. It's best if all requirements are talked about before the nanny is hired."

Greenbaum said difficulty is inherent in the nanny-employer relationship. "People do treat the work relationship in a relaxed manner," she said. "Sort of as a friend rather than employer-employee, and that's when issues come up."

Greenbaum has great empathy for families, who must learn so many different pieces that go into the employer role during a stress-filled time while trying to meet all of their professional and personal obligations. Plus, added Greenbaum, stress naturally arises when parents first leave their children with another adult.

Often referring parents to GTM for employer information, as well as wage and tax assistance, Greenbaum noted that the hiring process is both complex and lengthy, typically taking a while to find the right person for the right job and the right family. "[Hiring a nanny] is such a personal decision," she said. "People have to feel that it's right. It can be a very long process. Sometimes there's magic, and it all comes together. It could take one day to find the right nanny, but I tell families, if possible, give it at least two months."

Given all of the processes and pieces, Greenbaum is not surprised that a first-time hire does not often go smoothly. "People are busy," she said, "and the nanny process is time consuming, so all these pieces that need to be included in the work agreement form are pushed to the back burner. It's understandable why some serious problems happen."

> Household employers must take the same professional attitude toward job descriptions and work agreements in the household as do corporations. Doing so will greatly help establish the first-time, as well as the experienced employer, as a professional and put structure around the position.
>
> —Guy

Work Agreement Checklist

An experienced employment attorney should review your work agreement. As you are preparing the agreement, keep these few tips in mind.

- Think clearly about what to include in the work agreement, and if using an agency, get its input.

- Be concise. There is no room for ambiguity in the phrasing of the work agreement.

- If using a standard work agreement template, customize it to suit the household's specific needs.

- Leave no stone unturned. Include everything the job will involve.

- Once written, discuss the work agreement with the employee.

- Make sure the employee signs and dates the agreement, and receives a copy.

- Be sure the agreement is in place prior to the employee's start date.

- The agreement should be signed and dated by both the employer and employee, and it should be witnessed.

- An agreement should be written so it is understandable by a high school graduate.

- Font size must be a minimum of ten points.

- The agreement should cover all essential facts.

- Put important passages in boldface.

- Specify time periods and note reasonable limitations.

- A confidentiality clause may be included in the work agreement. This clause extends during and after employment with the household.

- If the employee expresses a concern, the employer should recommend that the employee seek his or her own legal counsel.

- Provide a signed copy to the employee and file a signed copy in the employee's personnel file.

- If working with a third party, such as a placement agency or attorney, send a signed copy to the third party for his or her records and for safekeeping.

7

Personnel Practices for the Home

The household employment industry is working to establish a professional structure around a very informal situation. The perception of the household occupation and the role within the home is often different for employers and employees. Many employers view hiring staff for their home as a personal responsibility, whereas household employees see it as employment. Even though the employment is not in an office or a retail setting, it is a worksite where employment laws prevail. Of course, for the employer, it also is a home and a sanctuary. It will take some effort for a household employer to view his or her home as another's workplace. Clear communication, respectful treatment, openness to discussion, and adaptability should be what everyone in the household works toward to maintain a satisfying workplace. This can be set in place from the start with an employee handbook.

An employee handbook can alter the at-will nature of the employment relationship. As discussed here, the employee handbook should outline the relationship, responsibilities, and duties. An employer must be very careful to not include binding clauses and promises to the employee that can shift the employment relationship from an at-will relationship.

The Employee Handbook

Like any employer, household employers must establish fair personnel practices and policies, and apply them equally to all staff. Providing each employee with an employee handbook that explains the household workplace's rules, practices, and policies is a necessity, and presents clear advantages to the employer.

While highly prevalent in the corporate workplace, employee handbooks are noticeably absent in the majority of households today. In tandem with the work agreement, the employee handbook cements the household's employment and personnel policies.

All new employees should receive a handbook immediately upon hire or on the employment start date. The employer should have the employee sign an *Employee Handbook Acknowledgment Receipt* (see Appendix E). The employer should file this in the employee's personnel file. The release states that the employee was provided with information on important household HR issues, such as:

- accommodation for individuals with disabilities (ADA, ADAAA)

- antiharassment and antidiscrimination policies

- Consolidated Omnibus Budget Reconciliation Act of 1985 (COBRA)

- discipline

- dress code

- educational assistance

- employee assistance

- employee benefits

- equal employment opportunity

- expense reimbursement

- household philosophy and conduct

- immigration law compliance

- in-home surveillance

- introductory or evaluation period

- labor laws and how they apply

- leave of absence

- medical insurance
- overtime
- payroll and taxes
- performance reviews
- personnel file (and access to same)
- references and background checks
- retirement
- salary increases, bonuses, and gifts
- short-term disability
- sick and personal days, holidays, and vacation time
- Social Security
- termination, resignation, and exit interview procedures
- timekeeping and work schedules
- unemployment insurance
- use of employer property
- workers' compensation insurance
- workplace safety policy
- zero tolerance of drug and alcohol use

Reference this list when developing your household's employee handbook.

When developing a handbook, address any questions an employee has or any information an employee wants to know about his or her job and the workplace. Obviously, this is a huge undertaking and is daunting for a household employer to develop. However, it is well worth the effort to avoid later disputes with the employee. Fortunately, there is also help on how to create an employee handbook. For more insight into how to develop an employee handbook and create a customized version, go to www.gtm.com.

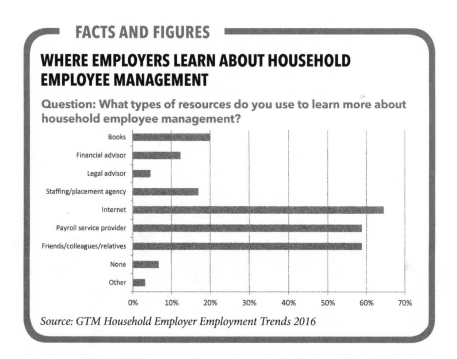

FACTS AND FIGURES

WHERE EMPLOYERS LEARN ABOUT HOUSEHOLD EMPLOYEE MANAGEMENT

Question: What types of resources do you use to learn more about household employee management?

Source: *GTM Household Employer Employment Trends 2016*

Introductory Elements for Employee Handbook

There are many elements important to an employee handbook. You may want to begin your employee handbook with a welcome letter to your employee and an at-will statement. Virtually all states are employment at-will states. To what degree states uphold the doctrine regarding employers' rights to discharge employees varies by state. The at-will statement may be included in the welcome letter to the employee, or it may stand alone as a separate written policy. Either way, it may be best for you to include the statement at the front of the employee handbook, thus clearly providing the employee with the at-will condition. Employers should be particularly careful to not create unintended liabilities in the language used in an employee handbook that creates an impression that employees can only be dismissed for cause. For example, by including procedures that will follow with regard to discipline or termination. To minimize this, it is advisable to include an unambiguous disclaimer in the handbook that says that it does not create contractual rights and that the employment relationship is at-will. This can also be done by using a sample at-will employment statement, as in the *Sample Employee Handbook Sections* following (also see Appendix E). Some states make this mandatory.

In today's world, there are many technologies used to keep you informed and in touch—and even entertained. However, not all technology should be accessed during the workday, and it is a good idea to include your policies about the use of technology in the home. As an employer, you need to set your policy on an employee's access to and use of your computer, the internet, text messaging, mobile phone, handheld devices, tablet computers, television, or digitally recorded movies or shows. The employee handbook should also include your preference on how much time an employee can use his or her own technological gadgets. No one wants a nanny who is constantly texting her friends rather than playing with the children. In addition, you may also need to set a policy for any equipment—your car, exercise machines, telephone—that is on the premises and may or may not be available to your employees. Take care in developing your policies, as your employee may need to use your equipment in order to perform his or her work duties.

It may be relevant to include policies on how to handle visitors to the home. During the course of the day or work shift, an employee may need to manage guests, visitors, service professionals, vendor, repair workers, or contractors that may need or request access to the employer's home or property.

Following are sample sections of an employee handbook taken from GTM's Household HR Document service that you may want to include in an employee handbook for your employee. It can be customized to suit your household and is intended as a guideline.

Sample Employee Handbook Sections

Welcome Letter

> Welcome to our home. We wish you every success here.
>
> Please familiarize yourself with this handbook. You are responsible for reading, understanding, and complying with the policies and procedures within it.
>
> The employee handbook is a policy guide and summary of employee benefits and working conditions. It is to be used as a reference tool and guide, and is not intended

to be all-inclusive. No employee handbook can anticipate all circumstances or questions. Therefore, we reserve the right to revise, supplement, or withdraw any policy or portion of this handbook as necessary. When amendments to the household employee handbook are made, employees will be notified.

It is our intent to provide the best possible employment for household employees to excel in their positions. Our open-door policy allows an employee to ask questions and to discuss concerns or suggestions regarding the household and his or her position. By developing and maintaining clear communication, we hope to resolve any difficulties that may arise.

The information provided in the household employee handbook applies to all employees within the household and is not a contract between the employer and the employee. This is not a work agreement or job description. The work agreement we developed and signed upon your hire details your role within the household. Your work agreement pertains only to you. This employee handbook is an overall guide to the household's employment practices and policies. If at any time the handbook and work agreement specify conflicting policies, the employee should view the work agreement as the superseding document.

The employee handbook does not constitute a contract or contractual commitment of continued employment.

Again, welcome to our household.

Regards,
(Name of Employer), Household Employer

At-Will Statement

The (Name of Employer) household does not offer tenured or guaranteed employment. Employment is at-will and entered into voluntarily.

You may resign at any time and for any reason without notice, and you may be terminated at any time—with or without cause—by (Name of Employer).

Equal Employment Opportunity

The (Name of Employer) household is committed to a policy of equal employment opportunity, and maintains a policy of nondiscrimination with employees and applicants for employment. Employment within the (Name of Employer) household is not influenced in any manner by race, color, religion, sex, age, national origin, physical or mental disability, or any other basis prohibited by law. (Name of Employer) household will reasonably accommodate a person with physical or mental disability, as long as the accommodation will not cause the (Name of Employer) household undue hardship.

Workers' Compensation Insurance

The (Name of Employer) household carries workers' compensation insurance to cover the cost of work-related and work-incurred injury or illness. Workers' compensation benefits help to pay for an injured or ill employee's medical treatment, as well as to cover a portion of the employee's income that may be lost while he or she is recovering.

Workers' compensation benefits are mandated by state law, and benefits depend on the circumstances of each incident.

Social Security

All employees are covered under the federal Social Security Act, which provides for future security in case of retirement, disability, death, survivor benefits to dependents, and Medicare benefits. Employees pay a portion of their earnings into Social Security from each paycheck, and the employer matches the employees' deduction.

Use of Employer Property

Equipment essential in accomplishing job duties is expensive and may be difficult to replace. Employees who use household equipment, machines, tools, and other property to perform their duties are expected to follow proper usage and care. When using equipment and property, employees are required to follow all operating instructions, safety standards, and guidelines. If any household equipment or property is broken or damaged during an employee's job performance, the employee is expected to report it to the employer as soon as possible. The (Name of Employer) household prohibits any household property to be removed from the premises. Unauthorized removal of household property or an employee's possession of household property off work premises will be considered theft, and the employee will be immediately dismissed and criminal charges will be made.

Use of Phone, Computer, and Other Equipment

Personal telephone calls and personal use of the household computer, internet, and other equipment is not permissible unless otherwise directed or approved. The (Name of Employer) household understands that employees will need to make personal phone calls (e.g., medical appointments) from time to time. If such phone calls are necessary, employees are required to keep them brief and to a minimum.

(Name of Employer) also understands that there are some occasions that merit personal use of household computer systems or tablet devices. Household employees using household communications resources do so knowing that the content of all internal and external communications utilizing household resources is the property of the (Name of Employer) household and that (Name of Employer) reserves the right to monitor and review the use and content of any such communications.

Use of Vehicle(s)

The (Name of Employer) household may require an employee to use the employer's car in order to complete job tasks. If driving is required, the employee will be permitted to use the employer's car. (Only employees with clean driving records will be allowed use of the employer's car.)

Employees need to be aware that (Name of Employer) is taking great expense to allow the household employee(s) to use (Name of Employer) household vehicle(s). Repairs may be costly and parts may be difficult to replace. Improper, careless, negligent, destructive, or unsafe use or operation of (Name of Employer) vehicle(s), as well as excessive or avoidable traffic and parking violations, may result in disciplinary action, up to and including termination.

Workplace Visitors

The household does not allow employees to have visitors on work premises during their working hours without prior permission. On occasion, in specific circumstances and only with prior authorization by the employer, employees may have a family member or friend visit during working hours. During these occasions, employees are responsible for the conduct and safety of their visitors.

If an unauthorized individual is observed on household premises, employees are required to immediately telephone the police and contact the employers at the listed emergency number(s).

Work Personnel and Contractors

The (Name of Employer) household will work directly with service and repair professionals and contractors concerning all household matters. (Name of Employer) will arrange an appointment and inform the household employee of the time and date of the scheduled appointment.

(Name of Employer) requests that while inside the house, the employee:

- require all contractors to sign in and out of a service visit book upon entrance to and departure from the house

- accompany the service technician, repairman, vendor, or contractor to the area in need of service

- while at the house, contractors and service technicians should use their own mobile phones; if they do not have a mobile, the employee should accompany the individual to the household's main telephone, which the technician may use for local calls only

- when work has been completed, the employee is to accompany the technician back to the entrance

- if a vendor or service bill is left with the employee, the employee will paper clip the bill or service information to the service visit book page the vendor signed. The employee is to inform (Name of Employer) that the service was performed and that the invoice or statement is included in the service visit book

Expense Reports and Reimbursement for Work-Related Expenses

An employer should detail—in the employee handbook—the process an employee must follow for reimbursement of work-related expenses or disbursement of spending money for an upcoming event. As part of the process, it is helpful to stipulate that an expense report must be submitted each month, fiscal quarter, or event, and whether the employer requires the original sales receipt or a photocopy of the sales receipt. Also, employers may include guidance on the minimum dollar amount when an original sales receipt or photocopy of the sales receipt is required (e.g., all expenses of $10 or more must be submitted with a receipt or photocopy of a receipt). For example, if a nanny spends $2 on an ice-cream bar for a child at the playground, then a receipt (or photocopy of the receipt) is not mandatory. However, if a personal assistant spends $12.50 on office supplies, then a receipt (or photocopy of the receipt) must be attached to the *Expense Report*. (See Appendix E.)

A list of approved employer-covered expenses should be included within the employee handbook and amended as necessary. To ensure clarity, some employers also include a list of expenses that are not covered. For instance, some employers may cover an employee's mileage, tolls, and parking, but not maintenance costs or gas (which is actually included in the mileage reimbursement rate). Some employers may cover the costs of work-related cell phone calls, but not the cost of the cell phone or its monthly service charge. The handbook and the expense reimbursement form may include a clearly worded sentence recommending that an employee with any questions regarding reimbursement and employer-covered expenses check with the employer regarding coverage approval prior to the event or task.

CASE STUDY

• •

TRISH STEVENS
NANNY
NEW YORK, NY

Trish Stevens said she became a nanny because she wanted to be Mary Poppins.

"I knew I wanted to take care of children," said Stevens, who has been a nanny for over 20 years and has worked in Indiana, Ohio, and New York. "Each job is different...Today, it is more of a profession, with more people thinking of it as a real job. Now, there are personal days and paid holidays. It's more than being a babysitter and more like being a teacher."

Stevens, who cares for three children in New York City, ensures that work agreements are in place with her employers to clearly describe the job requirements. "It's not easy finding [the right] nanny, and it's not easy to find [the right] nanny job," said Stevens.

The agreement helps, but Stevens offers some tips on how household employers should treat their employees, including the following.

- Say thank you.

- Remember that your nanny is there for the children, not to keep house.

- Offer the business standard of at least five paid personal days and five paid sick days each year.

- Pay for at least half of the employee's health insurance.

- If a nanny goes on vacation with the family, remember that it is the employers' vacation—not the nanny's (she or he still must care for the children)—and he or she still needs downtime.

- If an employer cannot afford a raise or a bonus, offer some time off, if appropriate.

- Pay a nanny on the books, with the correct taxes withheld.

- Understand that a household employee does not have the same resources as the employer. If an employer decides to take the next few days off, an offer for the employee to "get away" or use her or his vacation days during that time is not as generous as it may appear to the employer. Unexpectedly offering the employee an opportunity to take vacation time in just a matter of days does not allow for economical travel planning and scheduling.

For nannies, Stevens offers these tips.

- Speak English, or the language agreed upon by employer and employee.
- Support the parent, even if you do not agree.
- Be trained in CPR and first aid.
- Be sure to develop a work agreement with the employer.

A household employee's perspective is interesting to hear and is really no different from the expectations of those who work for large companies. All of these tips may be achieved by taking into account the employer's goals and the employee's needs when developing personnel policies, and by setting the stage for ongoing communication.

In this case, an employer would most likely provide an employee handbook stating the termination, personal time off, salary increase, payroll, and employment policies that promote achieving household goals.

—Guy

CASE STUDY

DENISE SHADE
HOUSEHOLD EMPLOYER
NEW YORK, NY

Denise Shade, first sought in-home child care so her children could be on their own schedules and not adhere to their parents' work timetables. "Primarily, the kids did not have to mold to our jobs," she said. "They could nap when they wanted and not be woken up by us to be transported someplace else. Plus, as newborns, in-home child care limited their exposure to germs, compared to a setting with many children."

Shade first hired a nanny when her daughter was born. Although they first intended to hire a nanny who lived outside the home out of concern for their privacy, the Shades hired a live-in nanny because they wanted to hire a particular candidate who needed a live-in situation. They have had live-in nannies ever since.

"It worked out better than we expected," said Shade, who takes great care to respect the nanny's time. "We ensure that the nanny is done with work at 6 p.m. If we need child care at night, we hire a babysitter, or, if we need to, we'll hire the nanny for the night as a babysitter if she is available."

Respect for the nanny and his or her abilities is the key to Shade's successful employee relationships—and is the foundation for close connections that continue today. Shade's first nanny was ideal for the care required for a single newborn. When Shade gave birth to her son three years later, another nanny with multitasking skills was hired. Unfortunately, when the Shades moved from Ohio to Connecticut, the second nanny did not relocate, preferring to stay in close proximity to her family.

In all, the family has had great experiences with nannies, and these have countered one poor experience—the result of the nanny having different expectations, said Shade.

Although already having enjoyed fantastic nanny relationships, Shade said that one was a "difficult experience for everyone in the family. We learned that small issues can quickly disrupt the functioning of the entire family." Along with unrealistic expectations, the nanny was a difficult and unhappy person, Shade said. She explained that the nanny complained about the water bottles purchased just for her because they had screw tops and not pop-up tops, the rug for her room was not soft enough on her feet, and she disliked the car provided for her to drive. Because the nanny held an associate's degree in child development, she believed she was the final authority when it came to the children. She also claimed that she was the "number-one nanny" the Shades could have.

What really ended the relationship, however, was the nanny's maverick manner. According to Shade, the nanny medicated her daughter three different times without informing either parent—despite the fact that the daughter's father was working from home during her illness. When confronted, the nanny claimed that during her work hours—despite a parent's presence in the home—she had the final say on child care. Also, the nanny caused an incident at her daughter's elementary school by taking her out of school early on a snow day without informing the staff. The nanny had removed their daughter from school when she was picking up their son at the end of his standard half day. (Her daughter's school, Shade said, locks down when a child is thought to be missing.)

Along with providing great respect to her nanny, Shade also strictly adheres to fair and honest financial dealings with her nanny. If anything, said Shade, she ensures that all financial circumstances are in the nanny's favor. For instance, Shade rigorously monitors the nanny's time worked. If Shade is late, she pays the nanny for all extra time worked. Also, if during a pay period Shade has come home from work early or taken a vacation day, then she will pay the period's full salary wage.

"We really try not to take advantage of her," said Shade, "and we don't dump extra tasks on her. If the chore is in our contract, she does it. If not, we don't want her to do it."

In exchange for respecting her in-home employee's time and workload, and for her compensating fairly and considerately, Shade said she receives enormous loyalty. "The nanny really makes an effort to be available, because she knows we need her help," she said.

A household employer improves with each new experience. Showing consideration for an employee's feelings helps even the playing field between employee and employer, and is the correct management approach when dealing with employment issues. Employees must understand that an employer needs to be a manager, which includes establishing initial goals, communicating the philosophy of the home, and fostering household culture, as well as supervising the household employee. Plus, employees need to know up front how you will measure their performance. Set periodic review meetings to evaluate those goals and the employee's performance, handle lingering communication issues, clarify household policy, and coach the employee to improve his or her skills during his or her employment.

—Guy

Medical Release Forms

For child care and senior care workers, an employer should prepare a medication release form, allowing the caregiver permission to administer medication for prescribed and over-the-counter medication. Also, employers need to prepare a temporary medical care release form that allows a child to be treated by a physician or health care organization without a parent present. The caregiver can present this medical care release form with the employer's health insurance card to obtain treatment. (See Appendix E, for a sample *Medical Care Release* form and a sample *Medication Permission* form.)

Maintaining an Employee Personnel File

Keeping an employee personnel file ensures that the employer obtains and maintains information required by law and establishes a documented work history for that particular employee. The file contains all information related to that employee, such as job description, job application, job offer letter, *Form W-4* (Appendix E), the state withholding certificate (if applicable), a signed statement that the employee received an employee handbook, the work agreement, *Attendance Record* (Appendix E), performance evaluations, benefit forms, compliments and complaints from co-workers, awards, and so on. Keep personnel records confidential and locked in a safe location so no one can access them without the employer's consent.

Some states require employers to allow both past and present employees access to their employment files. Employers usually can ask the employee to look through the file on the worksite, with the employer present, ensuring that nothing is altered or taken. Some states allow employers to copy parts of the file and provide them to the employee, enabling the employer to shield sensitive information from the employee. Employers should include information on employees' access to their personnel records in the employee handbook.

Performance Reviews

Companies of all sizes establish periodic (written) reviews and evaluations of employees. It is a good employment practice to implement, particularly for new employees, because it allows the employer and employee to communicate what the employee has accomplished and areas that may need development. With the reviews, employees are provided an opportunity to improve, and the employer has a documented history of the employee's performance and problems.

While informal employer-employee discussions relating to job performance and goals are encouraged and expected throughout an employee's tenure, it is common practice for an employer to perform a formal written performance review at the end of an employee's introductory period, and then on a scheduled basis. (See Appendix E, for a sample *Performance Evaluation Form*.) Many employers choose to review employees on a yearly basis. Some prefer to evaluate employees every six months. The work agreement and the employee handbook should detail expected review times.

When reviewing an employee's work performance, employers need to remember to focus on work performance and not on the employee's personality or characteristics. Employers should:

- be as positive as possible but very clear about situations—speak frankly and in a straightforward manner
- offer a review of both strengths and weaknesses
- cite specific examples of when the employee has exceeded, met, or failed job expectations

- set reasonable goals for the employee to work toward (and meet) in developing and improving skills

- schedule a second review to determine the employee's progress if her or his performance is weak (this could be done in three months or six months—whichever is considered a fair amount of time for the employee to improve and demonstrate better performance)

- list in the review any disciplinary actions, including termination, if the employee fails to improve his or her performance

Employees may thoroughly examine all performance reviews and may provide a written opinion to be placed in the personnel file. Some evaluation forms have a designated area for the employee's response. It is common practice for both the employer and employee to both sign the review. This documentation helps protect the employer from any false claim made by a current or former employee.

Performance reviews may or may not be accompanied by a salary increase consideration. Employers should clearly state that salary increases are awarded in light of an employee's significant performance and at the employer's discretion—and certainly are not guaranteed. Salary increases are evaluated by the employee's:

- ability to perform all job tasks and functions

- attendance and punctuality

- willingness to work

- ability to cooperate with other employees and household members

- adherence to all household policies

CASE STUDY

WILLIAM BRUCE REYNOLDS
FORMER OWNER/CONSULTANT
ESTATE CONSULTING AND MANAGEMENT, INC.
COLUMBIA COUNTY, NY

William Bruce Reynolds has spent much of his time working with the staffs of private homes, resorts, and restaurants, teaching them how to provide the utmost in customer service. A director of the International Guild of Professional Butlers, a chef trained at the Culinary Institute of America, a Certified Executive Protection Specialist, and an experienced household manager, Reynolds helps others find employment, and uses the wealth of his experiences to train others to succeed in the household and service professions.

Reynolds said he believes the industry is divided into two groups:

1. those people who are trained and highly motivated
2. those people who are untrained and poorly motivated

An employer who has spent millions of dollars creating his or her dream property looks to a professional household manager to train and supervise a staff capable of delivering the highest degree of professional service. The position of household manager is quite comprehensive and requires proper training and education.

The household manager is required to create a multifaceted program specific to the estate that he or she is managing. The plan will include, but not be limited to the following:

- safety and security

- property systems

- maintenance

- organization

- operations

- staff management

- vendor, trade, and outside laborer management

Reynolds reminds those working in the household profession that they do so at the whim of the individual or family. All questions should be answered beforehand, and both parties should know what is expected from the arrangement. The position will last only as long as the requirements set forth in the working agreement are carried out.

"For household help to be treated as professional, they must always conduct themselves as professionals," noted Reynolds.

Hiring a household manager to outsource the management responsibilities of an estate is similar to a growing company's founder hiring a chief operations officer to run the firm's operations. As multimillion-dollar companies have objectives and budgets to manage, so do households. Therefore, a household manager, who is tasked with keeping a close eye on the balance sheet and the estate's expenses, requires higher skill sets than typical household employees. For a maximum return on investment, an effectively run estate—whether a small, five-thousand-square-foot estate or a large, sixty-thousand-square-foot estate—benefits from a well-managed program featuring detailed policy and procedure manuals for all aspects of the estate and its operations.

—Guy

Discipline

While household employment is largely at-will employment (see Chapter 2) in most states, an employer will generally take disciplinary action before dismissing an employee. Such discipline can be implemented in progressively more serious actions, such as a verbal warning followed by a written warning, counseling, probation, suspension, and finally termination. By employing a progressive disciplinary practice, an employer can demonstrate that the employee knew about the problems and, for whatever reason, did not improve the situation. In the employee handbook, detail the disciplinary policy, but state that employees may be fired at will. Ensure, too, that not all employee actions will be spun through the progressive process; a serious infraction of household policy and serious misdeed will result in immediate dismissal. If an employee proves untrustworthy and instills fear that harm will be done to a household member, a co-worker, or employer property, by all means, remove the employee from the workplace *immediately*. In the employee handbook, state that the employer will decide which situation warrants what type of disciplinary action. (See the *Sample Offer Letter* in Appendix D.)

First Days

As an employer, you need to prepare for your nanny's (or other household help's) first days on the job. He or she needs to become acquainted with the household, its operations, its environment—even the household's culture. Be ready to spend some time with your new nanny during his or her first several days, perhaps spending the entire day with him or her the first day, and reducing the number of hours on the following day. You want to be there to help the nanny become accustomed to the nuances of the household, the children, and their schedules. To help, prepare a list of activities and information you need to cover with your new nanny during his or her first few days.

Some ideas to make the transition proceed smoothly include the following.

- Introduce your new employee to the members of the household. In particular, take whatever time is necessary for you to encourage your children to become familiar with the new nanny.

- Introduce your new nanny to your neighbors.

- Take your new nanny on a tour of the community, pointing out local drugstores, schools, your doctor's office, playgrounds, hospitals, and so on. Notify your children's school or day care center if the nanny will be picking the children up from either location, and perhaps visit the school or center to introduce your nanny to the staff.

- Make sure the nanny's name is on the list of authorized persons to pick up the children and that proper documentation is submitted.

- If the nanny will be using your vehicle, spend some time reviewing the vehicle with the new employee. Make sure he or she is comfortable driving the vehicle prior to transporting the children. Practice driving the car with the new hire, quietly observing his or her skills while you cover the typical route the nanny will be taking, such as the route from the home to the elementary school or from the home to the local public library. Also, be certain the nanny can properly install a child safety seat, if applicable. (Local fire departments often provide free training regarding proper child safety seat installation and usage.) Practice with him or her taking the seat in and out of the car, and practice proper restraint of your child.

- Review all household policies and procedures listed in the employee handbook. (Remember, now is a good opportunity to discuss household rules on visitors, as well as phone and computer use.) Be sure the new employee understands these policies, procedures, and rules.

- Address all emergency contact information, and post it in a designated area for the nanny.

- Review all safety procedures and appliances for the household. (First aid kit, alarm system, washer, dryer, and any other household equipment that the employee is expected to use.)

- During the first workweek, review job responsibilities detailed in the job description, and take the time to sit down and discuss with the employee how the first week went.

- Review the work agreement.

- After the first few days, drop by unannounced for a quick visit to see how things are progressing, or telephone at different times during the day to check in.

- Describe your performance review plan. Do periodic performance reviews for the first six months.

- Set aside time at the end of each workday to discuss the day. Remember, you want to have a ten- or fifteen-minute recap of the day's or night's events before handing over responsibility for the children.

- During these recaps, be sure to encourage the nanny, reinforcing the expectations you have while also boosting his or her self-esteem. Use these recaps to provide alternatives to how the nanny may have handled a situation. These constructive conversations will help in obtaining the household you have been working toward.

- Ask the nanny to keep a daily log, entering important events as well as questions that arise during the first several weeks, and ask the nanny to make note of any supplies needed. At the end of the workday, review the log with him or her, and take the opportunity to establish trust and mutual respect for one another.

To help you prepare for your new nanny, think about the following.

- What results are you seeking?

- What information, tools, and instruction does the nanny need to know to successfully do his or her job?

- What are the priority tasks and what are the secondary tasks?

- What support or assistance do you need to provide to your new nanny to make his or her adjustment to your household as quick and easy as possible?

A welcome practice is for the employer and employee to spend the first days of employment together for training. You can show the new nanny where things are, review household procedures, provide him or her with the established preferences for the household (e.g., keep all bedroom doors closed, put all notes and messages on a dry-erase board affixed to the refrigerator), demonstrate how to operate household equipment and where he or she can find operations manuals, review work and safety procedures, and so on. It is also an opportunity for both to get to know each other, to treat one another with respect and professionalism, and begin to establish trust.

Schedule a meeting for one week after the start date for a discussion on how the job is going, issues that have arisen or may arise, questions that need to be answered, and so forth. This will help ensure that any uncertainty is resolved and will establish the relationship with open and clear communication. An employer's efforts to be available to employees for reviews and discussions of the job, expectations, work environment, and the like will go a long way to foster a respectful and trusting relationship.

Q & A

Q. As a new parent, I am concerned with leaving my infant with my newly hired nanny. If I install a nanny cam in my home, am I required to inform the nanny that she may be monitored?

A. It is fair and proper for a household employer to fully disclose to a job applicant whether he or she will monitor the household. Check your local law for the legal use of these devices in your home and your employee's workplace. Disclose this information during the hiring process to ensure that the applicant is comfortable with this practice.

Personnel Practices Checklist

- Note that while household employment is largely a customized situation, it is often handled as an informal situation. In fact, it is a professional endeavor requiring human resources and personnel practices and policies.

- Write and update job descriptions.

- Establish household policies and procedures.

- Develop and maintain an employee handbook detailing all policies, including work schedule, performance reviews, dismissal, severance, references, and so on.

- Include an at-will statement with your employee handbook.

- Provide an orientation during the first few days of employment with on-the-job training for the household employee.

- Establish a performance review schedule for the first year and keep to it.

- Ensure the employee has all the necessary forms and releases that he or she may need to perform his or her job (e.g., medical release form, expense report form).

- Inform the necessary people about the employee's start date (e.g., schools, neighbors, relevant doctor's offices, special needs staff).

8

Determining Wages and Scheduling Hours

Wage and hour concerns are complicated; therefore, they create a lot of uncertainty within households that employ help. Through the job description and work agreement, wages and hours should be clearly defined and agreed on by both employer and employee. To even begin the interviewing process, employers should define a specific work schedule for the employee, as well as a policy for when work is required or performed beyond the specified regular workday. In addition, before beginning employment, wages should be negotiated and agreed on, and pay schedules should be clearly established. However, there is much more involved with wages and hours in the law. Employers must be aware of their legal requirements on federal, state, and local levels in order to lawfully hire and employ a household employee.

Uncertainty stems from the fact that there are many laws, as well as misinformation and anecdotal recommendations from friends and advisers who are not experts in household employment. In wage and hour issues, the problem exists of not knowing what the requirements are—and there is much to know and manage. This chapter discusses why employers must pay an employee according to the law, and provides information on how to properly plan for and manage wages and hours. With the following information, employers will be more informed—and more comfortable—with wage and hour legal requirements.

Discussing Gross Pay vs. Net Pay Payment Methods

It is extremely important that, from the beginning, all discussions about wages between household employer and household employee clearly state whether the wage will be gross pay or net pay. Many employees who work in the home are not aware of the tax deductions that are necessary for them to be legal and may have worked before off the books by receiving only cash when paid for their work. From the employer perspective, an employer just wants to know the total cost of hiring an employee. For the worker, they want to know what money they will be taking home at the end of the week. Because of the nature of the household employment industry and the history of so many employers hiring illegally and paying illegally, a minority of domestic workers are interested in the benefits of being paid according to the law. In some circles and among the more professional household employees, this is changing. And as more famous examples of exposure are publicized, employers are more aware of the risks involved in not paying an employee legally.

Employers do have a greater risk when using net calculations to pay employees as the employer is responsible for all taxes. Also, the tax amounts can change with tax law changes or if the employee chooses to increase or decrease his or her withholdings.

FACTS AND FIGURES

Note: the example used below includes the calculations: filing singly, zero allowances and zero deductions, from Massachusetts.

Scenario 1: Talking in gross pay terms

When gross pay is agreed to, the necessary withholding taxes (Social Security, Medicare, federal income tax, and state income tax—for example Massachusetts) will be deducted from this gross wage. The remaining amount is the net that is paid to the employee. So, if the gross pay is $500, the employer would pay the employee $500 of gross, *less* the deductions from tax (approximately $121.20

a week). This would result in the employee's take home, or *net* pay, as being $378.80.

The employer then has to remember that there are additional employer taxes to be paid on top of the *gross* pay of $500 (federal and state unemployment, matching Social Security, and Medicare), which calculates to about $50.60. When this is combined with the gross $500, the total employer responsibility is $550.60, in order to pay the employee $378.80 a week.

Scenario 2: Talking in net pay terms

Net calculations begin with an agreed-on net or take-home pay, which then has to be "grossed up" by the employee's Social Security, Medicare, withholding taxes, and other mandatory deductions. For example, using a net calculation of $500 agreed on by employer and employee would mean that the employee would take home $500. When this is grossed up by the employee's taxes, there is a gross payment of $668.00 (using Massachusetts as an example of state taxes).

For the employer, there are then the employer taxes on top of that $668.00 (federal unemployment tax, Social Security, Medicare, and state unemployment—MA here), which add up to $67.60. This has to be added on to the gross wage of $668.00 to give a total employer responsibility of $735.60.

Scenario 1 with a gross pay of $500 creates an employer's total responsibility of $550.60 per week.

Scenario 2 with a net pay salary of $500, creates an employer's responsibility of $735.60 per week.

An employer who does not understand the difference between gross pay and net pay can potentially find him- or herself in a situation where he or she is paying an additional $185.00 per week. Therefore, it is important to know the differences prior to negotiating the compensation with your employee.

Note: Calculations estimated from tax rates as of January 2017. Exact calculations may have changed from time of print. Up-to-date figures can be calculated using GTM's Tax Calculator at www.gtm.com.

Discussing Hourly Wages vs. Salary

Deciding to pay an employee an hourly wage or a salary is another key element of household employment. Generally, most household employees are paid an hourly wage, especially those who work part time. This allows for more accurate record keeping which is mandatory according to the *Fair Labor Standards Act* (FLSA) for hourly workers. This is especially true because, according to the FLSA and many state's labor standards, household employees are classified as nonexempt to overtime laws and therefore must be paid on an hourly wage basis and be paid overtime. However, salaries are sometimes appropriate for long-term employees who work full time and who generally have managerial or supervisory responsibilities (e.g., household managers). There are important considerations to both parties.

An employee paid an hourly wage is based on the actual hours he or she has worked in a given payroll cycle. In contrast, a salary employee is paid based on an agreed annual salary amount, divided by the number of payroll cycles in a calendar year. The most common payroll cycles are the following:

- weekly, for 52 cycles for the year

- weekly-lag, which lags your payroll by one week, for 52 cycles in the year

- biweekly, for 26 cycles in a year

- semimonthly, for 24 cycles

- monthly, for 12 cycles per year

For example, if an employer and an employee agreed to an hourly wage of $12.50. To compute the compensation, you would multiply the hours (40) times the rate of $12.50 to come up with a $500 weekly rate. For a salaried employee, you would take the annual salary (e.g., $26,000) and divide by 52 pay frequencies to come up with a $500 weekly salary. Once the agreed-on compensation has been discussed, employers should always communicate in writing an hourly compensation to their employee, keep proper time cards, and document the hours worked on the employee's pay stub each pay cycle.

Fair Labor Standards Act

The U.S. *Fair Labor Standards Act* (FLSA) establishes minimum wage, overtime pay, record-keeping, and child labor laws affecting full- and part-time workers. Under FLSA's individual coverage provision, domestic service workers—housekeepers, nannies, cooks, chauffeurs, and so on—are covered if their cash wages from one employer are at least $2,000 (2017) per calendar year.

According to the U.S. Department of Labor (DOL), the FLSA requires employers to pay employees at least the minimum wage (set by the federal government at $7.25 per hour for 2017) and overtime pay of one and a half times the employee's regular rate of pay. (See the table in this chapter on minimum wage rates per state.)

Overtime pay must be paid for hours worked over 40 hours in a work week—with some exceptions. (See the box below on what the FLSA does not require.) Overtime wages (as required by FLSA) are due on the regular payday for the pay period covered. Household employers with staff living *outside* the workplace must comply with the FLSA labor law.

Live-in domestic workers *not* employed by a third party are exempt from the FLSA's overtime pay requirement, although they must be paid at least the applicable minimum wage for all hours worked. The law provides that caregivers are not required to be compensated for times where they reside in the home but have complete freedom from all duties (meals, sleep, or other free time), if employee and employer agree. If the meal periods, sleep time, or other free time are interrupted by work duties, the interruption must be counted as hours worked. Some states, like California, New York, Maryland, Minnesota, and New Jersey, have laws that extend greater protection to live-in help, including overtime.

CASE STUDY

● ●

ANNIE DAVIS
OWNER/OPERATOR
ANNIE'S NANNIES, INC.
SEATTLE, WA

Annie's Nannies, Inc., a nanny referral agency based in Seattle, places nannies throughout Washington State. Most nannies, who are predominantly viewed as salaried employees, work 40-50 hours per week, said owner Annie Davis. However, even if they are treated as salaried employees, overtime pay still applies to domestic workers who live outside the workplace.

One nanny who Davis placed cared for a child for four years. At the job's outset, both nanny and employers agreed on hours and salary. After four years, however, the nanny decided to end the relationship because she was working longer hours than previously agreed on. She submitted one month's notice. The nanny and the child's father argued, and the father asked the nanny not to return to work.

The family blocked the nanny's unemployment insurance claim. The nanny, upset with being out of one month's salary and with being denied unemployment insurance, contacted her attorney.

The nanny took the family to court to obtain unemployment benefits. The family failed to attend the court proceedings, and the judge ruled in favor of the nanny to access unemployment. The judge, reviewing the nanny's hours worked, informed the nanny that she was entitled to overtime pay for the period she worked. The nanny then sued the family for all of the overtime pay she was entitled to during her four years of employment. According to Davis, the case was settled out of court for $15,000, and the nanny likely would have been awarded more money if her suit went through the court process.

It is an expensive lesson to learn. "My guess is most families do not abide by the overtime laws for domestic employees, and in fact, most do not even know domestic employees are covered by law," said Davis. "As an agency, you have to educate families on everything. Families need to know their legal requirements, including tax and payroll requirements."

Prior to hiring an employee, it is very important for any household employer to understand his or her obligations as an employer, as well as which laws apply to the household. Generally, employers do not look to take advantage of their help, but they often feel cheated when matters that adversely affect their financial expectations arise—whether the matter entails tax obligations, misunderstanding gross wages vs. net wages, or assuming that overtime rules do not apply to them.

—Guy

FACTS AND FIGURES
NOT REQUIRED UNDER FLSA

FLSA does not require (but please be advised that some local laws may require):

- vacation, holiday, severance, or sick pay
- meal or rest periods, holidays off, or vacations
- premium pay for weekend or holiday work
- pay raises or fringe benefits
- discharge notice, reason for discharge, or immediate payment of final wages to terminated employees

Source: U.S. Department of Labor, "Handy Reference Guide to the Fair Labor Standards Act," revised 2014.

FACTS AND FIGURES
WHAT EMPLOYERS PAY THEIR NANNIES (GROSS WAGES PER WEEK)

Question: Approximately how much does your nanny earn in pre-tax (gross) wages per week?

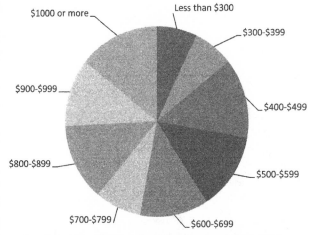

Source: GTM Household Employer Employment Trends 2016

FLSA Record Keeping

According to the law, employers are required to keep records on wages, hours, and other items as specified by DOL record-keeping regulations. Records to be kept for minimum wage and overtime pay include the following:

1. employee's full name and Social Security number

2. address, including zip code

3. birth date, if younger than age 19

4. sex and occupation

5. time and day of week when employee's workweek begins

6. hours worked each day

7. total hours worked each workweek

8. basis on which employee's wages are paid (e.g., "$9 per hour," "$440 a week," "piecework")

9. regular hourly pay rate

10. total daily or weekly straight-time earnings

11. total overtime earnings for the workweek

12. all additions to, or deductions from, the employee's wages

13. total wages paid each pay period

14. date of payment and the pay period covered by the payment

For more on FLSA, go to www.dol.gov or call the wage hour toll-free information and help line at 1-866-4USWAGE (1-866-487-9243).

A handy guide to FLSA regulations for homecare workers can be found at www.dol.gov/whd/homecare/homecare_guide.pdf

As a rule of thumb, the records should be retained for at least three years, but it is advised that seven years is better.

Employers subject to the FLSA's minimum wage requirements must post (and keep posted) in the workplace the federal minimum wage rate. Posters can be easily downloaded at www.dol.gov or obtained at state labor departments.

Also, the FLSA does not limit the number of hours in a day or days in a week an employee may be required or scheduled to work, including overtime hours, if the employee is at least 16 years old. These issues are to be agreed on by the employer and the employee.

In addition, many states set their own minimum wage and overtime pay laws. Employers need to ensure that they comply with the laws set in their locality. State labor departments can provide more information to employers on state and local requirements.

FACTS AND FIGURES

WAGE PROTECTION FOR HOME CARE WORKERS AND THE FINAL RULE

Under the Fair Labor Standards Act (FLSA) employees are protected for minimum wage and overtime worked. The FLSA exempts certain direct care workers from FLSA, most notably the live-in domestic worker who is exempt from overtime but must still be paid at least minimum wage. (Agencies and other third-party employers are not included in the exemption.) The Department of Labor's Final Rule which took effect January 1, 2015, revised some of the regulations surrounding domestic service workers: narrowing the meaning of companion services to fellowship, protection, and up to 20 percent of care services. The Final Rule brings important minimum wage and overtime protection to the workers working especially with those with disabilities, or elderly individuals in their homes. If more than 20 percent of a worker's hours during the work week is spent providing care services, companionship and protection cannot be claimed for that work week. In addition, the companionship exemption cannot be claimed if the worker performs any household work for other household members or any medically related service.

The main changes from previous regulations include:

(1) the tasks that comprise "companionship services" are more clearly defined

(2) the exemptions for companionship services and live-in domestic service employees are limited to the individual, family, or household using the services

(3) the recordkeeping requirements for employers of live-in domestic service employees are revised

For more information, see www.dol.gov/whd/regs/compliance/whdfsfinalrule.htm

FACTS AND FIGURES

WHERE EMPLOYERS LEARN ABOUT SALARY AND BENEFITS

Question: How did you determine what pay and benefits to offer your nanny?

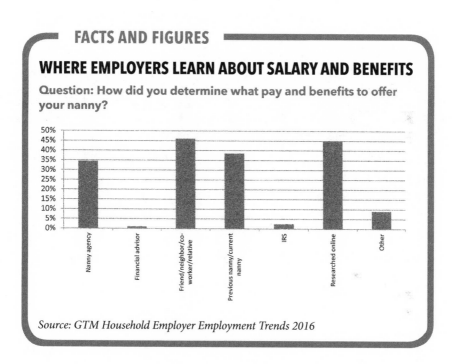

Source: *GTM Household Employer Employment Trends 2016*

Salaries and Minimum Wage

Salaries vary greatly in the household employment industry—just as household positions and workplaces differ. The household position is often customized to meet the needs of one particular household, and salaries reflect that fact. No standard salaries exist within the household employment industry other than the federal minimum wage requirements. The minimum wage in the United States is $7.25 per hour (2017), unless the state in which the household employee works mandates that it is higher. (The U.S. Congress has been considering raising the minimum wage. To ensure that you know the current minimum wage rate, go to www.dol.gov.)

A Philadelphia agency owner said she believes that a nanny's salary and compensation package should reflect her or his background and experience. "The more experienced, educated nanny typically is paid in the higher salary range," she said. "As in any industry, an individual who brings more to the job by way of a broader and deeper experience will be compensated accordingly."

A GTM partner agency owner added that she has little to offer families that want to underpay employees. When it comes to household employee pay, she lives by the maxim "you get what you pay for. Our children are worth more. Salary is not a place to cut corners."

Another GTM partner agency located in New York City agreed. "An employer is paying for one-on-one time with his/her child, with no downtime. One client who wanted to employ a nanny for 40 hours for four workdays flipped out over the suggested salary range of $450 to $550 per week that nannies were being paid. I told her, 'This is not your Mercedes Benz or Toyota Camry. You're trying to cut costs in the wrong place. You must think of it as an investment in your child's well-being.'"

FACTS AND FIGURES
MINIMUM WAGE PER STATE IN 2017

STATE	Rate
Federal	$7.25
Alabama	no state minimum; $7.25 for Federal
Alaska	$9.80
Arizona	$10.00
Arkansas	$8.50
California	$10.50 for employers with 26 or more workers, $10.00 for employers with 25 or less employees
Colorado	$9.30
Connecticut	$10.10

Delaware	$8.25
District of Columbia	$12.50* effective July 1, 2017
Florida	$8.10
Georgia	$7.25
Hawaii	$9.25
Idaho	$7.25
Illinois	$8.25
Indiana	$7.25
Iowa	$7.25
Kansas	$7.25
Kentucky	$7.25
Louisiana	no state minimum; $7.25 for Federal
Maine	$9.00
Maryland	$9.25* effective July 1, 2017
Massachusetts	$11.00
Michigan	$8.90
Minnesota	$9.00
Mississippi	no state minimum; $7.25 for Federal
Missouri	$7.70
Montana	$8.15
Nebraska	$9.00
Nevada	$8.25 with no health insurance benefits provided by employer/$7.25 with health insurance
New Hampshire	$7.25
New Jersey	$8.44

New Mexico	$7.50
New York	$9.70 (New York City, Long Island and Westchester have higher minimum wage. NYC: $10.50 for employers with 10 or less employees, and $11.00 for employers with 11 or more employees.)
North Carolina	$7.25
North Dakota	$7.25
Ohio	$8.15
Oklahoma	$7.25
Oregon	$10.25* effective July 1, 2017
Pennsylvania	$7.25
Rhode Island	$9.60
South Carolina	no state minimum; $7.25 for Federal
South Dakota	$8.65
Tennessee	no state minimum; $7.25 for Federal
Texas	$7.25
Utah	$7.25
Vermont	$10.00
Virginia	$7.25
Washington	$11.00
West Virginia	$8.75
Wisconsin	$7.25
Wyoming	$7.25

Note: Minimum Wage is subject to change, please refer to www.dol.gov/whd/min-wage/america.htm for the most recent information.

Source: www.dol.gov, 2017

FACTS AND FIGURES

THE CRIME OF WAGE THEFT

While household employees are often excluded from federal and state laws protecting against wage theft and overtime pay because of the limited number of employees within the home/business, a growing number of states are addressing the crime of wage theft by some employers—employers who pay workers below minimum wage or do not pay overtime, resulting in overworked, underpaid employees. Many (but not all) of these employees tend to be immigrants who come to the United States desperate for any work, and who therefore accept what is on offer—even if the job entails an infringement of worker's rights and federal and state law.

According to a 2013 briefing report, "Low Wages and Scant Benefits Leave Many In-home Workers Unable to Make Ends Meet", by Heidi Shierholz, in-home workers, such as nannies, housekeepers, and senior care workers, often receive such low wages that they are living below twice the poverty threshold. While the household employer must ensure his or her employee receives at least the minimum wage and other protections such as overtime pay, meal breaks, etc., domestic worker organizations are calling for action at the federal and state level as many employers are in violation of this.

According to the briefing report, in-home workers have a higher incidence of poverty than workers in other occupations.

- Nearly one quarter—23.4 percent—of in-home workers live below the official poverty line, compared with 6.5 percent of workers in other occupations.

- More than half—51.4 percent—of in-home workers live below twice the poverty line, compared with 20.8 percent of workers in other occupations. (Researchers commonly use twice the official poverty threshold as a measure of what it takes a family to make ends meet.)

In addition: in-home workers' hourly wages are nearly 25 percent lower than those of similar workers in other occupations (after accounting for demographic differences) and in-home workers' median weekly pay is 36.5 percent lower than similar workers in other occupations.

According to the report, in-home work is expected to grow 53.2 percent, compared with 14.3 percent for other occupations. All federal and state laws and efforts to protect domestic workers will add to the occupation's growth. Some states have enacted Domestic Workers' Bill of Rights laws that help with this protection. And, in mid-2016 the federal government updated the DOL's final rule regulating overtime. According to the DOL, the updated final rule automatically extended overtime protections to more than four million workers within its first year of implementation.

The 2012 report, "Home Economics: The Invisible and Unregulated World of Domestic Work", also documents "serious and widespread" mistreatment of domestic workers in the United States. Generally domestic workers, said the report, "are underpaid, in many cases less than the minimum wage, and often at levels too low to adequately care for their own families...Employed in private homes, behind closed doors, domestic workers endure long hours and substandard pay. There is little economic mobility and almost no financial security..."

The historic 2009 study, "Broken Laws, Unprotected Workers", (www.unprotectedworkers.org/brokenlaws) highlighted the low-wage workforce in Chicago, Los Angeles, and New York City, the nation's three largest cities. The study found that core employment laws—like minimum wage and overtime pay—were aggressively and systematically violated. It estimated that two-thirds of the 4,387 workers surveyed experienced pay violations and that the average worker lost more than $2,600 in annual income due to the violations, a full 15 percent of annual income. Broken Laws also found:

- one in four workers (26 percent) was paid below the minimum wage in a given workweek

- 76 percent of those who worked overtime were not paid the required time and a half

- 70 percent did not get any pay at all for work performed outside their regular shift

Private households yielded the highest minimum wage violations—exceeding 40 percent. Child care workers experienced the highest violations of any job, with 89 percent of in-home child care workers earning less than the minimum wage and 90 percent facing overtime violations. Wage theft appears to be widespread, particularly with low-wage workers and immigrant workers.

Examples of State Wage Theft Prevention Laws

A number of states protect workers with wage theft prevention laws. Wage theft prevention laws mandate that employers provide workers with written, detailed information on how much and when a worker is paid. These employer pay notices must generally be provided upon hire and when there is a change to the information provided.

New York State. The New York State Wage Theft Prevention Act (WTPA) went into effect in 2011 and was strengthened in 2014 to guard against employer wage theft. At the time of hire, all New York employers must provide all employees with written pay notices that include:

- the employee's rate or rates of pay

- the overtime rate of pay, if the employee is nonexempt

- the basis of wage payment (e.g., per hour, per shift, per week, piece rate, commission, etc.)

- the allowances to be claimed against the minimum wage (e.g., tip, meal and lodging allowances)

- the regular pay day

- detailed employer information

The law also requires that these notices be:

- provided to the employee both in English and in the employee's primary language (if DOL offers a translation)
- signed and dated by the employee
- maintained for six years

An employer who fails to provide the required notice within ten days of hire may have to pay damages of up to $50 per day per employee (up to $5,000/employee), unless the employer paid the employee all wages required by law.

The WPTA also increases the amount of wages that can be recovered as damages for nonpayment over and above lost wages—from 25 percent to 100 percent, and allows greater protection for workers who speak up against exploitative employers. The criminal penalties for wage violations is now far greater: up to a year in prison and a $5,000 fine.

In early-2015, the law was amended to extend protections, including stiffer penalties for retaliating against employee complaints, and more DOL enforcement power, including allowing DOL to order the employer or acting person to pay liquidated damages and payment up to $20,000, as well as order the employer to reinstate the employee's job.

California. California's Wage Theft Prevention Law became effective in 2012 and mandated that employers provide each nonexempt employee with a written notice containing specified information at the time of hire. In 2015, the law was updated to include California's Paid Sick Leave, which mandates all employees working 30 days or more within a year of beginning employment be entitled to one hour of paid sick time for every 30 hours worked.

Washington, D.C. Effective in 2015, D.C.'s law requires employers to provide employees with: the rate and basis (hour, shift, week, etc.) of pay, including tip, meal or lodging allowances; overtime pay and overtime exemptions; the living wage and exemptions; applicable prevailing wages; the employee's regular pay day; and other pertinent information about the employer (e.g. name, address, phone number). This notice must be in writing, signed and dated by both the employer and employee, and provided upon hire and when any information changes.

Penalties

Employers not following laws and regulations could find themselves facing penalties and even jail time. If you owe money to the Federal Government, a delay in filing may result in an IRS failure to file penalty as well as interest charges. The longer you wait to file your return, the more money you are going to be charged in penalties—the amount you owe could increase as much as 25 percent if you continue to delay. State tax penalties can be just as harsh as those imposed by the IRS if you fail to report wages for an employee. The worst case scenario, the state can prosecute you for a crime if it believes your failure to file tax returns was due to a fraudulent scheme. This could result in jail time. Usually, the result of not filing state returns is a penalty, interest, and other fees, added to the amount of tax due. But beware: some states can even put liens on your property, seize your assets, garnish wages, and intercept a federal tax refund if you wait too long before filing or paying your owed taxes.

CASE STUDY

• •

JUDI MERLIN
EXPERIENCED AGENCY PRESIDENT
KIM CINO
EXECUTIVE DIRECTOR
A FRIEND OF THE FAMILY
SMYRNA, GA, AND CHARLOTTE, NC

A Friend of the Family, which places child care and senior care workers in Atlanta, Georgia, sees a trend in the industry: caregivers are raising their salary requirements.

"Some caregivers have not made accommodations regarding the present economic conditions and are not skilled in making cost-of-living adjustments," said Judi Merlin, former president of the agency. "The caregiver salary is [generally] in a very good range, but we see cases where the caregiver inflates his or her worth for no other reason than he or she wants to. As an agency, we spend a lot of time educating those clients and caregivers [on how] to meet in the middle."

The agency invests a lot of time educating clients on fair compensation at time of hire and as the relationship progresses. In fact, the agency's staff will check in with recent placements about every four months to ensure fair wages are being paid for the number of hours worked.

According to Kim Cino, the agency's executive director, a key aspect of the agency checking in with clients and household help several times a year is to determine if a new employer-employee contract needs to be drafted to reflect new circumstances and fair compensation. "We feel this will make for happier clients and nannies," she said.

Despite the trend of rising costs to employ in-home caregivers, Cino said many caregivers who have worked with families for a while—and older nannies unsure of their current market worth—are unfairly compensated. She said one reason for this is that the employers, who have worked with a particular nanny for several years, are unaware of the current market rate for child care. An incident proves her point.

A nanny took a position caring for a three-year-old child and doing light housekeeping. She worked a 52.5-hour workweek. Three years later, the mother remarried, and a father with two children was added to the household. Still working 52.5 hours per week, the nanny then had a significantly heavier workload. Although she was provided with a raise during her employment, the nanny was never compensated for the additional responsibilities.

The nanny spoke with her employers about a pay increase to reflect her new duties, but the employers stated they did not believe the nanny should receive a higher salary. At the nanny's second request for fair compensation for the workload, the employer and nanny agreed to keep the nanny's salary the same but to reduce her hours to 45.5 per workweek.

While the nanny was satisfied with the solution, Cino maintains that the nanny remains underpaid, largely because employers working with one employee for many years are not familiar with current compensation practices or other household employment services.

Ensuring that a household employee is fairly compensated is one of the keys to retaining a household employee. To combat the double threat of an employee feeling underpaid or being pursued by a recruiter, employers must make sure that their employees are paid for all hours worked, including overtime, and that their wages are in line with the market. A good way to assess the market value is to ask agencies and other employers, as well as to participate in annual industry salary surveys.

—Guy

CASE STUDY

● ●

LIN TAYLOR-PLEIMAN
FORMER OWNER/PRESIDENT
AMERICAN DOMESTIC AGENCY, INC.
WHITEFORD, MD

As former owner-operator of American Domestic Agency, Inc., Lin Taylor-Pleiman placed many household employees who came to her agency because she required clients to submit a signed work agreement covering all aspects of work hours and wages. One nanny came to the agency after working without a work agreement. She had been caring for three children, one with significant behavioral and emotional problems. The nanny accepted a request to travel with the family on vacation, but when she asked her employer about payment for the vacation work, the employer angrily told her that the trip was on hold. "The family, it turns out, thought room, board, and air were compensation enough," said Taylor-Pleiman.

From that point on, the relationship deteriorated. According to Taylor-Pleiman, the nanny received nastily worded notes daily, and endured constant complaints and nitpicking. The family hired its former nanny to care for the children during the trip and did not pay the current nanny for the days they were away. After six months, the nanny left the position without having a chance to say goodbye to the children, with whom she had established a good relationship.

Household employers must remember that their vacation time is not their household help's vacation also. The employee traveling with the family and performing work responsibilities should be paid accordingly. Many times, employers view family vacations as a perk for the employee, when the employee views it as a continuation of his or her employment responsibilities, which is, of course, exactly what it is.

—Guy

CASE STUDY

● ●

SUSAN TOKAYER
OWNER-OPERATOR
FAMILY HELPERS
DOBBS FERRY, NY

Susan Tokayer, owner of a household employment referral agency in Dobbs Ferry, New York, said she has seldom seen nannies use sick time. Despite this, Tokayer experienced one incident regarding a nanny's sick time.

A nanny was out sick nine times during the four months that she was employed. The family thought this was excessive. A completed work agreement listed sick days "as needed," so a concrete number of paid sick days was not specified. Therefore, neither the nanny nor the family clearly understood what sick time compensation would be provided.

According to Tokayer, this occurrence demonstrates the need to be explicit in all areas of the work agreement. "Sometimes clients don't get detailed enough, even though we supply a work agreement," she said. "People don't see down the line that it could be a problem. Instead of writing 'sick time as needed,' put 'four days' down on the work agreement. Then, depending on circumstances, be open to compensation after those four days are used." Tokayer said household employees generally have three to six paid sick days (or sick or personal days) to use during an employment year.

According to Tokayer, household employers, particularly those new to household employment, want to start off the relationship congenially—so they behave delicately. "People say the work agreement seems too hard line, too firm," she said. "This relationship is unique. It's a work relationship, but it's an intimate, friendly relationship. Families don't want to come across as too intense or too formal. But if the work agreement isn't completed thoroughly, something could be misconstrued, or there could be a problem down the line."

Tokayer said her clientele is educated, affluent, and knowledgeable about the household employment industry. However, outside of help with a newborn or child, clients most likely have not had household help before. Tokayer still has advice for all potential household employers—know yourself. "Be honest," she said. "Know who you are, what your family needs, and present that honestly. Then, pay well… No matter how hard the job is, if the nanny is well compensated, she will stay forever."

Although not required by law, an employee benefit of sick or personal paid time is standard in the corporate workplace and should be considered in the household. Many household employers shy away from hiring temporary help when a household employee is off work, and it is often detrimental if a household employer misses work him- or herself to cover for his or her household help. This is why household employers must and do take great pains to stress the importance of reliability to their household help.

Household employers should consider implementing a sick- and personal-day policy that distinguishes between sick and personal days, and a plan that accrues available hours each pay period, up to a maximum allotted amount over a one-year period. It is then important to also consider allowing employees to borrow (or not borrow) against time yet to be accrued. A common policy that is not recommended is one that allots time-off hours to those employees who did not miss a workday the previous month. For example, perfect attendance in March translates to an extra day off to be used later. This is not a good policy because it places the motivation for the attendance on the wrong criteria. If an employee is contagiously ill, no one wants him or her on the worksite, exposing others to the illness.

Ultimately, a good policy benefits all, and a well-documented policy safeguards against most eventualities. Employers need to establish a policy that protects everyone within the household and covers all circumstances.

—Guy

Time-Off Payments

Time-off payments for sick, personal, or vacation days should be agreed on by the employer and employee prior to hiring, and should be written in the household employment work agreement and employment handbook. Be certain to specify if time off may be taken in full- and half-day amounts, and when a doctor's note regarding sick time will be required.

Employers are typically mandated to provide time off for voting, jury duty, and military and National Guard training or active service.

Debts Owed by Employee to Employer

Information about whether an employee may borrow money against future wages from the employer should be provided to the employee and included in the employee handbook. If such activity is permissible, then the employer should detail what needs to occur to necessitate an employer loan to the employee, what process an employee needs to follow to request an employer loan, and what steps will be taken to obtain payment of the loan. When considering granting a loan, the employer should take into account the length of time that is considered reasonable for the employee to repay the loan.

Employers should obtain a signed *promissory note* from the employee for any significant amount of money loaned (e.g., $25 or more). This note should include the following:

- date of loan

- loan amount

- payment method (e.g., loan payments taken directly from paychecks; some states, such as New York and Connecticut, do not allow this. It is important to research your state laws before offering this option. The promissory note should be filed in the employee's personnel file, and a photocopy of the note should be provided to the employee.)

- payment schedule

- the employee's and the employer's signatures

Q & A

Q. If I employ a household worker who is an immigrant—not a U.S. citizen—must I pay U.S. minimum wage?

A. Yes. Minimum wage, as well as federal and state labor laws, generally apply to domestic and household employees working in the United States or a U.S. possession or territory, regardless of employee citizenship or immigration status. You should also ensure that the worker is eligible to legally work in the United States.

Garnishment

The federal wage garnishment law limits the amount that may be legally *garnished* (withdrawn for payment to another, per legal direction, such as an ex-spouse for child care payments) from an individual's income, and protects an employee whose pay is garnished from being fired on account of owing a single debt. For the most part, these amounts cannot be more than 25 percent of an employee's disposable earnings. Both the employee and the employer receive copies of any garnishment. Specific guidelines will be listed on formal garnishment orders.

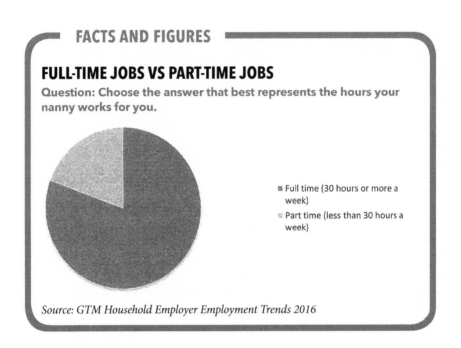

FACTS AND FIGURES

FULL-TIME JOBS VS PART-TIME JOBS

Question: Choose the answer that best represents the hours your nanny works for you.

- Full time (30 hours or more a week)
- Part time (less than 30 hours a week)

Source: GTM Household Employer Employment Trends 2016

Overtime

According to the U.S. Labor Department, the federal *Fair Labor Standards Act* (FLSA) requires employers (including household employers) to pay overtime pay of one and a half times the regular hourly pay rate. Domestic employees are nonexempt employees, according to FLSA, and therefore need to abide by minimum wage and overtime rules.

In most circumstances, FLSA requires employers to pay covered employees who live outside the workplace at least the minimum wage, as well as overtime pay at one and a half times the regular pay rate for hours worked beyond 40 in a week. Live-in employees are not subject to overtime regulations; however, state and local laws for overtime vary, and may supersede the federal FLSA. In addition, domestic service workers employed to provide babysitting services on a *casual* basis, or to provide companionship services for those who cannot care for themselves because of age or infirmity, are currently exempt from the FLSA's minimum wage and overtime requirements, whether or not they reside in the household where they are employed. The Department of Labor's Final Rule, which went into effect on January 1, 2015, revised the definition of 'companionship services' to clarify which duties are covered under this term. The final rule also clarifies that direct care workers who perform medically-related services for which training is typically a prerequisite are not companionship workers and therefore are entitled to the minimum wage and overtime. And, in accordance with Congress' initial intent, individual workers who are employed only by the person receiving services or that person's family or household and engaged primarily in fellowship and protection (providing company, visiting, or engaging in hobbies) and care incidental to such activities, will still be considered exempt from the FLSA's minimum wage and overtime protections.

Finally, it is important to note that some states impose their own requirements, which may differ from federal law and be more stringent. For example:

California differentiates between 'personal attendants' (most nannies and senior care providers) and other domestic workers. Personal attendants (either live-in or live-out, full time or part time) whose duties require mostly caretaking (i.e. not personal housekeeping, for example), have been awarded overtime rights as of September 2013 (Domestic Worker Bill of Rights, AB 241), where they are required one and a half times regular rate of pay for work over nine hours in a day, or over 45 hours in a week. Live-out domestic employees who are not personal attendants (butlers, cooks, gardeners, maids, chauffeurs, companions, housekeepers, tutors, valets, and so on) are entitled to one and a half times regular rate of pay for over eight hours in a day or 40 hours in a week and the first eight hours on the seventh consecutive day of the workweek. These employees are also entitled to double time (twice times regular rate) for hours worked over 12 in a day and hours worked over eight on the seventh consecutive day of the workweek. Live-in domestic workers who are not personal attendants have more stipulations. As of September 2016, the overtime protection for domestic workers in California has been made permanent. (SB 1015 was written in to law to continue the success from AB 241 (2013)—which granted overtime protections to California's privately hired domestic workers—by removing the 2017 sunset provision and making the law's provisions permanent).

In Massachusetts, the laws for live-out and live-in are the same and domestic workers must be paid overtime (one and a half times regular pay rate) for hours worked more than 40 in a given workweek.

In New York, live-out employees must be paid overtime (one and a half times regular pay rate) for hours worked more than 40 in a workweek, and live-in employees in New York must be paid overtime for hours worked more than 44.

In Texas, live-out employees must be paid overtime for hours (one and a half times regular pay rate) worked more than 40 in a workweek, and live-in employees are required to be paid overtime for hours in excess of 40 per week, but it can be at their regular rate of pay.

It is therefore wise to contact your state department of labor for your state's specific laws.

A household employer should specify in the work agreement when approved overtime can occur and what the specific rate of pay will be. There should also be specific details about whether overtime will be paid on weekends and holidays (and if so, which holidays). This will avoid any conflict when the issue arises and ensure that both employer and employee are on the same page. The employer should also keep track of all the hours worked by the employee and pay accordingly.

FACTS AND FIGURES

OVERTIME EXAMPLE

Employee works 55 hours per week and is paid a standard $700 a week.

To be overtime compliant, the suggested employee's hourly rate = $11.20.

First 40 hours should be at standard rate of $11.20 = $448.00.

Extra 15 hours of overtime at 1.5 x standard rate of $11.20 ($16.80) = $252.00.

So first 40 hours of $448.00 + extra 15 hours overtime of $252.00 = $700 in wages for the week.

FACTS AND FIGURES

PAID TIME OFF, FLEXIBLE HOURS, AND BENEFITS OFFERED TO NANNIES

Question: Please check any of the following benefits you provide to your nanny.

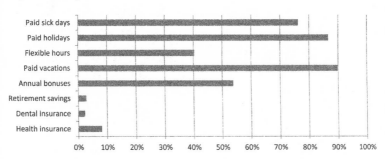

Source: GTM Household Employer Employment Trends 2016

Compensation During Travel and Off-Site Events

Before an employer hires an employee, the employee's compensation must be detailed fully, including vacation, mileage reimbursement, paid auto insurance, and so on. It is important to spell out what compensation a household employee will be paid when he or she travels with the family, or when he or she attends an off-site event as part of the workday.

Employees using their own cars for work tasks and work-related events should be reimbursed for mileage. The federal mileage reimbursement rate for 2017 is 53.5 cents per mile. It is useful to include a copy of an *Expense Report*, which includes a section on mileage in the employee handbook. (See Appendix E.)

While many employers defer to established federal rates, once again, employers need to be certain of what is required by their local laws. Some requirements are quite extensive. For instance, in New York State, the Department of Labor has set standard allowances for meals and lodging. According to New York State law, an employee's meal and lodging may be considered part of the minimum wage, but the employee must be provided with a written notification of any allowances claims of this kind.

Breaking Down the Paycheck

Employers should always pay employees by check, so both parties have a record of the payment. Checks need to be *net*—total wages after all taxes and benefit option payments are withheld. Even if an employer directly deposits paychecks per employee's request, a payment record or voucher should be supplied to the employee and kept on file for the employer to access if needed. (See Appendix D for a sample *Paycheck and Payroll Earnings Statement*.)

Taxes

Every employer is responsible for several federal, state, and local taxes. A household employer is responsible for the timely payment or deposit of employment taxes withheld from an employee, his or her matching share of Social Security and Medicare (the Social Security and Medicare taxes are combined into what is known as FICA—the Federal Insurance Contribution Act), and all Federal Unemployment Tax Act (FUTA) taxes. (See Chapter 10, for more information on payroll and taxes.)

FACTS AND FIGURES
RECOMMENDED PAY-STUB INFORMATION

An employer should include the following information on an employee's pay stub:

- employer name and address
- employee name
- pay period start and end dates
- check date
- check number
- current payroll information
- gross earnings
- total deductions:
    - o federal
    - o Old Age Survivors Disability Insurance (OASDI) (e.g., Social Security)
    - o Medicare
    - o state withholding
    - o local tax withholding
- net pay
- year-to-date payroll information

- sick time and vacation time accruals
- withholding allowances (according to withholding status)
- health reimbursement account

Note: some states may require more information on the pay stub so you should check with your state, or ask a payroll service like GTM Payroll Services Inc. (www.gtm.com). For example, New York State's Wage Theft Prevention Act (2011), asks that pay statements include many other details, such as, for non-exempt employees, employee's overtime pay rate, the number of regular and overtime hours that the employee worked, and the employer telephone number on the paycheck.

CASE STUDY

● ●

LEANN BRAMBACH
EXPERIENCED AGENCY OWNER
SEATTLE, WA

Leann Brambach formerly owned Home Details, Inc. (HDI), an agency that placed household employees in positions throughout Seattle. Citing an example of one nanny placement, Brambach said, "Both nannies and clients need to be educated from the get-go about their tax obligations and gross versus net."

Brambach placed a woman in a position as a part-time nanny and household assistant for $13 per hour. The employee asked her employer to raise her salary to $15 per hour after learning that the job was more work than anticipated and after comparing salaries with other nannies. The employer agreed and asked Brambach to update the work agreement. In updating the work agreement, another issue became apparent—both the nanny and the employer thought that the other was paying income tax on the nanny's salary. In the end, the employment failed. The employer was willing to pay $15 per hour gross, which equaled approximately $12 per hour net. The nanny resigned, believing that she was misled.

"This was one big misunderstanding that left both parties feeling frustrated, and trust was broken," said Brambach.

Household employers can opt to not withhold federal and state income taxes from their employee's pay, placing the burden on the employee to make estimated tax payments throughout the year. The rule is that both parties must agree that the employer will withhold these taxes; otherwise, the employee is responsible.

When an employee submits a completed W-4 form to the employer and the employer accepts it, the responsibility of withholding is then placed upon the employer. Withholding is commonly done through payroll deduction. Because this practice is so widespread, an employer who is unwilling to accept the responsibility must clearly spell out in the work agreement his or her stance, as well as notify the employee in person. If it is not, great friction can easily build to a breaking point in the employer-employee relationship—especially since employees frequently misunderstand the calculation and payment of their own income taxes.

—Guy

CASE STUDY

• •

DENISE SHADE
HOUSEHOLD EMPLOYER
NEW YORK, NY

Denise Shade, senior vice president of Key Bank's foreign exchange unit and mother of two, could easily be considered a financial whiz. Yet despite her obvious executive-level financial ability, Shade uses GTM's services for nanny taxes and payroll.

"We first did our taxes and payroll on our own," said Shade, "because we really wanted to understand it, but it is incredibly time-consuming on a weekly basis."

Along with the standard time required to attend to payroll and taxes, Shade said that twice issues arose with the IRS, causing payments to be tracked. While Shade was able to submit to the IRS proof of payments, she explained that the time required for this is particularly lengthy. Noting that such issues arise from time to time, she added that GTM's services were helpful in saving her from what could be stressful and painstaking record searches.

All employers, including household employers, must deal with the complexity of payroll and taxes, as well as the compounded legal requirements from federal, state, and local levels. Along with these concerns is the demand that employers are responsible for the timely payment or deposit of employment taxes. There are many things to learn and to consider, such as while deducting payroll taxes, an employer need only deduct the employee's share of Social Security and Medicare taxes, and not the employer's taxes (as Denise Shade noted). In addition, employers are, at times, questioned by the IRS or their state of residence, and need to submit necessary forms and records. All this is annoying and time consuming. Many household employers save themselves significant time and effort by using a third-party payroll firm to provide tax and payroll services. By relying on a knowledgeable payroll service, household employers and their employees can be assured that they are protected and will be eligible for assistance if needed.

—Guy

FACTS AND FIGURES

DEPENDENT CARE ASSISTANCE PROGRAM (DCAP)— A TAX-SAVING TIP FOR HOUSEHOLD EMPLOYERS

A major concern for families today is how to provide dependent care for family members while family providers are at work. Companies may deduct expenses from an employee's salary to assist the employee with his or her dependent care obligations. The dependent care tax credit also helps families with lower household incomes.

Household employers can access Dependent Care Assistance Program (DCAP) information at their company's human resources department. The DCAP may allow up to $5,000 in pretax earnings per year to be set aside for child care or senior care. This is especially important if the family has undergone a change of life experience (e.g., the birth of a new baby) that might affect its eligibility for the program. There are specific DCAP open enrollment periods during which to apply. A household employer can learn more through his or her company's HR department.

FACTS AND FIGURES

BENEFITS OF PAYING AN EMPLOYEE CORRECTLY

There are numerous benefits and protections to correctly paying an employee for both the employer and the employee, including the following.

Employer Benefits

- **Attract higher quality employees:** By doing payroll and taxes the right way, an employer can pick from a larger pool of qualified, professional candidates for the job.

- **Feel secure**: It is the law. Federal and state law mandates that each time a taxpayer signs his or her federal 1040 U.S. Individual Income Tax Return, he or she is answering the household tax question. Anything reported that is less than actual amounts is tax evasion.

- **Reduce the risk of an audit**: Once the federal government realizes an employer hasn't been compliant with household employment law, the chances of being audited skyrocket. So maintaining compliance decreases the likelihood of this happening.

- **Avoid state and federal fines and penalties:** An employer avoids steep fines (plus interest) and even jail time by paying above board and on the books. It's easy to get caught paying under the table. All it takes is an employee filing for unemployment after he or she leaves a job and listing the previous employer (the employee will be denied benefits and then the employer will come under scrutiny for not paying the proper taxes), or the employee is injured on the job and goes to the ER—this can trigger an investigation too.

- **Gain financial protection:** Employers in most states are protecting themselves if they pay into a workers' compensation insurance fund, which will help them cover expenses in the event that an employee is injured while working. Without it, an employer could be liable for an employee's medical expenses and lost pay.

- **Take advantage of tax savings:** Employers may be eligible for federal assistance programs, such as the Earned Income Credit Program, Child Care Tax Credit, and the Dependent Care Assistance Program (DCAP). These can help cover some of the qualified expenses associated with being a household employer.

- **Work with a happier employee:** Employees who know they are legally on the books feel more secure in their employment relationship, and the employer benefits by having happy and secure employees. The nanny will appreciate the benefits and protections of being paid legally and feel as if he or she is truly treated as the professional that he or she is. This helps create and maintain an easier working relationship between the employer and employee.

- **Enjoy peace of mind:** All of the above benefits lead to one major advantage...peace of mind. Employers will know that they are practicing good human resources and are legally operating a business. An employer will have a solid relationship with an employee and financial protection. There will be no worry about fines, penalties, audits, or lawsuits.

Employee Benefits

- **Avoids audits and penalties:** It is the law, so abiding by the IRS' rules provides peace of mind and reduces the likelihood that the employee will be audited for taxes.

- **Legal employment history**: Getting paid "on the books" creates a work history. Employees have a legal employment history to refer to when applying for future jobs, mortgages, loans, credit, and so on.

- **Social Security and Medicare benefits:** Employees and employers paying payroll taxes mean employees are eligible for Social Security and Medicare credits that can help pay for living and medical expenses upon retirement.

- **Unemployment benefits:** If an employee is out of work for any period of time, unemployment benefits will partially replace lost wages as he or she looks for a new job.

- **Verifiable income:** An employee needs to show that he or she can pay monthly installments if he or she applies for a car loan, student loan, mortgage, or even a credit card. Being paid legally provides that, as it shows the documentation of the employee's pay which he or she can show to creditors.

- **Workers' compensation benefits:** With a workers' compensation policy in place, an employee will receive assistance with medical expenses and lost wages if he or she is injured or becomes ill on the job. Workers' compensation is required for household employees in many states.

- **Earned Income Credit:** Employees may qualify for the Earned Income Credit, which enables them, in some instances, to claim more money from the government than their payroll taxes if their payroll taxes were calculated without the credit.

- **Health Care Subsidy:** The Affordable Care Act requires everyone to have health insurance or pay a fine. A health insurance marketplace has been created to help people find coverage. If an employee buys a policy through this marketplace, he or she could qualify for a subsidy and cut the costs of insurance, but only if he or she is paid legally.

Family Medical Leave Act

The *Family Medical Leave Act* (FMLA) generally requires employers of 50 or more people to provide up to 12 weeks of unpaid, job-protected leave to eligible employees for the birth or adoption of a child, or for the serious health condition of a spouse, child, or parent. Leave is also available for reasons associated with military service. (Under the FMLA, employees must have worked for the employer for at least 12 months and have at least 1,250 hours of service in the 12 months before taking leave to be eligible for the protected leave.) While FMLA does not apply to the majority of household employers because of the stipulation of 50 or more employees, family medical leave—or a variation of it—is a valid consideration for employers to offer their domestic help.

Some states have family and medical leave acts, but like the federal law, most apply to employers with at least several employees, generally not to a one-employee business. However, it is best to check on individual state and locality medical leave requirements.

California

In 2002, California became the first state in the country to create a Paid Family Leave (PFL) program, making it easier for employees to balance the demands of the workplace and family care needs at home. This program provides vital support to workers who are bonding with a new child or caring for a family member with a serious health condition.

Workers (including those in household employment and noncitizens) who contribute to the State Disability Insurance (SDI) fund are entitled up to six weeks of partial pay each year while taking time off from work to bond with a newborn baby, adopted, or foster child; and to care for a seriously ill parent, child, spouse, or registered domestic partner. Workers may receive up to approximately 55 percent of their weekly wages up to a maximum weekly benefit amount. The benefit amount is determined by weekly wages in the base period. Workers do not need to take all six weeks consecutively as PFL can be taken intermittently on an hourly, daily, or weekly basis as needed. Before receiving benefits, workers must serve a seven-day nonpayable waiting period.

According to the National Conference of State Legislatures (NCSL), while only California, New Jersey, and Rhode Island offer paid family and medical leave (with New York offering paid family and medical leave, effective January 1, 2018), states with their own family leave laws include: California (paid and unpaid), Connecticut, DC, Hawaii, Maine, Minnesota, New Jersey (paid and unpaid), Oregon, Rhode Island (paid and unpaid), Vermont, Washington, and Wisconsin.

Planning and Scheduling Wages and Hours Checklist

- Abide by all laws—local, state, and federal.

- Check your state's minimum wage laws, as some state and local minimum wage laws supersede the federal minimum wage ($7.25 per hour, 2017).

- Check special living wage ordinances and requirements in your locality to ensure that you meet those wage rates and are not faced with a penalty.

- Check to be sure you file your wage reports accurately and on time to avoid penalty.

- Clearly communicate, in writing, during pre-employment discussions whether wages are gross or net.

- Clearly identify whether the employer or employee will pay income tax from wages.

- Know your overtime requirements and make sure these are detailed in the work agreement.

- Research the standard salaries for the employee's job in your area and ensure you are paying the expected wage (this avoids you losing your employee to another position).

9

Employee Benefits to Help Retain the Best

While providing employee benefits is largely optional and seldom required by law, employee benefits greatly help the household employer attract and retain high-level employees. To get and keep the most talented employees, employers must treat employees like professionals. Therefore, offering employee benefits is an important consideration for all household employers. By providing an attractive employee benefits package, the employer is helping to maintain a satisfied workforce. Satisfied employees equal a happy workplace, which in turn equals a happy family and life for the employer.

The most popular household employee benefits include medical or dental insurance, paid time for vacation, holiday, sick or personal leave, bonuses, annual pay increases, flexible hours, housing allowance or live-in arrangement, vehicle use or vehicle allowance, education reimbursement, cell phone or allowance, and a computer or tablet device.

Health insurance and other employee benefits covered in this chapter are instrumental in recruiting and retaining talented employees. It is prudent for an employer to take the time needed to secure a valuable employee benefits package by reviewing with his or her employee what benefits he or she requires.

Medical Insurance Coverage

Health insurance is often the first benefit requested by any employee and one that is increasingly popular for household employers to provide. While health care is a benefit provided by most employers in the United States, the household employment industry has been slow to provide household help with medical benefits and health care coverage (although this is increasing). Health care insurance coverage is a priority for many workers, including those in household employment, because of the high cost of coverage and medical fees. The cost can be high for the employer as well—especially since most household employers have only one employee or just a few employees. However, various options are now on the market that make coverage more affordable than ever before.

Today, an employer's choice to provide health care coverage as an employee benefit remains optional for those with less than 50 employees, except for employers in the state of Hawaii, which mandates that all employees achieving a specific monthly income must be covered. Hawaii's Prepaid Health Care Act was the first in the nation to set minimum standards of health care benefits for workers. Hawaii mandates that every employer paying a regular employee monthly wage amounting to at least 86.67 times the minimum hourly wage and who has an employee who works at least 20 hours per week for four or more consecutive weeks must provide that employee with coverage by a prepaid group health care plan. Hawaii has mandated that minimum wage be set at $9.25 per hour (2017). Therefore, the employee earning a minimum of $801.70 (86.67 x $9.25) a month is eligible for health care coverage. Coverage commences after four consecutive weeks of employment.

In Massachusetts, there is also a health care insurance reform law, enacted in 2006, which mandates that nearly every resident of Massachusetts obtain a state-government-regulated minimum level of health care insurance coverage and provides free health care insurance for residents earning less than 150 percent of the federal poverty level (FPL) who are not eligible for MassHealth (Medicaid). The law also partially subsidizes health care insurance for those earning up to 300 percent of the FPL.

The law established an independent public authority, the Commonwealth Health Insurance Connector Authority, also known as the Health Connector (www.MAhealthconnector.org). Small employers who wish to contribute toward their employees' group health coverage can purchase health insurance through the Health Connector. Among other roles, the Health Connector acts as an insurance broker to offer private insurance plans to residents. The reform legislation also included tax penalties for failing to obtain an insurance plan. Massachusetts tax filers who failed to enroll in a health insurance plan which was deemed affordable for them lost the personal exemption on their income tax.

In general, employers with fewer than 11 full-time equivalent employees (i.e., most household employers) are exempt from most requirements of the law. However, their employees who live in Massachusetts are still required to have health insurance. (Under the Massachusetts Health Care Reform Law, in 2015, if a resident could afford health insurance but did not enroll, he or she may face a tax penalty for each month uninsured.)

FACTS AND FIGURES
THE AFFORDABLE CARE ACT AND HOUSEHOLD EMPLOYEES

Regarding the Affordable Care Act, commonly known as Obamacare, and household employees, household employers may be wondering what, if anything, they need to do in order to comply with changes in health care laws.

Household employers are generally NOT required to offer health insurance to their employee(s). Any employer with fewer than 50 full-time employees is not required to provide health insurance coverage to staff.

Household employers MUST provide a Notice of Coverage Options. All employers must provide this notice to all current and any future employees. This will inform your employees about the coverage options that are available and the Health Insurance Marketplace. The Marketplace allows individuals to compare health insurance plans offered by private insurance companies. There are two sample notices that the Department of Labor provides, depending on whether you currently offer your employees health coverage or not.

Your employee may be subject to a penalty if he or she can afford health insurance, but chooses not to obtain it. While the law does not require you to provide coverage, your employee must be covered or pay a fee, unless an exemption applies. Employees can purchase insurance through the Health Insurance Marketplace. To be eligible for health coverage through the Marketplace, your employee must live in the United States and be a U.S. citizen or national; if not a U.S. citizen, coverage can still be obtained, provided certain requirements are met. Plans and coverage may vary greatly from person to person; all of the information needed to get insurance can be found at www.healthcare.gov/quick-guide/

If you wish to provide insurance for your employee(s) as a "sole proprietor", with at least one full-time employee that is not an owner of the business or a family member, you may acquire health insurance through the Small Business Marketplace for your employees. Group coverage can sometimes be obtained outside of the Marketplace for Sole Proprietors with one or more employees.

Should you not wish to offer coverage to your household employees, they can apply for coverage through the Health Insurance Marketplace (also known as the Individual Exchange). Household employees may qualify for a tax credit on their monthly premiums. Depending on income level and size of household, individuals may qualify for premium tax credits and other savings on an Individual Exchange plan. Employees can apply part or all of this tax credit each month to their premium payments. Any earned tax credit not applied towards the monthly premium can be claimed by filing Form 8962 with the individual's federal income tax return. Use the chart at www.healthcare.gov/lower-costs/ to help your employees see if they qualify.

Types of Health Plans

Employers may offer employees certain types of health plans. The four most popular plans are the following.

1. *Health Maintenance Organization* (HMO)—a member-based organization that provides health care at affordable costs and, in general, emphasizes preventive care. An HMO is a specific type of health care plan found in the United States. Unlike traditional health coverage, an HMO sets out guidelines under which doctors can operate. On average, health care coverage through the use of an HMO costs less than comparable traditional health insurance, with a trade-off of limitations on the range of treatments available.

2. *Closed Panel HMO*—HMOs that own their own facilities or clinics and employ the medical staff who work in them.

3. *Preferred Provider Organization* (PPO)—much like HMOs in their operation, PPOs formed as a way to control managed care and health care costs. PPOs are groups of medical professionals and hospitals that may be controlled independently or by insurance companies and which provide health care services at a reduced fee. A PPO is similar to an HMO but care is paid for as it is received instead of in advance in the form of a scheduled fee. However, unlike HMOs, in PPOs doctors are not employed by the PPO, and facilities or clinics are not owned by the PPO. Another PPO advantage is that there are no referral requirements. A member can see any doctor he or she chooses at any time. A member may use doctors who are part of the PPO network, but it is not required. However, using a PPO-member doctor, provider, or facility usually offers financial incentives.

4. *Exclusive Provider Organization* (EPO)—An EPO is an insurance plan that is a network of individual medical care providers or groups of medical care providers who have entered into written agreements with an insurer to provide health insurance to subscribers. Basically, an EPO is a much smaller PPO.

5. *Major Medical*—a health insurance policy with high deductibles to cover most serious health problems and conditions, up to a specific limit or reimbursement maximum. Although most major medical policies contain lifetime limits of $1 million or more, meeting the lifetime limit usually is not an issue. Major medical policies are indemnity-type policies, in which the insurer covers most medical services with a significant cost-sharing element for the employee.

6. *An Indemnity Plan*—also known as a mini-med plan. This covers basic expenses, such as doctor's visits and hospital benefits, but does not extend to catastrophic expenses.

Health Reimbursement Arrangement

A *Health Reimbursement Arrangement* (HRA) is a creative option available to the household employer, regardless of budgets, who wants to offer a contribution program for health-related expenses as an employee benefit. Growing in popularity, an HRA is an employer-sponsored plan that reimburses an employee for eligible medical care expenses, as defined by the IRS. Based on IRS guidance issued in 2015, employers with two or more employees cannot set up or fund a HRA to pay for an employee's individual healthcare plans. Only those with one employee can continue to set up an HRA for this purpose.

The employer funds a predetermined amount of money for each eligible employee. Monies in the account are not subject to employment taxes. Health Reimbursement Arrangements allow employees and employers to take advantage of the lower premiums offered by high-deductible major medical plans and help keep health care costs under control.

The HRA advantage is that monies can roll over each year. Therefore, an employer does not lose a contribution if an employee does not use up the account in any given year. Health Reimbursement Arrangements mandate an employee-employer relationship, so independent contractors paid by a Form 1099 are not eligible. For more information on setting up an HRA, go to www.gtm.com.

Flexible Spending Account

A *Flexible Spending Account* (FSA) provides an important tax advantage that can help pay health care and dependent care expenses on a pretax basis. An employee anticipates the annual cost for the individual or family health care and dependent care costs for the next plan year and can actually lower his or her taxable income. This plan allows the employee to set aside a portion of his or her pretax salary in an account, and that money is deducted from the employee's paycheck over the course of the year. The amount that is contributed to the FSA is *not* subject to Social Security (FICA), federal, state, or local income taxes, which effectively adjusts the employee's taxable salary. The employee is given a benefit card which is a debit card that will immediately have the annual amount of the contribution in the account. These accounts may be used to cover the health insurance deductible and co-payments for medical services and prescriptions. Usually the employee has to furnish receipts to the provider to prove eligibility of the expenses covered by the account's plan. Although the FSA is in the employee's name, the employer can arrange for the account to be set up which provides a useful employee benefit that is advantageous to the employee but does not cost the employer anything.

FACTS AND FIGURES

OFFERING EMPLOYEE BENEFITS HELPS THE EMPLOYER TOO!

Emotional Benefits

- Attracts high-level employees

- Practices preventative care, which reduces absenteeism

- Creates a happy, satisfied employee, a happy family, and a happy employer

- Helps retain valued employees: often employees work better and longer for a job they are happy with

Financial Benefits

- Saving tax on premiums paid through employee deductions for health or dental insurance through an approved pretax plan

- For every dollar of premium deducted from gross pay, the employer and employee will see tax advantages

- Employers can save 7.65 percent payroll tax savings on Social Security and Medicare tax

- Employer avoids costs for replacing employees who are not happy with their job (e.g., placement search fees, hiring temporary help, and new employee training)

FACTS AND FIGURES

A COMPARISON: EMPLOYER OFFERING HEALTH BENEFITS TO A NANNY THROUGH AN APPROVED PRETAX PLAN AND AN EMPLOYER WHO DOES NOT

Nanny's weekly wage = $500	Nanny's weekly wage = $500
Employer provides health benefits through an approved pretax plan. Nanny has $50 of pretax health benefit	Employer provides no health benefits
Nanny and employer save the taxes which would have been paid on the $50 • 7.65 percent for employer • 7.65 percent for the employee	No tax saving on pretax health benefit plan for employer or employee.
Pay = $500 Pretax health plan premium = $50 Taxable amount = $450 Employer tax liability 7.65 percent on $450 Employee tax liability 7.65 percent on $450 Employer saves 7.65 percent on $50 per week Employee saves 7.65 percent on $50 per week	Pay = $500 Employer tax liability 7.65 percent on $500 per week Employee tax liability 7.65 percent on $500 per week

Note: Employee tax liability is usually 7.65% (2017)

Retirement

Like medical coverage, retirement plans are a standard part of U.S. corporate employee benefit packages. While not legally mandated to offer employees a retirement plan, employers may consider doing so in order to attract and retain the best employees. If a retirement plan is offered, the employer must comply with IRS tax requirements and administrative requirements as set forth in the U.S. *Employee Retirement Income Security Act* (ERISA).

Individual Retirement Account (IRA)

Two popular retirement options for household employees are the *Individual Retirement Account* (IRA) and the *Roth IRA*. Both are fairly simple programs to establish as an employee benefit, and therefore, suitable as a household employee benefit.

An IRA is a special savings plan authorized by the federal government to help people accumulate funds for retirement. Traditional IRAs and Roth IRAs allow individual taxpayers to contribute 100 percent of their earnings up to the IRA's plan-specified maximum dollar amount. Each year, the IRS sets maximum annual contributions for IRAs, with *catch-up* contributions for people age 50 and over. For 2017, maximum contributions are $5,500, with an additional catch-up of $1,000 for those age 50 or older.

Traditional IRA contributions may be tax deductible, whereas Roth IRA contributions are not. Roth IRA principal and interest accumulate tax-free. A Roth IRA usually is preferred by those ineligible for the tax deductions associated with the traditional IRA or by those who want their qualified Roth IRA distributions to be tax- and penalty-free, which depends on all conditions being met. Some people prefer a Roth IRA as a means to simply build a retirement egg without the worry of paying taxes at a later date (Roth contributions have already been taxed).

401k Retirement Plan

The *401k Retirement Plan* is the option most workers choose when it comes to saving for their retirement. Historically, there has not been a solution that provides Americans that work within the home access to a 401(k) Plan. In 2012, GTM Payroll Services Inc. introduced a 401(k) Profit Sharing Plan for household workers. Employees can save pretax, via payroll deferral, up to $12,500 a year (2017). If they are 50+ years old they can invest another $3,000 as a catch-up contribution. They cannot go over the limits imposed by the IRS, but can modify the amounts they choose to defer, which offers them flexibility. In addition, their employer may choose to make employer contributions into the Plan in the form of Profit Sharing Contributions. These contributions can be used to reward and retain valuable domestic workers. Employees are able to self-direct their investments from a list of monitored, low-cost mutual funds and have access to advisors who can help choose which fund is best for them. They are always 100% vested in their account balance. If they change employers, but continue to use GTM Payroll Services, their new employer can continue contributions or roll the money to another qualified retirement plan or individual retirement account (IRA). This helps the household employee have a consistent, tax-deferred retirement plan account throughout his or her career.

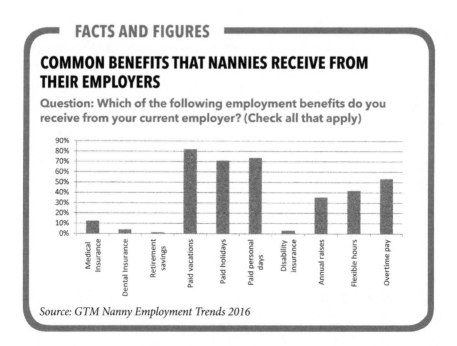

FACTS AND FIGURES

COMMON BENEFITS THAT NANNIES RECEIVE FROM THEIR EMPLOYERS

Question: Which of the following employment benefits do you receive from your current employer? (Check all that apply)

Source: GTM Nanny Employment Trends 2016

Life Insurance

Some employers offer their employees life insurance coverage. The main purpose of life insurance is to provide a death benefit to the employee's dependents or beneficiaries, in order to help replace lost income and protect against the financial losses that could occur from the insured's untimely death.

Generally, there are two types of life insurance: term and permanent (whole). *Term life insurance* pays a death benefit to beneficiaries if the insured dies during the term the policy exists, in return for regular premium payments. *Permanent (or whole) life insurance* generally is designed to provide long-term life insurance coverage for the insured's entire life—up to age 121. It has two components:

1. the death benefit

2. a cash value benefit, which differentiates it from term insurance, and accumulates cash value that the policy holder may withdraw or borrow against

The coverage may vary, but commonly term policies offer either a set amount of insurance (e.g. $10,000 policy for each employee) or are based on the employee's salary (for example: one full year of an employee's salary (up to a specified limit) or double an employee's salary). Many employers limit group term coverage to $50,000 as a policy with a death benefit up to $50,000 which is tax deductible to the employer, but not includable in the income of the employee and an employee's beneficiary will not pay federal income taxes on the death benefits (state may require so). This helps protect the policy's designated beneficiary in the event of an employee's death.

Educational Assistance

Another common benefit for employees is educational assistance for education or training pursued outside of working hours. Although optional for an employer to offer, educational assistance is beneficial in providing a satisfying workplace. The employer may tailor the assistance to best suit him or her. Guidelines provided in the employee handbook may include educational pursuits that will be covered (e.g., classes must be provided by an accredited educational organization and relate to the employee's occupation); the limit available for educational assistance per year; educational expenses that are covered (e.g., tuition only, tuition and books, etc.); and the requirements the employee must meet to receive assistance (e.g., the employee must achieve a passing grade as defined by the educational organization).

With these guidelines, an employer should include information on the process the employee must follow for assistance. Consider whether the employee needs to:

- provide the employer with a course description and a written request for assistance prior to the start of class

- obtain a signed approval from the employer prior to the start of class in order to be reimbursed for expenses (see Appendix E)

- achieve a specific grade or higher to obtain reimbursement

Be precise to ensure that the employee understands what is required. Also, employers may consider paying for professional membership fees, industry conferences, or trade journal subscriptions.

CASE STUDY

• •

MARY STARKEY
FOUNDER, OWNER
STARKEY INTERNATIONAL INSTITUTE FOR HOUSEHOLD MANAGEMENT
DENVER, CO

Mary Starkey opened the first household service management educational institute in the United States and has mentored household employment professionals for more than 35 years.

"Private service is experiencing an awakening and renaissance into the professional world," said Starkey. "With a new paradigm for private service in hand, certified household management graduates are bringing standards and professionalism to the American household employment industry."

Starkey noted that service management education for employers and staff is taking household service out of a crisis mode of operation into a defined process of identifying service expectations and performing accepted service etiquette practices. Household service management education guides employers to articulate overall household standards and to identify individual needs. Starkey suggested that employers utilize her service management tool, the Day in the Life. With this, employers can plan and communicate with staff about their expected daily activities, slotting them into a time-oriented weekly schedule. Then, the employees carry these tasks out for a week or two. Next, the employers review their weekly plan to determine whether expectations were met and whether the tasks are functional and feasible for the family and the home.

"Private service has become a recognized and well-paid career path," she said. "Now, service professionals must focus on educating themselves and growing our industry in professional standards, state-of-the-art practices, and industry ethics."

> Continuing education, training, seminars, and conferences play an important role in corporate employment. This education, as well as online learning courses that educate employees, help promote professional growth and elevate employee performance—making the educational benefit a win-win proposition for both the employer and employee. It is important for a household employer to decide whether access to education is an important employee benefit and, if so, how often.
>
> —Guy

Flexible Work Hours

Flexible work hours—an often overlooked employee benefit—enable an employee to work different (flexible) hours during the workweek. Flexible work hours can be an important employee benefit for staff with significant personal obligations, such as the need to attend to regular medical treatment (e.g., physical therapy, chemotherapy, etc.), or family needs (e.g., children, parents, or other dependents who need assistance at variable hours throughout the week). Flexible work hours are not an alternative to personal or sick time. A flexible work schedule is often a long-term arrangement, with the employee working the full workweek but at nonstandard hours. It is generally not to be used for the occasional doctor's appointment or parent-teacher meeting.

Although this may not suit all household schedules, employers willing to consider flexible working arrangements (when requested in advance) are likely to establish a more loyal, stable, and happy household workforce. Recognizing and remembering that employees have a personal and social life outside of work is important to any employer-employee relationship. Many household employers allow for part-time work, time off during the week if the employee worked during the weekend, or time off for the occasional personal commitment or infrequent sick day—with each potential circumstance being discussed in the work agreement, in the employee handbook, and at the start of employment. Clear communication is essential for mutual understanding. Therefore, employers offering permanent flexible work arrangements should carefully plan schedules with the employee, particularly if the household help member is tasked with dependent care.

Employers should be aware of their state's policies on mandatory time off, especially when considering a flexible working arrangement. For example, in New York State, the Domestic Workers' Bill of Rights (2010) requires those who employ domestic workers to provide, at least, the following time-off:

- for unpaid time off: one day of rest is required in each calendar week

- if employees choose to work on their day of rest, they must be paid at one and a half times their hourly rate of pay

- after one year of work with the same employer, employees are entitled to at least three days off each calendar year, paid at their regular rate of compensation

FACTS AND FIGURES
POPULAR JOB PERKS FOR NANNIES
Question: What job perks does your current employer provide?

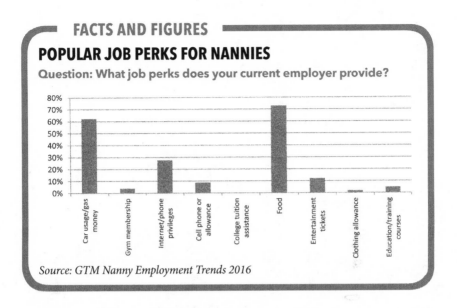

Source: GTM Nanny Employment Trends 2016

FACTS AND FIGURES
RECEIVING A HOLIDAY GIFT OR YEAR-END BONUS
Question: Do you receive a year-end bonus/holiday gift?

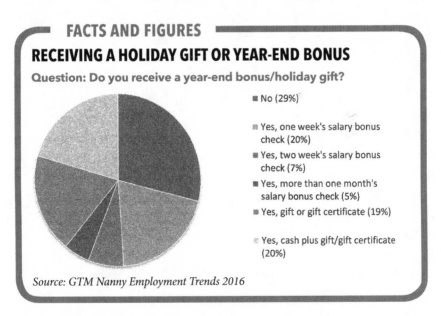

- No (29%)
- Yes, one week's salary bonus check (20%)
- Yes, two week's salary bonus check (7%)
- Yes, more than one month's salary bonus check (5%)
- Yes, gift or gift certificate (19%)
- Yes, cash plus gift/gift certificate (20%)

Source: GTM Nanny Employment Trends 2016

Prepaid Legal Services

Some employers offer employees prepaid legal services as an employee benefit. Prepaid legal services may involve citizenship, divorce, adoption, and so on, and create a unique value to employees who require legal advice and representation. Prepaid legal services may be available through a subscription plan. Employers need to clearly state in the work agreement and the employee handbook the premium requirements for prepaid legal services, and if such services are provided at the employer's discretion.

CASE STUDY

● ●

ARLINE RUBEL
EXPERIENCED AGENCY OWNER
NEW YORK, NY

Arline Rubel, former owner and president of a New York City-based agency relies on a lifetime of experience—from orchestrating home care for family members, to teaching mentally challenged adults independent living, to referring employees to work positions in the home. Growing up with a brother with cerebral palsy, and then as an adult helping eight ailing family members obtain care in their homes, enabled Rubel to hone her skills and expertise in this area.

Many caregivers believe that working in a private home or on a one-on-one basis offers tremendous benefits, noted Rubel. Many enjoy the close relationships that develop, and derive pride and satisfaction from seeing first hand the results of their work. "Many frequently work closely with family and professionals, and develop a team approach to ensure the client receives the best care possible," said Rubel. "The work is challenging and difficult. Those who do it well are to be admired and appreciated."

Rubel and her staff use lengthy and detailed interviews to learn as much as possible about applicants, including work history, personality, level of responsibility previously held, communication skills, motivation, ability, and work preferences. "An appropriate, consistent, and checkable work history with written references is the best place to begin," said Rubel. "References communicate important and reassuring information particular to the position."

Employers, advised Rubel, should be candid about their expectations, job duties, and difficulties that may arise on the job. In addition, Rubel said, employers need to discuss with job applicants how emergencies should be handled, who the decision maker is, who to call in certain situations, which professionals need to be involved, household expenses, meals, sick time, personal calls, and visitors.

"A successful and long-term employment relationship is generally a two-way street," she said. Rubel offers a friendly ear to both her client and the caregiver she places—even years after the initial placement—because she believes that most jobs fall apart when issues are ignored or not dealt with constructively. According to Rubel, she encourages each party to find a workable solution. Most issues are solvable, she noted, when both parties use constructive communication.

> Professionalism includes open communication throughout employment to ensure employee and employer happiness. Some household employees look for no more employee benefits than just a few extra days off, extra pay on working holidays, and professional treatment. Employee benefits are not necessarily all perks that an employer must purchase for the employee.
>
> —Guy

Use of Employer's Personal Property and Facilities

Use of personal property and facilities normally unavailable to the employee outside of work can be considered a great employee benefit. Many employers allow household employees to use certain household property or facilities not required to perform their jobs. This may include use of the home computer, television, exercise equipment and/or gym, swimming pool, and so on. The employee handbook needs to clearly list what is available for employee use and to whom this can extend in terms of friends and family of the employee. The employee handbook must also clearly state which parts of the property and facilities are off limits.

Employees should be reminded that the employer owns the property or facility, and that the employer has the right to inspect and monitor usage—including, for example, user history files on the internet and sent email messages. The employee handbook should outline procedures for reporting needed repairs or any damage or misuse of property and facilities to the employer. (Please see sample policy in Chapter 7.)

Holiday Club Savings Account

An employer may choose to establish what is commonly known as a *holiday club savings account*, which works like other savings plans. Employees may authorize in writing that a specified amount be deducted from their paycheck and deposited into a holiday club savings account. This account usually runs just a few weeks short of a full year and enables the employee to collect his or her savings in the fall (generally mid-October), when he or she may require extra spending money for the holiday season.

Q & A

Q. I would like to be as clear as possible when instructing my household help on what is available to them for use at my home while they are performing their duties. What is the best way to do this?

A. Employers should detail all relevant information in the employee handbook. This includes not only wages, hours, and job requirements, but also information on auto insurance coverage when a staff member is required to drive to complete a work task and use of an employer's facilities (e.g., television, computer, etc.). Odds are that not every question will be answered, so be sure to meet with the employee to discuss any question or item that arises—particularly during the first week of employment. Once questions are answered, remember to update the employee handbook to clearly specify what has been agreed upon.

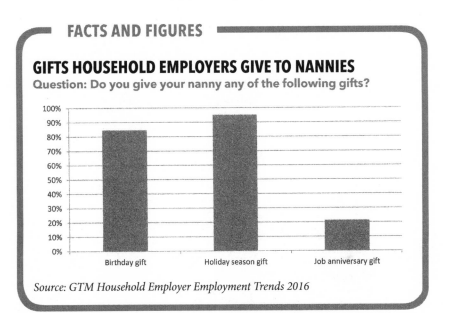

FACTS AND FIGURES

GIFTS HOUSEHOLD EMPLOYERS GIVE TO NANNIES
Question: Do you give your nanny any of the following gifts?

Source: GTM Household Employer Employment Trends 2016

FACTS AND FIGURES

20 IDEAS FOR BENEFITS OR PERKS

1. Sick, personal, and/or vacation time
2. Cell phone use
3. Tuition waivers
4. Education, seminar, or conference expenses
5. Annual bonuses
6. Sponsorship of employee's family from other countries
7. Health Reimbursement Arrangement
8. Frequent flyer miles
9. Entertainment tickets to ball games, movies, or shows
10. Time share or use of a vacation home
11. Gas card
12. Gift certificates
13. Purchase of a laptop computer, tablet, or cell phone
14. Workers' compensation

15. Housing allowance

16. Health insurance

17. Retirement funding

18. Education of a dependent

19. Life insurance

20. Clothing allowance

Benefits Checklist

- Investigate health and insurance coverage options thoroughly to see which one best fits an employee's needs and an employer's budget.

- For the benefit of the family and household help, calculate the amount of personal time to be offered to employees.

- Set regular review periods for salary changes and salary bonuses, and make sure employees know when these might occur.

- Be clear on the extra perks the employee receives while working within the household—including use of facilities and property.

- Consider providing your employee with mileage reimbursement or a gas card to help with his or her commute or with transporting children.

- Think about developing a transportation policy. You may, perhaps, provide an auto club membership to your employee who drives as part of his or her job, or periodically provide for the vehicle in use to be maintained with a tune-up and oil change.

- Consider adding special perks to help your employee. You may establish an employee assistance plan or gift certificate to a spa or health club as a way to help your employee reduce stress.

- Consider providing your employee with some scheduled free time each week for him or her to make personal errands and phone calls.

10

Managing Payroll and Taxes

In the United States today, GTM Payroll Services Inc. estimates that there are more than 2.5 million household employees. Exact figures on household help are difficult to obtain. The U.S. Internal Revenue Service (IRS) Schedule H form filings can sometimes provide a glimpse into the numbers and trends in household employment. The IRS Schedule H form must be completed and filed by household employers with their income tax statements. It is used (among other things) to figure household employment taxes. In 2013 (the latest year that numbers for Schedule H filings are available from the IRS media liaison department), the number of returns with a Schedule H attached was 201,591 and was actually down from 2008 when 219,000 household employers paid taxes via Schedule H ("Household Employer Payroll Tax Evasion: An Exploration Based on IRS Data and on Interviews with Employers and Domestic Workers," by Catherine B. Haskins). Even accounting for the percentage of household employees with more than one employer, this amounts to a startling number of household employers in noncompliance—whether or not intentional—with paying payroll taxes.

Many people do not pay payroll taxes because they believe that:

- they will not be caught
- they know friends or neighbors who are noncompliant
- their employees do not necessarily want to be paid above board
- the employees will realize more income
- it costs the employer more
- it is not considered a *real* employment situation

Although household payroll taxes may be confusing to many, this chapter describes an easy-to-follow, step-by-step guide to managing household employment payroll and taxes. (For the latest information on payroll and taxes, visit www.gtm.com.)

Employer Responsibilities

It is your duty to clearly and fully understand what your responsibilities are as a household employer and for reporting and paying required payroll taxes. (See Appendix A, for a calendar on employer tax responsibilities.) Ignorance is no excuse or defense for not complying with laws and regulations.

Household employers who choose to pay their nannies off the books are putting themselves and their nannies at risk. By not paying payroll taxes (dubbed the *nanny tax*), the employer is risking hefty fines, penalties, and even jail time, and the employee is losing valuable protection mandated by law, such as unemployment insurance, Social Security credits, Medicare, and disability coverage.

Household employers are not obligated to withhold federal or state *withholding* taxes from the employee's gross wages unless the employer and employee mutually agree to it. For more information, see IRS Publication 926. If these taxes are not withheld by the household employer, the employee can pay these annually if the employee qualifies.

A household employer must understand the federal, state, and local employment laws that pertain to his or her household. Knowing the risks of noncompliance is part of fully understanding your employment laws. Depending on your location, you may have plenty of requirements to meet.

Many laws require the employer to obtain, file, and submit necessary paperwork. For instance, for each person hired, an I-9 Form must be completed. Tax laws also have paperwork requirements, such as reporting wages to the Department of Labor or a state's Wage and Hour Division. While some laws require employers to submit forms to a designated department or division, others require employers to file completed forms and be ready to produce the paperwork when requested by government officials.

Dealing with taxes and payroll is time-consuming, nerve-racking, and complicated. GTM Payroll Services Inc. calculates that a household employer spends more than 60 hours a year handling payroll and tax administration. It is not easy, and many household employers choose to use the services of a professional payroll service. Many household employers find security in knowing that their household payroll and taxes are taken care of by experienced and qualified professionals.

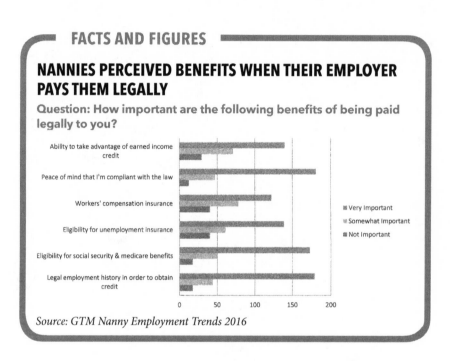

FACTS AND FIGURES

NANNIES PERCEIVED BENEFITS WHEN THEIR EMPLOYER PAYS THEM LEGALLY

Question: How important are the following benefits of being paid legally to you?

Source: GTM Nanny Employment Trends 2016

FACTS AND FIGURES

HOUSEHOLD EMPLOYERS' TAX GUIDE

IF you	THEN you need to
A. Pay cash wages of $2,000 or more in 2017 to any one household employee Do not count wages you pay to: Your spouse Your child under age 21 Your parent Any employee under age 18 at any time in 2017	Withhold and pay Social Security and Medicare taxes: The taxes are usually 15.3 percent of cash wages. Your employee's share is usually 7.65 percent* (You can choose to pay it yourself and not withhold it.) Your share is 7.65 percent

B. Pay total cash wages of $1,000 or more in any calendar quarter of 2017 to household employees Do not count wages you pay to: Spouse Child under age 21 Parent	Pay federal unemployment tax. The tax is usually 0.6 percent of cash wages (2017) after the FUTA tax credit of up to 5.4% if you paid state unemployment taxes in full on time, and the state is not determined to be a credit reduction state* Wages more than $7,000 a year per employee are not taxed. You also may owe state unemployment tax.

NOTE: *If neither A nor B above applies, you do not need to pay any federal employment taxes, but you may still need to pay state employment taxes.*
*See IRS Form 940 to determine credit.
Source: IRS Publication 926: Household Employer's Tax Guide for wages paid in 2017.

CASE STUDY

• •

HILARY LOCKHART
PRESIDENT
A+ NANNIES, INC.
MESA, AZ

Hilary Lockhart of A+ Nannies said a nanny she placed learned the importance of being paid above board. This nanny was working in a position for nine months and was told by her employer that her services were no longer needed. The employer and nanny agreed at the outset to payment under the table. So, when the nanny was let go, she was five months' pregnant and unable to collect unemployment insurance benefits. She looked for work for six or seven weeks unsuccessfully before her doctor ordered bed rest until she delivered her child.

"The nanny couldn't collect any [unemployment] money at all because there was no record of her ever working," said Lockhart. "So, the nanny—five months' pregnant—is unable to find work being a nanny. No one seems to want to hire a nanny for four months and then give six weeks off for maternity leave."

Now, Lockhart tells clients and nannies to follow the law and pay all taxes. "Number one, I tell them it's against the law to pay under the table," said Lockhart, whose business places an average of four to ten child care workers a month. "I give all my clients a lot of information on taxes and the law. I used to ask clients if they were going to pay cash. I don't ask that any more. I tell [nannies] to get the taxes done right, especially in light of situations like this."

As a former nanny for seven years, Lockhart brings to her business a well-rounded perspective—a nanny, mother, and president of a referral agency. Constantly learning, she said she considers her clients' wishes and requirements against her own litmus test of placing herself as the nanny in that situation, which is why she now strongly advocates proper payroll and tax payments.

Paying household employment taxes involves a lot more than adherence to the law. Unemployment coverage also protects employees in instances when they become involuntarily unemployed. If a former employee files a claim for unemployment insurance coverage, then the state unemployment fund, which the employer had paid into through payroll taxes, pays the employee his or her unemployment insurance payment, which is a percentage of the employee's average weekly wage. The employer is not subject to additional or ongoing payments once the employee leaves the household. However, the household employer may incur higher payroll taxes (i.e., a higher unemployment insurance rate) with future employees.

—Guy

FACTS AND FIGURES

PAYING OFF THE BOOKS—THE RISKS

There is no doubt about it; paying off the books is risky business. It puts the employer and employee in peril by not providing the payroll coverage employers and employees are entitled to by law.

Liability to household employer:

- increased exposure to an IRS audit
- a considerable penalty fine for failing to file (or attempting to evade or defeat tax payments) and potential jail time
- a false or fraudulent statement or failure to furnish a tax statement could result in a minimum $1,000 fine
- payment of all back employment taxes, interest, and penalties
- no eligibility for tax breaks, Dependent Care Assistance Program (DCAP), or Child Tax Credit

Liability to household employee:

- IRS penalties due to failure to file timely income taxes
- no unemployment insurance benefits
- no legal employment history or credit history
- no contributions to Social Security and Medicare, and therefore no eligibility to these benefits
- no workers' compensation or disability coverage

Getting Caught Paying Off the Books

Many employers mistakenly assume that because the employment of domestic work is within their home they are unlikely to get caught paying their employee illegally. Because there is a long history of household employment being paid in this way, many employers assume that this is the accepted way of paying for work in the home. Even if they are aware of the consequences, many believe getting caught is so unlikely to happen that the risk is worth it. This is not the case. Paying a household employee off the books may mean an employer is investigated by the IRS. Some of the circumstances where this can occur are as follows.

- If you have formerly paid payroll taxes on past household employees but then do not with a new employee.

- You use an agency or an online registry and the IRS audits that entity for information about household employers not reporting payroll taxes.

- You terminate an employee who has not been paid legally and they complain to the IRS.

- You have mistakenly assumed the employee is an independent contractor and not an employee, so have not withheld the correct tax obligations.

- A former employee files for unemployment benefit but cannot get it because you have not paid unemployment tax.

- An employee is injured on the job so tries to claim worker's compensation and has to name you as the employer.

- A retired employee wants to claim Social Security and reports working for you.

Understand the Laws

Ignorance is no excuse for breaking the law. As an employer, it is critical for you to understand the laws and regulations governing household employment, payroll taxes, hiring, and so on. This handbook aims to help you do so.

Employee vs. Independent Contractor

As detailed in Chapter 2, determining whether your household help is an employee or an independent contractor is important in household employment.

The majority of nannies and household employees are just that—employees. Therefore, they need to be accurately paid according to applicable labor and tax laws and receive a W-2 at the end of the year. More information on employee vs. independent contractor status is available in *Independent Contractor or Employee? (IRS Publication 1779)* and *Supplemental Tax Guide (IRS Publication 15A)*.

Researching Tax Laws

The IRS states that a household employer who pays an employee $2,000 or more (as of 2017) in gross wages during the calendar year must comply with all state and federal laws. For more information, see IRS Publication 926, *Household Employer's Tax Guide*, at www.irs.gov or www.gtm.com.

Follow Payroll Regulations

According to the *Fair Labor Standards Act* (FLSA), all household employees must be paid at least the federal or state minimum wage, whichever is higher. The federal minimum wage is $7.25 per hour (in 2017), but state minimum wages may be higher. Under certain conditions, benefits such as room and board can account for a portion of the employee's wage. Overtime pay is required for most live-out employees (according to FLSA) and there may be additional requirements for household employees, including live-ins, depending on the state in which the household resides. Paid vacations, holidays, and sick days are not required by law, and are at an employer's discretion, in most states. Some states have laws in place that do require paid time off. See the Domestic Workers' Bill of Rights laws for New York, Hawaii, California, Massachusetts, Oregon, Connecticut, and Illinois.

Expert Advice

"I cannot imagine trying to do my own tax payments. To me, doing payroll and tax payments yourself is pennywise and pound foolish. I am a strong believer in having professionals do the work. These people are professionals, and this is what they're good at."

> —Stephanie Oana
> Household Employer
> Oakland, CA

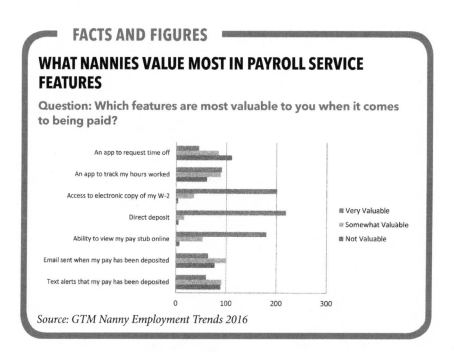

FACTS AND FIGURES

WHAT NANNIES VALUE MOST IN PAYROLL SERVICE FEATURES

Question: Which features are most valuable to you when it comes to being paid?

Source: GTM Nanny Employment Trends 2016

Comply with Tax Laws

GTM Payroll Services Inc., which provides tax and payroll services to household employers through its EasyPay Service, estimates that *employers* can expect to pay 9 percent–12 percent of the employee's gross pay for the following:

- federal unemployment insurance (usually 0.6 percent)

- Social Security and Medicare (7.65 percent)

- state unemployment insurance (about 2 percent–5 percent in most states)

- other state and local taxes (e.g., employment training or workforce taxes)

GTM estimates that, according to average salaries, *employees* can expect to pay 10 percent–30 percent of their gross pay for:

- Social Security and Medicare (usually 7.65 percent)

- other state and local taxes (e.g., disability), if applicable

- federal and state income taxes, if they choose (estimated at 15 percent–25 percent)

Though tempting to many, not paying taxes is illegal. By not paying an employee lawfully, the employer is liable for all unpaid taxes, interests, and penalties, and may face a potential jail term.

Obtain the Necessary Paperwork

Save for the SS-4, which is discussed below, before you can complete any of the necessary paperwork, you must ensure that your employee has a Social Security number. Do not assume that the employee has one, especially if he or she is not a U.S. citizen, and be sure to verify every employee's number with the Social Security Administration. This can be done online at www.ssa.gov/employer/ssnv.htm. If an employee does not have a Social Security number and is a legal U.S. citizen, then he or she can apply for one with Form SS-5 (Application for a Social Security Card). If an employee is not a U.S. citizen, an Individual Tax Identification Number (ITIN) can be obtained by using IRS Form W-7 (Application for IRS Individual Tax Payer Identification Number). An ITIN is only used for federal withholding tax purposes.

It is extremely important that you obtain all the necessary paperwork needed when you hire your household help. This includes several federal and state forms. Some of the documents you will be familiar with, probably having filled them out yourself when starting a job. Others are more unique to this type of employment or are documents you would probably not be familiar with unless you have been an employer before. From your employee's perspective, these are the forms needed to ensure he or she is getting paid and getting paid properly. To properly pay an employee, an employer should obtain the following documents (all the forms that follow are discussed in detail later in this chapter).

Federal Requirements

- Form SS-4 *Employer Identification Number* from the IRS
- Form W-4 *Employee's Withholding Allowance Certificate* to provide to newly hired employees
- Form I-9 *Employment Eligibility Verification* to provide to newly hired employees
- Form W-10 *Dependent Care Provider's Identification and Certification* for DCA Dependent Care Assistance (DCA)
- Form 1040 Schedule H *Household Employment Taxes*, an annual form
- Form 1040ES *Estimated Tax for Individuals*, optional

State Requirements

- Registration form for a state unemployment identification number
- Registration form for a state withholding number (if applicable)
- State withholding certificate (if applicable)
- State's new hire report (if necessary)

Federal Taxes

There are several federal taxes that apply to the household employer's payroll. Known as *payroll taxes*, these federal taxes are paid to the federal government via the employee's pay and are established to protect the employer and employee in the event the employee is no longer employed by the employer. For instance, if the employee is no longer needed by the employer, he or she may be covered by federal unemployment insurance. Key federal taxes include Social Security, Medicare, federal income tax, and the Federal Unemployment Tax Act (FUTA).

Social Security

Social Security tax, otherwise known as Old Age Survivor's Disability Insurance (OASDI), is required to be paid by both the employer and the employee. Each pays half of the Social Security taxes owed to the federal government. This usually calculates to 6.2 percent of the employee's gross salary. (Employee is withholding 6.2 percent, plus 6.2 percent from the employer as matching contribution, totaling 12.4 percent.) The tax is capped at a gross salary of $127,200 in a calendar year as of 2017 (for both the employee and the employer).

Paying into Social Security is an important benefit to your employee, as it provides retirement coverage when he or she becomes older. Protection for his or her future years is a valuable benefit and shows your employee that you respect his or her position.

Medicare

Like Social Security, Medicare taxes require the employer and employee to contribute equally. This tax is 2.9 percent, so both pay 1.45 percent of the employee's gross salary. There is no salary limit earned for this tax.

As with Social Security, Medicare is an important benefit for your employee to have when he or she is older and retired, providing basic medical insurance when many need it the most.

Federal Income Tax

Withholding federal income tax (FIT) from an employee's paycheck is optional, but if agreed to by employer and employee, then the employer must withhold income taxes based on the employee's completion of Form W-4. This is an employee-only withholding, and the employer does not incur any additional expenses. The FIT amount owed by each employee varies according to his or her income and filing status.

Paying federal income tax from each paycheck helps the employee disburse payment across the year, and not face paying the total federal income tax all at once. It also ensures that both employer and employee are complying with the law.

Federal Unemployment Tax Act

If an employer pays cash wages to a household employee, totaling $1,000 or more in any calendar quarter, then he or she is responsible for paying the *Federal Unemployment Tax Act* (FUTA). This is an employer tax and is not withheld from an employee's pay. It is calculated on the first $7,000 of gross wages per employee at the usual tax rate of 0.6 percent (2017), if an employer has paid his or her state unemployment taxes on time. (FUTA tax is 6 percent on the first $7,000 of gross wages. There is a FUTA tax credit of up to 5.4% if state unemployment taxes are paid in full on time, and the state is not determined to be a credit reduction state, thus decreasing the tax rate to 0.6 percent.) An employer must report FUTA with the Schedule H form, which is filed with his or her 1040 personal income tax return. Federal unemployment, while an employer tax, benefits an employee if he or she finds him- or herself to be out of work.

FACTS AND FIGURES

AN EXAMPLE OF HOW TO FIND OUT WHAT EMPLOYER TAXES TO PAY:

Facts:

Wage = $500 (gross) per week

State = New York

Filing = Single, No allowances

1. Federal Unemployment = $3 per week (2017)
2. Social Security = $31 per week
3. Medicare = $7.25 per week
4. New York State Unemployment = $20.50 per week.

Those four taxes add up to $61.75 per week. $61.75 (above taxes) plus $500 (gross wages) gives a total out-of-pocket cost, or the employer responsibility, of $561.75 per week.

Note: it may actually cost you a little bit less if you can qualify with your Dependent Care Assistance Plan (DCAP) at work, or use the Child and Dependent Care Tax Credit.

For more information, see GTM Tax Calculator at www.gtm.com.

Necessary Federal Paperwork

Form SS-4

All employers must have an employer identification number (EIN). This is generally the first document you will complete and gives you a specific tax number, much like your personal Social Security number, for dealing with the IRS and other parties. It is provided by the IRS through Form SS-4 *Application for Employer Identification Number*. An SS-4 form may be obtained by telephoning the IRS at 1-800-829-4933 or visiting www.irs.gov and completing it online.

Form W-4

If an employer and an employee have agreed to withhold income taxes, then employers should provide employees with a Form W-4, *Employee's Withholding Allowance Certificate*, and the employee must complete it. Form W-4 can be downloaded from www.irs.gov or www.gtm.com. The W-4 documents how much income tax is withheld from an employee's salary. If the W-4 is not submitted, then the employer must withhold the employee's income tax at the highest rate—as a single person with no allowances. (See Appendix E, for a sample *W-4 Form*.) Refer to IRS Publication 505 for more information.

Form I-9

Employers need to provide employees with a Form I-9, *Employment Eligibility Verification*. All employers in the United States must obtain a completed I-9 for every employee hired. The I-9 attempts to ensure that only people legally authorized to work in the United States are hired.

Employers can use the I-9 to verify the identity and employment eligibility of employees or can register and complete the USCIS e-verify system at www.uscis.gov/e-verify (See Appendix E, for a sample *I-9 form*.) More information about the I-9 process can be found at www.uscis.gov/i-9central.

Considering the rapid way in which immigration policies are changing and becoming stricter, it is vital that all employers complete the I-9 and keep it on file with appropriate copies of documentation in the employee's personnel file. In short, this proves your employee is eligible to be employed in the United States.

Form W-10

Form W-10 *Dependent Care Provider's Identification and Certification* is an optional form that any taxpayer can use to obtain information about the dependent care provider (household employees or even day care centers). This is the same information that the taxpayer reports on Form 2441 *Child and Dependent Care Expenses* with the 1040 Personal Tax Return. The IRS states that the taxpayer can use Form W-10 or any of the other methods of due diligence to collect this information, including:

- a copy of the dependent care provider's Social Security card or driver's license that includes his or her Social Security number

- a recently printed letterhead or printed invoice that shows the provider's name, address, and taxpayer identification number (TIN)

- if the provider is your employer's company's dependent care plan, a copy of the statement provided by your employer under the plan

- a copy of the household employee's W-4, if the provider is the household employee and he or she gave the employer a properly completed Form W-4 *Employee's Withholding Allowance Certificate*

Form 1040 Schedule H

Starting in 1995, the Schedule H (Household Employment Taxes) form was added to federal Form 1040 U.S. Individual Income Tax Return for employers who paid more than a total of $2,000 during the calendar year (as of tax year 2017) to household employees, or for employers who paid all employees more than $1,000 in any one quarter during the calendar year. Schedule H enables employers to report wages and taxes withheld for household help to the federal government with their own 1040 form.

Form 1040-ES

The option of transmitting taxes quarterly versus paying at the end of the year with Form Schedule H (Household Employment Taxes) allows a household employer to make estimated tax payments to cover household employment taxes. These vouchers allow you to make payments and pay all of the employment taxes at once or in installments. This form is due on a quarterly basis. (Refer to 1040-ES filing instructions for due dates.)

FACTS AND FIGURES
HOUSEHOLD EMPLOYER PAYROLL TAX EVASION

Probably the only dedicated thesis on this subject to have ever been written, Catherine B. Haskins at the University of Massachusetts wrote her 2010 dissertation, "Household Employer Payroll Tax Evasion: An Exploration Based on IRS Data and on Interviews with Employers and Domestic Workers," that reported the first-ever household employer payroll tax noncompliance estimates. Even though the data collection years (1996-2006) are a long time ago, the information she presented helps to document tax evasion in the household employment industry and present some of the trends involved. In all likelihood, it has not improved since. Despite the impossibility of accurately determining the true number of household employers who owe nanny taxes, Haskins found that the amount of estimated noncompliance per year was astounding. This evasion rate was calculated as the gap between the number of returns that should have been filed per year (based on government estimates of the number of household workers) and the number of Schedule H returns that were actually filed (from the IRS).

Haskins estimated that for every year surveyed, "the count of household payroll tax returns is never more than half and sometimes only one quarter as large as the estimate of household employees."

Using American Community Survey and Household Data Annual Averages data for the entire eleven years, Haskins calculated an overall noncompliance rate of 70 percent-71.3 percent for that period.

Haskins also stated that because these results can be considered as "reasonable lower bound estimates" she believed the actual noncompliance rate could be as high as 90 percent. She cited that many in the industry believe that government statistics understate the actual number of household workers which could mean that there is a national domestic worker population in the millions.

Source: Catherine B. Haskins, "Household Employer Payroll Tax Evasion: An Exploration Based on IRS Data and on Interviews with Employers and Domestic Workers" (2010). Open Access Dissertations. Paper 163. http://scholarworks. umass.edu/open_access_dissertations/163

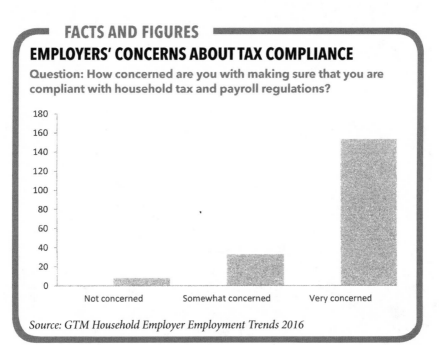

FACTS AND FIGURES
EMPLOYERS' CONCERNS ABOUT TAX COMPLIANCE

Question: How concerned are you with making sure that you are compliant with household tax and payroll regulations?

Source: GTM Household Employer Employment Trends 2016

FACTS AND FIGURES
INDIVIDUAL TAXPAYER IDENTIFICATION NUMBER

Regardless of whether a person is legally employed, an IRS Individual Taxpayer Identification Number (ITIN) can be used by those who are ineligible to obtain a Social Security number but who need to pay taxes on wages earned; these people include certain nonresident and resident aliens, and their spouses and dependents. The ITINs are nine-digit numbers beginning with the number nine and formatted like a Social Security number (9XX-XXX-XXXX). They are not to be used for nontax purposes (e.g., proof of identity for a driver's license, residency claim or employment, or to apply for welfare and health benefits). The IRS Form W-7 (Application for IRS Individual Taxpayer Identification Number) is used to obtain an ITIN and may be submitted to the IRS. According to the IRS, people using an ITIN cannot claim the earned income tax credit.

CASE STUDY

ZUZKA POLISHOOK
HOUSEHOLD EMPLOYER
PACIFIC PALISADES, CA

Zuzka Polishook hired her first nanny after the birth of her second daughter. With a two-and-a-half-year-old daughter and a second daughter just a few months old, Polishook transitioned her babysitter into a full-time nanny and housekeeper to help care for the two girls, as well as for a large house and two dogs.

Although Polishook knew from experience that the employee was responsible and a hard worker, she still painstakingly drafted an employee contract signed by both the nanny-housekeeper and herself. She did this to formalize this existing relationship but, more importantly, to clear any potential problem areas and resolve any unspoken questions. "The nanny knows where she stands with it, and I know where I stand with it," said

Polishook. "It's peace of mind for me. No matter how obvious, I wrote it down. It acts as a checklist for both parties."

However, even though she was exceedingly capable of preparing the paperwork and doing the subsequent necessary payroll and tax responsibilities, she quickly was surprised by the amount of paperwork involved in employing a domestic employee.

"Time is my most valued currency, and I was clueless where to start. I didn't even know what I needed to know." Thus, Polishook took advice from a friend and contracted with a tax and payroll service to manage the payroll and tax piece of the household employment equation. "I'm in the know and in control," she said, "but I don't have to figure the details out." By using a payroll service, she was buying peace of mind, and stated, "now, I am able to dedicate the hours I would have spent figuring payroll and taxes to my children."

Polishook advises families considering a payroll and tax service to calculate the value of their time per hour with the number of hours per month spent addressing tax and wage requirements. Once you determine the value of your time against how much time it takes away from spending with your children, using a payroll service may seem like a cost saving.

> As a household employer going it alone, it can be difficult to devote the time and energy needed to stay abreast of the changing employment regulation and tax laws. Using a payroll and tax service is an inexpensive way to save busy household employers valuable time and money.
>
> —Guy

Q & A

Q. Can we put our household employee on our company payroll?

A. Generally, no. Your company payroll should be reserved for those employees who work for your company.

Equally important, you cannot deduct your household employee's wages from your company's expenses. In most cases, you must pay your federal household employment taxes on your own federal income tax return, either annually or quarterly. The only exception to reporting your federal household employment taxes on your personal federal income tax return is if you are a sole proprietor or your home is on a farm operated for profit. In either of these instances, you may opt to include your federal household employment taxes with your federal employment tax deposits or other payments for your business or farm employees. (See IRS Publication 926 for more information.)

Reporting and Filing Federal Payroll Taxes

There are two options for filing federal payroll taxes: annually or quarterly. Household employers must report and file all federal taxes by using Form 1040 Schedule H, which is an annual reconciliation form that is used by the employer to report to the IRS wages paid to the household employee throughout the year.

Alternatively, employers may pay estimated taxes on a quarterly schedule to help alleviate the tax burden at the end of the year. In addition, Schedule H must be filed annually with the employer's personal 1040 federal tax return. To do this, an employer will need to file the 1040 Estimated Tax Form. This calculates an estimate of the following:

- employee federal income tax (FIT)
- employer and employee Social Security and Medicare
- employer federal unemployment tax (FUTA)

This sum is an estimated amount for each quarter. The due dates for submitting this form are explained in the box below.

■ FACTS AND FIGURES ■

FEDERAL TAXES FILING DEADLINES

Quarter	Due
First (January-March)	April 15
Second (April-May)	June 15
Third (June-August)	September 15
Fourth (September-December)	January 15

Note: some years, estimated tax deadlines can be adjusted a little, due to date falling on a weekend or a holiday.

If estimated tax payments are not made quarterly, then an employer may want to arrange to have additional federal income taxes withheld from his or her own salary. This will help to avoid owing a significant sum on his or her personal federal tax return and also to avoid a possible 10 percent under-payment penalty.

Each year, an employer must provide employees with Form W-2 (Wage and Tax Statement) on or before January 31. This provides a breakdown of all withholding and income throughout the previous calendar year and helps the employee submit her or his individual income tax forms.

By January 31, whether filing by paper or electronically, the employer must also file the employer copy of the employee's W-2 and W-3 (a wage transmission report) forms to the Social Security Administration. A W-3 is a reconciliation of all W-2s for each employee, even if an employer is only employing one employee.

It is extremely important for your employee to be able to prove that he or she has a source of income in establishing credit, getting a loan or a credit card, or benefiting from any tax credits. Plus, both employer and employee may benefit from tax credits: an employer may benefit from credits and from a dependent care account at work, whereas an employee may benefit from the federal earned income tax credit.

Q & A

Q. I am nervous about dealing with the IRS and all federal, state, and local tax forms that I need to complete. What can I do to ensure that I'm doing all I need to be doing, particularly since two friends of mine do not file the same paperwork that I do?

A. Given the circumstances, you're right to be anxious. Following all tax requirements can be confusing and time consuming, but it must be done. Refer to IRS Publication 926 and Publication 15, as well as relevant state and local labor and tax guides. Many household employers contract with payroll services firms like GTM to handle taxes and paperwork and to consult with experts regarding the precise, timely, and lawful handling of wages. Many who choose not to adhere to the tax law unfortunately risk heavy penalties and jail. Paying a household employee under the table puts the household employee in a very vulnerable spot, as he or she is without the protection of unemployment insurance, Social Security, and so on. The important thing is to make sure you pay the correct taxes.

State Taxes

Along with federal taxes, household employers are responsible for complying with their state and local tax laws. Be sure that you cover all payroll taxes—federal, state, and local.

Necessary State Paperwork

State Unemployment Identification Number

Household employers are required to obtain a state unemployment identification number with the state where the physical work will be performed. Refer to IRS Publication 926 for a list of State Unemployment Tax Agencies (also available online at www.irs.gov). This ID number is needed to pay state unemployment taxes on a quarterly basis and will appear on the W-2 (Wage and Tax Statement) form for each employee.

State Withholding Certificate

It is optional for an employer to withhold taxes from an employee's paycheck. If an employer and employee decide to withhold state income taxes, then the state's registration form should be completed by contacting the state's withholding agency. This provides an employer with an ID number, a coupon booklet, and instructions on how to submit withholding taxes according to the state's laws. This number will also appear on Form W-2 for each employee.

State New Hire Report

New hire reporting is a process by which an employer has to register any newly hired employee with the state within a certain time of the hire date.

This report usually gives contact and basic identification information for each new employee to the state's department of labor, which then transmits the report to the National Directory of New Hires (NDNH). (The most common use of this information is to help the child support collection unit track down debtors for child support payments.)

Workers' Compensation and Disability Insurance

Most states require household employers to carry a workers' compensation and/or disability policy if employing someone full time or part time. These policies provide compensation to an employee who is injured on the job. It is recommended that even if your state does not require employers to have a policy, you should consider obtaining appropriate coverage for peace of mind. Some states also require insurance coverage for nonoccupational injury or illness. If you do not cover yourself for an employee injury, you set yourself up for possibly a very costly lawsuit if your nanny, senior caregiver, housekeeper, or other employee is injured on the job. Homeowner's insurance policies often *do not* cover these situations. With the proper insurance coverage, you will protect yourself and your home—while also protecting your employee from the added costs of the injury and potential loss of work.

States that mandate workers' compensation and disability insurance are discussed in Chapter 11.

State Unemployment Insurance

State unemployment insurance is an employer tax and is not withheld from an employee's pay. It is normally due on a quarterly basis. Unemployment insurance contributions are accumulated in every state's unemployment insurance fund for workers who can claim eligibility. State unemployment insurance is generally calculated between 2 percent and 5 percent on a certain amount of each employee's gross wages for the calendar year, which varies state by state. For example, for new employers, Virginia's state unemployment insurance is set at 2.53 percent on the first $8,000 per employee, whereas Arizona requires 2 percent on the first $7,000 (in 2017).

Unemployment is an important factor for any worker. Sometimes, a new employee just does not work out, or perhaps circumstances change and you no longer need a nanny or other household worker. Unemployment insurance would protect your nanny and his or her family, paying a percent of the income, until he or she is hired elsewhere and no longer needs assistance.

Q & A

Q. Is there a difference between being covered by Social Security and being eligible for Social Security?

A. Yes, and the difference is significant. To be eligible for Social Security, an employee must work 40 calendar quarters to be fully insured and eligible for retirement, disability, death, and survivor benefits. To be covered, you must work at least ten calendar quarters to be insured and eligible for limited death benefits.

State Income Tax

State income taxes are employee income taxes based on filing status and wage level. Withholding state income tax is not required, unless agreed upon by the employer and employee, but it generally helps employees distribute their owed income taxes throughout the year at regular intervals, rather than requiring a total payment at the end of the tax year. The employee may want the employer to withhold state income taxes from his or her paycheck.

Also, much like federal taxes, paying state withholding taxes documents an employee's legal employment history and is critical in establishing and improving him or herself financially.

Disability Insurance

Some states may require the employer to withhold additional taxes for disability insurance from the employee's pay. For example, New Jersey, California, Hawaii, New York, and Rhode Island have a state disability tax. California State Disability Insurance (SDI) is a partial wage-replacement insurance plan for California workers. The SDI program is state mandated and funded through employee payroll deductions. It provides affordable, short-term benefits to eligible workers who suffer a loss of wages when they are unable to work due to a non-work-related illness or injury, or a medically disabling condition from pregnancy or childbirth.

Q & A

Q. I am a housekeeper and my employer is paying my Social Security and Medicare but asked me if I would like income taxes withheld. I am uncertain whether to have income tax withheld from my paycheck. What is the best scenario?

A. What is best depends on you. First, choosing to withhold income tax from your paycheck is not the same as choosing whether to pay it. You must pay it. The option is whether you want your employer to withhold income tax from your paycheck or whether you want to pay the income tax yourself. So, this becomes a budgeting and convenience issue. We strongly discourage employees from trying to pay taxes on their own.

Local Income Tax

Some localities require an employer to withhold local income tax, based on either the place of employment or residence of the employee. Such localities include some in Ohio and Pennsylvania, as well as New York City.

Filing State Taxes

Most states require the quarterly filing of state taxes (state unemployment and other taxes). Unfortunately, state tax quarters do not coincide with federal tax quarters.

Instead, states require taxes to be submitted every three months—typically one month after the quarter ends. After an employer has registered with the state to file taxes, the state sends blank quarterly forms with instructions. If an employer uses a payroll service, then he or she may avoid the hassle of signing checks and filing taxes accurately and timely. If they so choose, the employer and the employee may file state income taxes (state withholding taxes) that are typically due each quarter. However, each state has specific filing frequencies based on how much income tax is withheld. The amount withheld from an employee's wages during a quarter generally determines the filing frequency in any given state (e.g., semiweekly, monthly, quarterly, annually). When an employer registers with the state, state tax officials will inform her or him of the filing frequency. Another way to determine filing frequency is to refer to the welcome letter in the correspondence received with the state withholding income number.

More and more states are requiring electronic filing for state taxes, so it is best to check with your state if this is mandatory or not. Penalties may be applied to employers who remit payment by check and do not e-file.

FACTS AND FIGURES

STATE FILING DATES

Quarter	Due
First (January-March)	April 30
Second (April-June)	July 31
Third (July-September)	October 31
Fourth (October-December)	January 31

Although these dates do apply for most states, they can vary from state to state. Be sure to double-check your state's due dates with your state's tax agency.

Q & A

Q. What state taxes am I required to pay as a household employer?

A. State employment laws are similar for a worker in the home or in the corporate office. All states have a state unemployment insurance tax, which employers must pay.

This amount is a percentage (2 percent–5 percent) of the household employee's gross salary and is capped at an annual wage amount. For example, Illinois requires 3.45 percent on the first $12,960 (2017) of the gross wage per employee. Some states, such as California, New Jersey, Hawaii, New York, and Rhode Island require the employee to contribute a small amount to disability or unemployment out of her or his own gross pay in addition to employer payments.

Record Retention

An employer should make sure that all hiring, tax, and payroll documentation regarding an employee's hire, including all IRS and state forms, is kept in a safe place. It is recommended that these forms be kept on file for at least seven years, in case the IRS or Department of Justice needs to check who is, or has been, employed by the employer.

Employee Responsibilities

The employee who works in your home is responsible for reporting and paying required payroll taxes too. It is worth making sure that employees are aware of their responsibilities at the start of employment, if they do not already know. Nannies and other household employees are liable for four key taxes:

1.   Social Security (OASDI) at (usually) 6.2 percent (2017). If the household employee is getting paid $2,000 gross or more in 2017, he or she is required to withhold and pay Social Security

2. Medicare at 1.45 percent. If the household employee is getting paid $2,000 gross or more in 2017, they are required to withhold and pay Medicare

3. Federal income tax is not required to be withheld by the employer but must be paid by the employee*

4. State income tax is not required to be withheld by the employer but must be paid by the employee*

*Federal and state income taxes are not required to be withheld unless agreed on by the employer and the employee. It is advantageous to withhold them though because it

- helps employees distribute their owed income taxes throughout the year, rather than as a lump sum at the end of the tax year

- helps to document an employee's legal employment history

- ensures both employer and employee are in compliance with the law

FACTS AND FIGURES

AN EXAMPLE OF HOW TO FIND OUT WHAT EMPLOYEE TAXES TO PAY.

Facts:

Nanny's wage: $500 gross wage per week

Nanny's tax classification: claiming single zero

Location: New York City, New York

Federal income tax = $59.40

Social Security = $31*

Medicare = $7.25

State income tax = $14.59

Local income tax = $9.88

Total tax to be withheld = $122.12 per week. Take this from the gross wage of $500, would leave the employee with a net take home pay of $377.88 per week.

For more information, use GTM's tax calculator at www.gtm.com.

*calculated at the usual rate of 6.2%

All calculations based on tax rates for 2017

Paying an Employee

Unless an employer already has a firm idea of when he or she wants an employee to be paid, it is probably best to talk to the employee to see what best suits his or her needs and to agree on a regular pay interval. Generally, workers must be paid at least twice a month; however, some states require a weekly pay frequency for household employment.

Wages should always be paid by check so both the employer and the employee have an earnings and deduction record for the current pay period and year-to-date accumulated totals (see Appendix D, for a sample *Paycheck and Payroll Earnings Statement*). The amount on the check should always be net (after all applicable taxes are withheld).

An employer can also offer the option of direct deposit, which is a convenient payment method for both the employer and the employee.

Some states require more detailed pay rate information, such as under the *New York State Wage Theft Prevention Act*. This law requires the employer to provide in writing how the employee is paid by the hour, shift, day, week, salary, piece, commission, or other, on his or her pay statement and pay rate notice at time of hiring and keep a copy signed by the employee. In 2014, the law was revised to remove onerous employer annual wage notices while stiffening employer penalties allowing employees to recover from $50/week up to $2,500 to $50/day up to $5,000.

Employer Benefits of Paying Nanny Taxes	Employee Benefits of Paying Nanny Taxes
Tax savings which can help underwrite much of the employer's payroll tax expense	Eligible for Social Security credits
	Legal employment history
Eligibility for federal assistance programs e.g. child care tax credit and Dependent Care Assistance Programs (DCAP). This may allow up to $5,000 in pretax earnings per year that can be set aside for child care or eldercare expenses	Coverage for Social Security, Medicare, unemployment, and workers' compensation
	May qualify for earned income credit
	Ensuring tax compliance
Ensuring tax compliance	Peace of mind—knowing you are doing the right thing and abiding by the law
Avoiding state and federal fines and penalties	
Family financial protection, such as workers' compensation in the event the worker is hurt while working on the job	
Peace of mind—knowing you are doing the right thing to protect your family and your employee	

Payroll Tax Checklist

- Understand and abide by all federal, state, and local laws.

- Be aware of applicable state and local laws.

- Be clear about household tax needs and the importance of lawful tax payments for all household employees.

- Even if an employee asks to be paid under the table, do not do so. Explain that tax withholding is for the employee's benefit and will ensure unemployment and Social Security coverage.

- Ensure that the employee knows about his or her tax obligations as a household worker.

When a household employee is hired, the following applies.

- Obtain an employer identification number (if not obtained previously).

- Have household employees complete Form W-4 if the employer is withholding income taxes.

- Obtain Form I-9 for employee eligibility verification.

- Apply for a state unemployment ID number.

- Apply for a state withholding number (if applicable).

- Apply for a state's new hire report (if necessary).

- Obtain Form 1040-ES for estimated tax payments (if desired).

- Check workers' compensation policy requirements for the state.

- Establish a regular pay period schedule following any applicable state laws, and inform the employee.

When a household employee is paid, the following applies.

- Withhold Social Security and Medicare taxes from employee's pay.

- Pay on time federal, state, and local taxes that may apply.

- Withhold federal and state income taxes, if agreed.

- Provide your employee(s) with Form W-2 (Wage and Tax Statement) on or before January 31 each year.

- Send Copy A of Form W-2 with Form W-3 to the Social Security Administration by January 31 each year (whether filing electronically or by paper).

- File Schedule H with the employer's federal income tax return (Form 1040) by April 15 each year.

- Keep records in a safe place for seven years.

Source: IRS Publication 926 Household Employer's Tax Guide

11

Health, Safety, and Insurance

A satisfying workplace is only obtained in a healthy and safe environment. This is of paramount importance to the employee and will be discussed in this chapter with regard to the Occupational Safety and Health Act (OSHA) and other safety issues in the household that will help make the home a better and safer workplace. It is also of utmost concern when the household employee is taking care of family members, particularly children and seniors who are more susceptible to household injuries and accidents.

The leading report on childhood injuries is still the Center of Disease Control and Prevention (CDC) Childhood Injury Report, *Patterns of Unintentional Injuries among 0-19 Year Olds in the United States 2000-2006*, which states that the foremost cause of death among children is injury. About 20 children die every day from a preventable injury—more than die from all diseases combined. Although the majority of unintentional injuries involve a motor vehicle accident of some kind, there are still considerable numbers of unintentional injuries to children from drowning, falls, fires/burns, poisoning, and suffocation. These injuries and accidents can happen in and around the home. Similarly, each year, according to estimates by the U.S. Consumer Product Safety Commission (CPSC), nearly one million people over age 65 are treated in hospital emergency rooms for injuries associated with the products they live with and use every day. This chapter will discuss how the home can be made a safer place for the health of the entire household—including the household help—and how the employer should be aware of key circumstances to make it so.

Occupational Safety and Health Act

The Occupational Safety and Health Act (OSHA) ensures that employers provide employees with a workplace that is free from recognized hazards that cause or could cause serious harm or death to employees. Under OSHA, employers must provide safety training to employees, inform employees about hazardous chemicals to which they may be exposed, and notify regulators about workplace accidents.

Household employees often come in contact with a variety of workplace hazards in the home, such as exposure to harmful cleaning chemicals and potential injury from lifting children, seniors who have limited mobility, or heavy objects. While OSHA regulates worker health and safety, it does not protect household workers who are employed by individuals in their own residences to perform "for the benefit of such individuals what are commonly regarded as ordinary domestic household tasks, such as house cleaning, cooking, and caring for children" (www.osha.gov).

However, the household employer needs to provide a safe, hazard-free workplace and, therefore, may choose to follow OSHA requirements, such as providing employees with safety equipment like gloves and masks, maintaining safe equipment, listing any chemicals with which employees may come into contact, conducting safety training such as the correct way to lift, etc. The home environment can provide health hazards and safety concerns for the domestic employee or nanny and especially for senior care workers who help care for the elderly and disabled. Many households wish to remedy this situation and ensure that the home is a safe environment for their employee, as well as their family. This chapter offers advice on how to provide a safe work environment along OSHA guidelines.

Under OSHA, employers must follow requirements to ensure a healthy work environment, which include providing training, medical examinations, and record keeping. Some employer requirements follow:

- provide a workplace free from serious hazards, and comply with OSHA rules and regulations
- ensure that employees have and use safe tools and equipment

- use color codes, posters, labels, or signs to warn employees of potential hazards
- establish or update operating procedures, and communicate them to employees
- keep records of work-related injuries and illnesses (employers with ten or fewer employees and employers in certain low-hazard industries are exempt from this OSHA requirement)

Some OSHA workplace concerns include:

- exposure to hazardous chemicals
- first aid and medical treatment required as a result of a workplace injury
- noise levels
- protective gear (e.g., goggles, work shoes, ear protectors)
- workplace temperatures and ventilation
- safety training

Because OSHA is so broadly written, household employers may want to contact a local OSHA office to determine specific requirements. Housekeepers might be instructed to wear protective gloves when in contact with cleaning solvents, or gardeners might be instructed to wear goggles and earplugs when performing landscaping work with certain equipment.

Employers also should follow OSHA record-keeping rules, which include maintaining a log of workplace injuries that require treatment beyond first aid.

A good practice is for employers to keep a written safety policy in the employee handbook, which could offer instructions on where the house's first aid kit is kept, a list of emergency service telephone numbers, protective gear required for specific tasks, and an employee requirement to report all health and safety issues immediately to the employer. In addition, the safety policy could provide instructions that improper use of equipment (e.g., using equipment for purposes other than what it is intended or using equipment that is not properly connected) is prohibited within the household.

Along with federal OSHA requirements, an employer may need to meet state and local health and safety requirements. To obtain information on state and local requirements, contact your state and local health departments, chambers of commerce, business bureaus, and so on.

Q & A

Q. I recently argued with my full-time nanny about what I needed to provide her with to care for my five-year-old daughter with chicken pox. The nanny was concerned that she was exposed to the illness and was carrying it home to her husband, who had never had chicken pox. What types of protective gear am I liable for?

A. Every employer in the United States must ensure that a workplace—even one in the home—is a safe and healthy environment in which to work. As a household employer, you could provide your housekeeper with gloves and a face mask when using a chemical cleaner; a gardener with eye goggles and ear plugs when using landscaping equipment; a senior care worker with medical gloves when injecting medication; or a child care worker with medical gloves and a face mask when caring for a child with the flu, measles, chicken pox, and so on. Such universal precautions are standard in any work environment and are an ideal topic for employers to discuss with employees during the development of a work agreement and review of the employee handbook.

FACTS AND FIGURES
TOP FIVE WORKPLACE INJURIES

While these are the top workplace injuries for all workplaces—not just the home—many are relevant to the home environment. These show that when someone is employed in the home it is still his or her workplace and therefore workplace safety is just as relevant as in another location. Here are the top five workplace injuries based on the 2016 Liberty Mutual Insurance Workplace Safety Index.

1. Overexertion: Household workers have to do a lot of manual handling. Sometimes this involves a lot of lifting or other activities that require the use of hands and limbs required for elderly caregiving and work activities related to nursing, carrying children or gardening, to name just a few. Incidents that can relate to overexertion involve hand and arm strain and back pain.

2. Falls on Same Level: This pertains to falls that have happened on same level surfaces. Common injuries filed in this category are slipping on wet floors and falling on snow-covered surfaces. If an employee falls on your property and is injured because of a slippery sidewalk, or a wet bathroom, he or she has a workplace injury.

3. Falls to Lower Level: Falling from stairways, roofs, ladders, and other elevated areas are common injury-related occurrences. Homes that contain stairs or household work that requires ladders (such as gardening) can therefore cause these types of workplace injuries, and care should be taken to prevent falls with the proper installation of handrails and so forth.

4. Other Exertions or Bodily Reactions: Slips and trips are, without a doubt, among the most common accidents occurring in the workplace. Slips and trips can happen anywhere, including the home. Household employers should protect themselves against liability of them occurring in their home with regard to their employee.

5. Struck by an Object: This is usually from a tool falling on the head of the employee from above, and it can be relevant to the household industry if the employee works outside, such as a gardener, or sometimes in the home, such as a chef.

Source: www.libertymutualgroup.com/researchinstitute

Emergency Preparation

It is wise to familiarize a household employee with any home emergency procedures (e.g., in case of fire) and to provide a list of medical personnel for each family member, especially if there is a child with special needs or a senior with specific medical issues.

All household employees that are caregivers, such as nannies, should ideally be certified in CPR. If the nanny has not completed such training before hiring, it is very easy to find an infant or child CPR course in your local area by contacting the American Red Cross (www.redcross.org).

All homes should have a family fire escape plan that you should review with your household employee, as well as your family, on a regular basis. See www.nfpa.org for advice on fire safety. Other emergency situations that should be discussed with your employee depend on where you live. For example, if you live in a state where there are hurricanes, tornados, or earthquakes, the employee should be informed of any special procedures.

A new employee in the home should be given a list of emergency contacts and this should be easily located in the house for everyone to see. The nanny should keep a copy with her at all times, or save the numbers in her cell phone contacts, when leaving the house with the children. The list of emergency contacts should include:

- parents' home, work, and cell phone numbers, and work addresses and email addresses
- friendly, helpful neighbors' home, work, and cell numbers, and home addresses
- relatives' home, work, and cell numbers
- number for the local Poison Control Center
- 911 in your area and whether the 911 procedures are different for the employee's cell phone or any digital and line numbers that are not in the 911 system
- numbers for pediatrician, dentist, and any other medical specialist required for the family member who is being cared for
- the local hospital number
- school main office and school nurse numbers if any of the children are at school

- list of children's school friends' home numbers, if appropriate

The Home Medical Kit

Every home should have a well-stocked first-aid kit. A home with a household employee should have one all ready for the employee's first day on the job. This prepares the employee for every eventuality and means that if an accident occurs in the home the employee knows exactly where to look for the right supplies. If the first-aid kit is all ready to go, this could save valuable time and hassle in the event it is needed. Ideally, you should prepare one kit for the home (storing it within easy reach but out of harm's way) and one for the car that the employee will be using when working with your family.

Good medical kits can be purchased easily, or you can make one yourself. General requirements for a first-aid kit follow:

- instructions on CPR and choking prevention or a first-aid manual
- sterile gauze pads (different sizes)
- adhesive tape
- band-aids (different sizes)
- a cloth or elastic bandage
- antiseptic wipes
- antibiotic ointment
- hydrocortisone cream (1 percent)
- acetaminophen and ibuprofen (appropriate to family members' ages)
- anti-histamine (appropriate to family members' ages)
- tweezers
- sharp scissors
- safety pins
- disposable instant cold packs
- calamine lotion
- alcohol wipes
- thermometer

- plastic, nonlatex gloves
- flashlight and batteries
- list of emergency phone numbers
- a blanket

Home Safety

Aside from federal, state, and local laws governing a healthy and safe workplace, household employers may take some basic steps to ensure household safety. These home safety measures apply to any home or household member, and can easily apply to household workers. This list is not exhaustive, but it does offer some general guidelines that employers may want to consider for their home.

Home Safety Checklist

There are many measures you can take to ensure that your home is safe, and an easy checklist reviewed occasionally can help you protect your family, friends, employees, and visitors from injury and harm.

Kitchen

- Are the exhaust hood and duct on the kitchen stove cleaned frequently?
- Are cleaners, disinfectants, poisons, and so on, stored away from food and out of children's reach?
- Are utensils and knives stored neatly and kept out of children's reach?
- Are pot and pan handles turned away from stove fronts?
- Are cupboard contents stored neatly to prevent falling?
- Are spills wiped up immediately?
- Are plastic grocery and shopping bags out of children's reach?

Entrances and stairways

- Are entrances, halls, and stairways adequately lighted to prevent trips and falls?

- Are steps well maintained?

- Are steps cleared of objects and tripping hazards? Are there at least two exits that are designated fire exits and always kept clear?

- Is a child's gate used at the top and bottom of stairs if a toddler is living in the home? (Accordion-type gates are dangerous; children's heads can easily get trapped in them.)

- Are steps and railings sturdy and in good condition?

- Does the employee know when and who to open the door to? (The household policy on this should be reviewed with the employee—any arranged visits by service people should always be told to the employee ahead of time.)

Living areas

- Are electrical cords kept away from carpets? Are cords in good condition (not frayed or overloaded)?

- Are long electrical blinds and drapery cords beyond a child's reach? (Excess cord can be bound with a twist tie, or a holder or spool specially designed to hide the extra cord.)

- Are all wires in the house properly insulated?

- Are there safety outlet covers in all of the unused electrical outlets?

- Are throw rugs secured to prevent tripping?

- Is furniture kept away from windows to prevent children from falling out? (Window screens will not prevent a child from falling out of the window.)

- Are sharp furniture edges covered?

- Are radiators and pipes covered to protect against burns?

- Are lamps located near beds to prevent tripping in the dark?

- Is there ample walking space between furniture and objects?

- Are all plants safe? (Some plants are toxic and need to be placed out of children's reach.)

Bathrooms

- Are medicines and vitamins stored out of children's reach?
- Is the home's hot water temperature set at the safe temperature of 120°F? (If the temperature cannot be altered, then install an antiscald device on the faucet.)
- Is there a toilet-lid locking device in households with small children?

Nursery

- Does the crib mattress snugly fit against the crib's sides? (No more than two fingers' distance should exist between the mattress and the crib railing.)
- Are crib bars two inches or less apart? (Any more space and a child could be caught or strangled between the crib's bars.) A good tip is to use a soda can. If you can fit the can between the bars, the crib is not safe.
- Are crib side rails kept up?

Garage

- Are all tools, including those used for gardening, automotive, and lawn care, stored in a locked container?
- Are recycling containers holding glass and metal far from children's reach?

Yard

- Is outdoor play equipment safe with no loose parts or rust?
- Are surfaces around swing sets and play equipment soft to absorb shock from falls? (Good surface equipment can be sand or wood chips; concrete and packed dirt are not adequate to absorb shock from falls.)
- Is access to the swimming pool blocked for small children? Are dangerous cleaning chemicals kept locked away?

Fire Safety Checks

- Are there smoke and carbon monoxide detectors on each level of the home and near the sleeping area?
- Are detectors checked monthly to ensure that they are operating?
- Are batteries replaced at least once a year?
- Are detectors cleaned monthly to clear away dust and cobwebs?
- Are detectors replaced every ten years? (Detectors become less sensitive over time.)
- Does the home have one or more fire extinguishers and do all household members and employees know how to operate them? (The local fire department can provide training on how to properly use an extinguisher.)
- Does the home have an automatic sprinkler system? (Automatic sprinkler systems are a good consideration— even in the home.)
- Is there a clearly written fire escape plan for the home? Is the plan practiced at least twice a year?

Home Security

Nothing is more important than protecting your loved ones. Keeping a household and family safe and sound can be complicated, expensive, and involved. Depending on the nature of the household and the location, an employer should make sure that the employee hired is aware of all necessary security systems, keys and locks, spotlights, and video surveillance that may be required knowledge for the job. For example, if the employer is away during the day, the employee should know how to lock up the house, turn on the alarm system, and so forth. It is advised that the employee have his or her own security code, if possible. It is a good idea, during the orientation of the employee in the first few days, to go over all security procedures and what needs to be checked if the house is left unattended during the day (e.g., closing and locking windows, locking doors, turning lights on, setting the alarm system).

Security Professional

If full-time personal security protection is warranted, then identifying the security professional for use in the household is not as difficult as it may seem. Some overall areas to consider include the following:

- experience in personal protection, business security, and estate and asset protection

- background in estate management practices, public relations, and personnel management

- personal demeanor, including personable countenance, flexibility, and discretion

A professional should have this experience and skill set before being considered for a household security position. Without them, the individual is either lacking the security skills necessary to protect the household or is missing the public relations skills needed to interact in a smooth, balanced, and relaxed manner with both the client and the household staff.

Driving Safety

If the employee is going to be driving your car, you need to check your insurance policy and make sure that he or she is a listed driver. This is especially important if the employee will be regularly driving family members to and from appointments, school, and for outings. Other safety precaution measures that should be done with regard to driving safety include the following:

- checking the employee's driver's license validity and for any record of violations and accidents (this is done prior to hire)

- asking about an employee's driving experience at the interview (especially if the employee is not from, or has limited driving experience in, the United States, or is particularly young)

- ensuring that the employee knows how to safely install child seats and all the regulations required for doing so according to child ages, if necessary

- making sure the car is safe, clean, and ready for the employee to use

- informing the hired worker that there is a zero tolerance policy with texting while driving and the safe procedures that should be followed to check or receive cell phone calls and messages when using the car

It may also prove useful to go on a driving test run, before you hire the employee, so you can experience his or her driving skills yourself.

NOTE: According to the International Nanny Association, auto accidents are probably the most common type of claim involving a nanny and his or her employer. So, employers need to fully understand what and who is covered by their insurance policies. To be safe, employers may want to consider adding the nanny or other household worker to their auto insurance policy.

Q & A

Q. I am a busy mother and working professional in New York, and I employ both a full-time child care provider and occasional babysitters. To what extent does my auto insurance protect me and my employees when they use my car during their work hours?

A. Check with your insurance agent about what your particular policy covers. Major liability could exist if your household employee is not properly covered under the household's auto insurance policy. While states' and carriers' requirements vary, the following is a summary of New York's auto insurance.

For occasional users (babysitters) driving the family's car, protection is offered through the liability and medical insurance segments of the insured's (the family's) car insurance. An occasional user driving his or her own vehicle is protected under the liability and medical insurance segments of the employee's car insurance.

A regular user (full-time child care provider) driving your car should be listed as a driver with the insurance company. This protects the employer in the event that an accident occurs when the employee is driving the family's car. An employer who does not notify his or her insurance agent of the regular user risks the insurer not renewing the insurance policy.

A Drug-Free Workplace

A written drug-free workplace policy is the basis of the workplace's drug-free program. Included in the employee handbook, the policy needs to clearly state why the policy is being implemented—to ensure a safe and healthy workplace. Prohibited behaviors should be clearly outlined within the policy. Use, at a minimum, language that states that the use, possession, transfer, or sale of illegal drugs or controlled substances by employees is prohibited. Include consequences, such as immediate dismissal, but take care that these consequences are consistent with other existing personnel policies and, of course, any applicable laws. For instance, if a personnel policy states that any illegal act performed by an employee on workplace premises will result in immediate dismissal, then it follows that any illegal drugs or controlled substances found on the employee will result in immediate dismissal.

In the drug-free workplace policy, an employer may want to include information on drug testing. While most private employers have the right to test for a wide variety of substances, federal, state, and local regulations may apply. However, according to the U.S. Department of Labor, employers who drug test without a drug-testing policy are exposed to liability. Employers may request that employees take a drug test after a job is offered and that employment is contingent on a successful outcome. Local drugstores sell drug-testing kits for about $20.

According to the U.S. Department of Labor, employers may be able to identify workers with substance abuse problems by noting aspects of their performance and behavior. While these symptoms may not mean that a worker has an alcohol or a drug abuse problem, employers should be alert to any of these aspects.

Remember, it is not the employer's job to diagnose substance abuse, but it *is* the employer's job to ensure health and safety within the work environment. Clear and firm communication with the employee focused on his or her job performance is key, as is explaining the drug-free workplace policy, performance policies, and what will occur when performance expectations are not met.

Some states have workplace-related substance abuse laws. To learn what states mandate, go to www.samhsa.gov/.

Q & A

Q. How can I tell whether my nanny is using drugs?

A. There are some signs and behaviors you can watch for to detect or raise your suspicion regarding drug use, or other questionable behavior, by your nanny. Signals to watch for include the following:

- frequent requests for early dismissal or time off
- frequent lateness or unreliability
- inconsistent work performance and behavior
- exhibited confusion, memory lapses, or difficulty recalling details and difficulty following directions
- progressive deterioration of personal appearance and hygiene
- anxiety, moodiness, and personality changes

It is a fairly standard business practice for new hires to take a drug test and for employers to ask employees to repeat drug tests periodically.

FACTS AND FIGURES
IDENTIFYING PERFORMANCE BEHAVIOR ISSUES

Performance	Behavior
Inconsistent work quality	Frequent financial problems
Poor concentration	Avoiding friends and colleagues
Lowered productivity	Blaming others for own problems
Increased absenteeism	Complaints about own home life
Unexplained disappearances from job site	Deterioration in personal appearance
Carelessness, mistakes, judgment errors	Complaints of vaguely-defined illness
	Needless risk taking
	Disregard for safety

Small Businesses and Household Employers

Large companies tend to have programs in place to combat workplace substance abuse. Small businesses and, especially, households do not. Some individuals who can't adhere to a drug-free workplace policy may seek employment at places that don't have one, including household employment. The good news is that small businesses and places of work have enormous power to improve the safety and health of their workplaces and employees by implementing drug-free workplace programs that educate employees about the dangers of drug abuse and encourage individuals with related problems to seek help. Some small businesses, including household employers, do not effectively address the issue due to a lack of resources. To help small businesses benefit from being drug-free, the Department of Labor and OSHA's Working Partners for an Alcohol- and Drug-Free Workplace program offers a range of free and easy-to-use tools to help them maintain safe, healthy, and drug-free workplaces.

Expert Advice

"Intelligence is recognizing possibilities; wisdom is preparing for those possibilities. The wise take steps before an unsavory event occurs. Well-planned security measures cause the nefarious to look elsewhere for their illicit gains. Thus, the wise protect their families and loved ones."

—Barry Wilson
President and certified protection specialist
Anlance Protection, Ltd.

Workers' Compensation

Many states require an employer to pay workers' compensation insurance. An employee can receive workers' compensation benefits to replace income and to cover medical expenses resulting from work-related illness or injury and the employer is protected from liability. Employers need to exercise caution—if state law requires workers' compensation insurance, be aware that a household liability insurance policy (or homeowner's policy) may not be adequate for state workers' compensation requirements and may not cover any injuries, court awards, or other penalties. In some states, homeowner's insurance policies may cover a domestic worker, depending on the number of hours worked, particular insurance carrier policy forms, and state regulations for the type of work performed. It is necessary to check with each individual insurance company and its policy terms and conditions. For example, in California, a homeowner's policy may include workers' compensation coverage if the nanny is injured on the job, while other states do not have any coverage for a domestic employee's work-related injury or work-related illness. For example, New York homeowner's policies never pick up workers' compensation for domestic employees. Mandatory regulation and compliance is regulated by each state and is determined by the number of hours an employee works, and therefore whether the employee is full time or part time. These specifications vary by each state. However, all states require that a workers' compensation policy is in effect *prior* to the employee's start date. It is important to note that a policy may be purchased, on a voluntary basis, regardless of mandatory requirements and that all policies may be available for part-time employees. Coverage can be obtained by the employer, thus eliminating the chance of lawsuits by an injured employee for lost wages and medical expenses. Obtaining workers' compensation coverage can be very reasonable and well worth the cost in the face of a work-related accident.

Some individual local and state workers' compensation requirements directly refer to household employees (i.e., domestic workers). A domestic worker is defined as someone employed and paid by a single person or a couple in a domestic partnership within a private household. These states require workers' compensation coverage in certain situations. It is therefore advisable to check with your local state authority for specific state requirements.

Examples of individual state differences:

> Maryland workers' compensation requirements
>> Under Maryland workers' compensation provisions, any domestic worker whose earnings from a private employer are $1,000 or more in any calendar quarter, may choose with the employer for the employee to be covered by workers' compensation, even if the individual does not meet the state earnings requirement.

New York workers' compensation and disability
New York workers' compensation laws cover domestic employees employed 40 or more hours per week by the same employer, including full-time sitters or companions, and live-in maids.

Massachusetts workers' compensation requirements
Massachusetts workers' compensation is required for all employees in domestic service working at least 16 or more hours per week.

Washington, D.C., workers' compensation requirements
Washington, D.C., calls for employers to carry workers' compensation coverage for domestic workers employed by the same employer at least 240 hours during a calendar quarter.

As always, you need to be aware of all statutes and requirements—federal, state, and local. It is best to consult your insurance agent and state insurance department, as many states offer employers a state insurance fund option, and laws requiring coverage may change.

FACTS AND FIGURES
WORKERS' COMPENSATION BY STATE

State	Voluntary/Mandatory
Alabama	Permits employers to provide voluntary coverage.
Alaska	Any domestic worker except part-time babysitters, cleaning persons, harvest help, and similar part-time or transient help.
Arizona	Permits employers to provide voluntary coverage.
Arkansas	Permits employers to provide voluntary coverage.
California	Any domestic worker—including one who cares for and supervises children—employed 52 or more hours, or who earned $100 or more, during 90 calendar days immediately preceding date of injury or last employment exposing such worker to the hazards of an occupational disease. Excludes workers employed by a parent, spouse, or child.

Colorado	Mandatory for all domestic workers working 40 hours or more in a week, or working five days or more in a week.
Connecticut	Any domestic worker employed 26 hours or more per week by one employer.
Delaware	Any domestic worker who earns $750 or more in any three month period from a single private home or household.
District of Columbia	Domestic workers employed by the same employer at least 240 hours during a calendar quarter.
Florida	Permits employers to provide voluntary coverage.
Georgia	Permits employers to provide voluntary coverage.
Hawaii	Any worker employed solely for personal, family, or household purposes whose wages are $225 or more during the calendar quarter and during each completed calendar quarter of the preceding 12 month period.
Idaho	Permits employers to provide voluntary coverage.
Illinois	Any worker or workers employed for a total of 40 or more hours per week for a period of 13 or more weeks during a calendar year by any household or residence.
Indiana	Permits employers to provide voluntary coverage.
Iowa	Any employee working in or about a private dwelling who is not a regular household member, whose earnings are $1,500 or more during the 12 consecutive months prior to an injury.
Kansas	Any domestic worker if the employer had a total gross payroll for the preceding year of $20,000 or more for all workers under his employ.
Kentucky	Two or more domestic workers regularly employed in a private home 40 or more hours a week. (Law has no numerical exemption for general employments.)
Louisiana	No specific provisions for domestic employers.
Maine	No specific provisions for domestic employers.
Massachusetts	Domestic workers employed 16 or more hours per week by an employer.
Maryland	Any domestic worker whose earnings are $1,000 or more in any calendar quarter from a private household. Domestic servants and their employers jointly may elect for the employee to be covered, even if the individual does not meet the earnings requirement.

Michigan	Any household domestic worker except those employed for less than 35 hours per week for 13 weeks or longer during the preceding 52 weeks.
Minnesota	Household workers are excluded from the workers' compensation coverage requirement. This includes a domestic, repairer, grounds keeper, or maintenance worker at a private household who earns less than $1,000 cash during a quarter of the year unless more than $1,000 was earned in any quarter of the previous year.
Mississippi	Mandatory with five employees or more.
Missouri	Permits employers to provide voluntary coverage.
Montana	Permits employers to provide voluntary coverage.
Nebraska	Permits employers to provide voluntary coverage.
Nevada	Permits employers to provide voluntary coverage.
New Hampshire	All household employers in New Hampshire must obtain coverage for any part-time or full-time domestic employee.
New Jersey	All household employers in New Jersey must obtain coverage for any part-time or full-time domestic employee.
New Mexico	Permits employers to provide voluntary coverage.
New York	Any domestic worker employed (other than those employed on a farm) by the same employer for a minimum of 40 hours per week.
North Carolina	Compulsory coverage. Covers domestic service if employer employs more than ten full-time non-seasonal laborers.
North Dakota	Workers' Compensation is not mandatory for household domestic workers.
Ohio	Any domestic worker who earns $160 or more in any calendar quarter from one employer.
Oklahoma	Any person who is employed as a domestic servant or as a casual worker in and about a private home or household, which private home or household had a gross annual payroll in the preceding calendar year of more than $10,000 for such workers.
Oregon	Permits employers to provide voluntary coverage.
Pennsylvania	Domestic workers are exempt. Voluntary coverage.

Rhode Island	Domestic workers are exempt. Voluntary coverage.
South Carolina	Covers domestic service if employer employs four or more employees.
South Dakota	Any domestic worker employed more than 20 hours in any calendar week for more than six weeks in any 13 week period.
Tennessee	Permits employers to provide voluntary coverage.
Texas	Permits employers to provide voluntary coverage.
Utah	Compulsory Coverage. Any domestic worker employed for 40 or more hours per week by the same employer.
Vermont	Not required for private households. Voluntary coverage.
Virginia	Domestic employees are excluded. Voluntary coverage.
West Virginia	Permits employers to provide voluntary coverage.
Washington	Compulsory coverage for two or more domestic workers if regularly employed in a private home for 40 or more hours per week. (Law has no numerical exemption for general employments.)
Wisconsin	Permits employers to provide voluntary coverage.
Wyoming	Domestic employees are excluded. Voluntary coverage.

Source: www.gtm.com/household/resource-center/workers-comp-requirements/ (2016). Please note that these rules are subject to change and you should check with the local state websites for up-to-date information.

Disability Insurance

Disability insurance is a form of insurance that insures the beneficiary's earned income against the risk that a disability will make working, and therefore earning, impossible. It only covers a portion of the salary. Disability benefits are temporary cash benefits paid to an eligible earner and are for injuries or illness occurring off the job. The process works by providing weekly cash benefits to replace, in part, wages lost due to injuries or illness that do not arise out of, or in the course of, employment. They are also paid to an unemployed worker to replace unemployment insurance benefits because of illness or injury. Premiums and available benefits for individual coverage vary considerably according to occupation and by state. Some states are now requiring that employers provide disability insurance for domestic employees. The New York Domestic Workers' Bill of Rights specifically includes the requirement that employers provide disability insurance for domestic workers who work more than 40 hours per week. These employers need to ensure they are providing their employees with the requisite insurance coverage. As well as New York, state mandatory disability applies in California, Hawaii, New Jersey, and Rhode Island.

CASE STUDY

ILO MILTON
EXPERIENCED AGENCY PRESIDENT
BEDFORD, NY

When clients and candidates ask Ilo Milton about the advantage of above the table pay, she readily describes a real-life incident that puts it all into perspective.

A family and its nanny mutually agreed that the nanny would be paid off the books. The nanny, playing with the two boys she was hired to care for, tripped, fell, and severely injured her back, which required at least three weeks of bed rest and subsequent physical therapy.

Since the employee was paid off the books, she was not covered by workers' compensation insurance. The nanny expected her employer to pay her full salary while she recovered—and even asked the employer to illegally submit a liability claim against the homeowner's insurance.

"All were complicit in going outside of the law," said Milton. "The family was terrified the nanny would sue. The nanny thought the family should pay her while she was out of work. The solution would have been easy if the nanny was on the books." They felt that the nanny was trying to take advantage of them without taking on any of the risks. They did not feel that they could trust the nanny any longer.

So the family paid the nanny four weeks' severance pay, and then replaced her.

"Everyone took a risk here," noted Milton. "While I have my belief that all should pay on the books, people live at their own risk tolerance level. I'm certain [this story] has an impact. It makes household employers aware of the realities and possibilities."

> As a household employer, you should ensure that you are adequately covered in the event that an accident occurs in the workplace. Most states require a workers' compensation insurance policy that covers accident-related medical expenses, and even if you do not meet the required standard for your state, you should consider obtaining a workers' compensation policy. Many household employers fail to see that an attempt to save a few dollars in the short term could result in a huge liability later, putting stress on both the employer and the employee.
>
> —Guy

Health, Safety, and Insurance Checklist

From time to time, incidents will occur with employees. It is a good practice to document the incident and discuss the matter with the employee in the hope to correct the behavior. (See Appendix E for a sample of an *Incident Report*.)

- Establish a safety policy, and provide protective gear and equipment.
- Enforce universal precautions and use of safety equipment.
- Conduct a home safety check to ensure a safe household and healthy work environment.
- Equip your house with a good first-aid kit and keep it in a handy location.

- Ensure your employee is knowledgeable about emergency procedures, including fire safety precautions.

- Write out an emergency contact list and keep it near the house phone.

- Check with an auto insurance company if your employee is going to be driving your dependents.

- Ensure the employee knows your home is a drug-free workplace and record this in the employee handbook.

- Call an insurance agent or the state insurance department for the contact information for your area's workers' compensation administration.

- Find out if your state requires workers' compensation insurance coverage and if it offers a state insurance fund option.

- Check if your state mandates disability insurance for domestic employees.

- Injuries happen. Consider workers' compensation insurance coverage even if it is not mandated by your state or locality.

12

Illegal Discrimination in the Home

The U.S. government enforces many laws and regulations that protect workers against discrimination. Employers need to be aware of all laws and regulations affecting them, including federal, state, and local. Often, antidiscrimination laws are required for businesses with a specific number of workers. Although many federal laws require five, fifteen, or even twenty employees for a law to apply, discrimination laws (especially state and local laws) could apply to household employers. A common best practice is to set fair hiring and employment procedures as if they do apply to any workplace. This creates a professional hiring attitude, while also designating the household as an equitable, unbiased work environment.

Federal law prohibits discrimination on the basis of the following:

- race, color, religion, sex, and national origin (Title VII of the Civil Rights Act)
- age (Age Discrimination in Employment Act)
- pregnancy (Pregnancy Discrimination Act)
- citizenship (Immigration Reform and Control Act)
- gender (Equal Pay Act)
- disability (Americans with Disabilities Act and Americans with Disabilities Act Amendments Act)
- union membership (National Labor Relations Act)
- bankruptcy (Bankruptcy Code)

- genetic information (Genetic Information Non-Discrimination Act)

In some circumstances, federal law may also be interpreted to prohibit discrimination against workers based on other factors, such as testing HIV positive, alcoholism, marital status, and obesity.

Federal Laws

The *U.S. Civil Rights Act* of 1964 (Title VII) protects employees from being discriminated against based on their race, color, religion, sex, or national origin. Federal law also prohibits discrimination based on age, pregnancy, disability, genetic predisposition, and U.S. citizenship status.

While Title VII applies only to those who employ 15 or more people, all household employers should act fairly to avoid any workplace discrimination charge. Remember that federal, state, and local laws may apply. For more information, go to the Equal Employment Opportunity Commission's (EEOC) website at www.eeoc.gov.

Immigration Reform and Control Act of 1986

The *Immigration Reform and Control Act* of 1986 (IRCA)'s core prohibition is against the hiring or continued employment of aliens whom employers know are unauthorized to work in the United States. The act requires employers to ensure that employees hired are legally authorized to work within the United States by verifying the identity and employment eligibility of all new employees, whether U.S. citizens or not, using Form I-9 (see Chapter 3). This has to be completed within the first three days of hiring the new employee and cannot be used to prescreen an employee for hiring. At the same time, the law prohibits employers with four or more employees from committing document abuse or discrimination when hiring, discharging, or recruiting on the basis of national origin or citizenship status (unless the person is an unauthorized alien).

Expert Advice

"All of us really do have two selves: our public selves and our home selves. It's the home self-psyche that the household employee deals with. I remind my clientele that even though their home is their private domain, it is now also the work environment of another. As private employers, they have an obligation to provide a safe and healthy work environment, abiding by labor laws, at a minimum, but also establishing clear professional boundaries."

> —Leann Brambach
> Experienced agency owner-operator
> Seattle, WA

Document Abuse

All U.S. citizens, legal immigrants, and certain other groups are protected from document abuse under IRCA. According to the U.S. Department of Justice's Office of Special Counsel, document abuse occurs when an employer (or potential employer) asks an employee (or an employee candidate) to produce a specific document to establish employment authorization, rather than allowing the employee to select what document to produce from the list of acceptable documents under IRCA. It can also occur if an employer or potential employer requests a different document other than the one the employee has selected from the authorized list. In addition, document abuse includes an employer's (or a potential employer's) rejection of valid documents that appear genuine and related to the individual. For instance, document abuse can occur when an employer, upon hiring an immigrant employee, asks that person to produce proof of employment eligibility but then refuses to accept an unrestricted, legitimate-looking Social Security card with the employee's name, and instead requires the employee's green card.

The employee must produce proof of employment eligibility and identity within three business days after she or he begins work. Proof of employment eligibility may be a green card or any U.S. Citizenship and Immigration Services (USCIS)-issued document. According to IRCA, employers must accept any document or combination of documents listed on the USCIS Form I-9 to establish identity and employment eligibility.

Such documents can include the following:
- a U.S. passport or U.S. passport card, an alien registration receipt card, or a permanent resident card (Form I-551)
- an unexpired foreign passport containing an I-551 stamp
- an unexpired employment authorization document issued by the USCIS that contains a photograph (Form I-766)

The list of documents to establish employment eligibility and identity is extensive. For a complete list of I-9 acceptable documents and for more information on Form I-9, go to www.uscis.gov, or see Appendix E, for a sample I-9 Form.

Employers who have failed to complete Form I-9 will be sanctioned by the USCIS if they hire aliens not authorized to work within the United States. Fines may be up to $3,000 per employee and/or include a six-month prison sentence if the employer demonstrates a persistent pattern of hiring unauthorized aliens. However, an employer who has completed Form I-9 correctly for an employee is protected from liability, even if the employee turns out to be not authorized to work. The nature of the documents that are acceptable under Form I-9 does mean that, on occasion, an alien without work authorization will be able to produce documents that comply with Form I-9, even though the alien is, indeed, not authorized to work.

Citizenship Discrimination

Title VII of the *Civil Rights Act* of 1964, the *Immigration Reform and Control Act* of 1986 (IRCA), and other antidiscrimination laws prohibit discrimination against individuals employed in the United States based on citizenship. However, all workers must have legal authorization to work in the United States (see Chapter 3). Title VII applies to employers with 15 or more employees, and IRCA covers employers with four or more employees. Although many household employers with one, two, or three household employees may not be required to follow the antidiscrimination rules put forth by these laws, it is best practice not to discriminate against any person lawfully admitted to the United States and authorized to work within the United States. It should be noted that an employer should not ask the candidate's country of origin or native language or treat employees differently on the basis of his or her last name, skin color, or accent.

State and Local Laws

Some states and localities protect employees with separate laws. For instance, the *California Department of Fair Employment and Housing Act* (FEHA) protects all workers from discrimination in all aspects of employment, including hiring, firing, and terms and conditions. While Title VII generally exempts employers with 14 or fewer employees, the California FEHA applies to employers with five or more employees.

Another example is the City of New York's Local Law No. 33 (see Chapter 2) which requires that licensed employment agencies provide to applicants for employment (as household employees) a written statement of employee rights and employer obligations under local, state, and federal law. Passed in 2003, the law is premised on the legislative finding that "the majority of domestic or household employees in New York City are immigrant women of color who, because of race and sex discrimination, language barriers, and immigration status, are probably vulnerable to unfair labor practices."

Similarly, the groundbreaking New York Domestic Workers' Bill of Rights, created in 2010, reforms New York State law to guarantee basic work standards and protections for nannies, caregivers, and housekeepers and is a comprehensive response to domestic workers' vulnerability to abuse and mistreatment (see Chapter 2). This law counters the historical exclusion of domestic workers from federal labor protections and amends state labor discrimination and disability laws for household employment. There are now seven states with Domestic Workers' Bill of Rights' laws: New York, Hawaii, California, Massachusetts, Oregon, Connecticut, and Illinois.

All employers must comply with all laws pertaining to them—federal, state, and local. Local law often supersedes the federal, and the onus is on you, the employer, to know all the laws and regulations by which to operate your household employment. For instance, the District of Columbia discrimination regulation (*DC Human Rights Act*) applies to all employers—any employer with one or more employee—and prohibits discrimination based upon the actual or perceived race, color, religion, national origin, sex, age, marital status, personal appearance, sexual orientation, gender identity or expression, family responsibilities, genetic information, disability, matriculation, or political affiliation of any individual.

Sexual Harassment

Sexual harassment policies stipulate that no employee should be subject to unwelcome verbal or physical conduct that is sexual in nature or that shows hostility to the employee because of his or her gender. Sexual harassment can have devastating effects on the workplace. Therefore, household employers need to take every step necessary to prohibit sexual harassment from occurring. Many workplaces have a zero tolerance policy, which means an employer will not tolerate any sexual harassment whatsoever.

It is best for an employer to include an antiharassment and/or antidiscrimination policy in the employee handbook, which specifically addresses sexual harassment. Such a policy should clearly state words to the effect that:

- all employees and employers within the household are expected to treat one another with respect to maintain a positive working environment
- the employer will act immediately upon learning of a sexual harassment complaint
- an employee should promptly file a formal complaint if the employee experiences behavior that is unwelcome, offensive, or inappropriate
- employers need to assure employees that all complaints of sexual harassment will be handled in confidence
- the employer mandates a workplace free from all forms of discrimination, as per the law

A sample policy document on anti-harassment procedure in the workplace can be found at www.shrm.org/templatestools/samples/policies/pages/cms_000551.aspx

An employer must be prepared to respond to sexual harassment in the workplace—just as he or she is responsible for preventing any harassment or discrimination within the workplace. The employee handbook should cover what actions will be taken when a sexual harassment complaint is filed. In addition, the policy must state that no employee will experience retaliation for submitting a sexual harassment complaint.

As well as federal laws that prohibit harassment for all employers, some states have particular laws that may be more stringent and apply to household employment, especially if a state has a Domestic Workers' Bill or Rights that stipulates that it is unlawful discriminatory practice for any domestic employer to engage in harassment of an employee.

Bill of Rights laws for domestic workers are currently in these states: New York, Illinois, California, Connecticut, Oregon, Hawaii, and Massachusetts.

FACTS AND FIGURES
CROSSING THE LINE

The line between home and work, domestic and business, personal and professional, has been blurry for a long time. Unfortunately, sometimes it becomes more than a story of cheating and closed door liaisons and becomes much more serious. As a result, domestic workers are frequently exposed to verbal and physical abuse.

Many household employees are immigrants who do not know their legal rights or the recourse to any legal protections. Domestic workers are also overwhelmingly nonwhite women, who are immigrants and not U.S citizens (95 percent of domestic workers were women, 46 percent were immigrants, 54 percent were non-white, and 35 percent were noncitizens, according to the American Community Survey (ACS) conducted by the Census Bureau). Many household employees are excluded from Title VII of the *Civil Rights Act*, which bans sexual harassment in the workplace, unless they work for an employer who employs 15 of more workers. Hence some states are developing bills of rights for domestic workers (see Chapter 2) which include protections against sexual harassment for those working within the home.

Coupled with the historical prejudice of household workers being "servants," domestic physical, verbal, and sexual abuse is still occurring in a number of U.S. households. The 2012 National Domestic Workers' Alliance report, "Home Economics: the Invisible and Unregulated World of Domestic Work", revealed that surveyed domestic workers often endured verbal, psychological, and physical abuse on the job—without recourse. This is especially true of live-in employees where 36 percent of live-in workers reported that they were threatened, insulted, or verbally abused in the past 12 months. One of the issues is that many domestic workers (especially undocumented illegal immigrants) are afraid of losing their jobs if they complain about any harassment or seek legal action. Of the workers who encountered problems with their working conditions in the prior 12 months, 91 percent said they did not complain because they were afraid they would lose their job and 42 percent reported that they did not do so due to fears of employer violence.

This same report depicts this situation thus: "U.S. domestic workers share conditions that leave them especially vulnerable to abuse on the job. While some employers are terrific, generous and understanding, others, unfortunately, are demanding, exploitative, and abusive. Working behind closed doors, in isolation, domestic workers are subject to the whims of their employers."

Americans with Disabilities Act

The *Americans with Disabilities Act* (ADA) prohibits discrimination against any qualified person with a disability. If an applicant is qualified to perform the job or can perform the work with reasonable accommodation, the ADA requires employers to consider that applicant equally with other non-disabled, qualified applicants. The ADA prohibits discrimination on the basis of disability in all employment practices—not only hiring and firing. Employment practices covered under the ADA include recruitment, pay, hiring, firing, promotions, job assignments, training, leave, layoffs, benefits, and all other employment-related activities.

Under the ADA, employers must ensure that people with disabilities:

- have an equal opportunity to apply for jobs and to work in jobs for which they are qualified

- have an equal opportunity to be promoted

- have equal access to benefits and privileges offered to other employees

- are not harassed because of their disability

The ADA covers employers with 15 or more employees, as well as applicable employment agencies. However, all employers should be aware of ADA regulations.

Under the ADA the following applies.

- A person with a disability is defined as someone who has a physical or mental impairment that substantially limits one or more of the major life activities of such an individual (e.g., walking, seeing, hearing, speaking), has a record of such an impairment, or is regarded as having such an impairment.

- A qualified employee or applicant with a disability is someone who satisfies skill, experience, education, and other job-related requirements of the position held or sought and who can perform the position's essential functions with or without reasonable accommodation.

- Reasonable accommodation may include (but is not limited to) making existing facilities readily accessible to and usable by people with disabilities, such as a specially designed computer keyboard or software, or perhaps just lowering a bulletin board to make it readable or lowering a paper cup dispenser in the employee break room for all to easily reach. Other accommodations could include allowing an employee to begin work at 10 a.m. instead of 9 a.m., in order for her or him to attend physical therapy appointments.

- Reasonable accommodation must be made if it would not impose undue hardship on an employer's business. Under the ADA, *undue hardship* is defined as an action requiring significant difficulty or expense when considered with an employer's size and financial resources, and the nature and structure of the business' operation. According to the federal government, most accommodations are not expensive. The Job Accommodation Network (JAN), an information service sponsored by the President's Committee on Employment of

People with Disabilities, reported in 2010 that a high percentage (56 percent) of accommodations cost absolutely nothing to make, while the rest typically cost only $600 for a onetime expenditure. In addition, to help businesses offset the cost of accommodations, tax credits may apply, such as the ADA Tax Incentives and the Small Business Tax Credit.

The ADA offers equal access and opportunities to people with disabilities. It does not offer people with disabilities an unfair advantage; an employer may hire a person without a disability who is more qualified than another applicant with a disability. While the ADA prohibits employers from asking about a disability, employers may ask whether an applicant will require a reasonable accommodation if it seems likely that he or she may need it. It is generally unlawful for an employer to ask an applicant whether she or he is disabled or to inquire about the nature or severity of her or his disability. Also, it is unlawful for an employer to require an applicant to take a medical examination before a job offer is made. However, an employer *can* ask an applicant questions about his or her ability to perform job-related functions (as long as the questions are not phrased in terms of a disability). The ADA strictly limits questioning; employers may first check with an ADA specialist to determine what is allowable under the law.

Go to www.eeoc.gov or www.ada.gov for more information, or call the ADA Information Line at 1-800-514-0301, where an ADA specialist may be reached. Information on the ADA and its tax codes and incentives may be reached at www.irs.gov or 1-800-829-1040.

Employers also should be aware of state and local laws pertaining to employment discrimination on the basis of disability. For instance, the Massachusetts Commission Against Discrimination (state law chapter 151B) works with the federal ADA to protect people with disabilities against employment discrimination. However, the Massachusetts law also extends to prohibit disability discrimination in housing, public accommodations, and credit.

A household employer needs to be cautious about imposing certain requirements on the position. He or she may prefer to employ an older, unmarried, Christian woman, but implementing such preferences may violate federal, state, and local law.

The Americans with Disabilities Act Amendments Act

In 2008 this act made important changes to the definition of the term *disability* to make it easier for an individual seeking protection under the ADA to establish that he or she has a disability within the meaning of the ADA. The ADAAA revises the definition of *disability* to more broadly encompass impairments that substantially limit a major life activity. The amended language also states that mitigating measures, including assistive devices, auxiliary aids, accommodations, medical therapies and supplies (other than eyeglasses and contact lenses) have no bearing on determining whether a disability qualifies under the law. Changes also clarify coverage of impairments that are episodic or in remission that substantially limit a major life activity when active, such as epilepsy or post-traumatic stress disorder.

The ADAAA overturned several Supreme Court decisions that had made it difficult for people with disabilities to qualify for protection under the ADA. As a result of these decisions, people with conditions such as epilepsy, diabetes, bipolar disorder, post-traumatic stress disorder, cerebral palsy, intellectual disabilities, muscular dystrophy, and other disabilities are now covered by the ADA.

For more information about the specific details of this law, visit www.eeoc.gov/laws/statutes/adaaa_info.cfm.

Equal Employment Opportunity Commission

The federal *Equal Employment Opportunity Commission* (EEOC) enforces most federal laws prohibiting job discrimination. These laws include the following:

- Title VII of the Civil Rights Acts of 1964, outlawing job discrimination based on race, color, religion, sex, or national origin
- Pregnancy Discrimination Act of 1978, prohibiting discrimination against a woman because of pregnancy, childbirth, or a medical condition related to either

- Equal Pay Act of 1963 (EPA), protecting against sex-based wage discrimination for men and women performing substantially the same work in the same establishment

- The Genetic Information Nondiscrimination Act of 2008 (GINA), which makes it illegal to discriminate against employees or applicants because of genetic information (from genetic tests or any information about any disease, disorder or condition of an individual's family members)

- Age Discrimination in Employment Act of 1967 (ADEA), protecting people age 40 or older

- Titles I and V of the Americans with Disabilities Act of 1990 (ADA), prohibiting discrimination against qualified individuals with disabilities in employment and the Americans with Disabilities Act Amendments Act (ADAAA), as above

These laws offer a wide range of protection to employees. EEOC oversees and coordinates the large majority of federal equal employment opportunity regulations, practices, and policies. Some antidiscrimination laws apply to employers with at least four employees, while some apply only to employers with 15 or more employees. (Household employment agencies may be subject to many of these laws; therefore, discrimination by such agencies is illegal.) Even employers not subject to antidiscrimination laws should use such laws as guidelines to ensure equal opportunity employment. In all, the federal antidiscrimination laws and the EEOC work to outlaw discrimination in employment, including hiring, firing, compensation, promotions, layoffs, recruitment, testing, job advertisements, use of company facilities, fringe benefits, retirement plans, disability leaves, and other terms and conditions of employment. Employers are required to post notices to all employees advising them of their rights under these laws.

It is important to note that Title VII of the *Civil Rights Act* of 1964 prohibits intentional discrimination and practices that have the effect of discrimination against individuals because of their race, color, national origin, religion, or sex.

State and Local Agencies

The EEOC has cooperative relationships with the vast majority of the state and local Fair Employment Practices Agencies (FEPAs). The EEOC and FEPAs have work-share agreements that separate common workload to avoid duplication of charge processing. (Go to www.eeoc.gov or call 1-800-669-4000 for more information.)

Commonsense Practices

Some commonsense practices can help employers prevent illegal discrimination in the workplace, such as the following:

- treat all employees equally

- hire, promote, and fire without bias

- review employment policies for unfair and negative impact on a protected class (e.g., race, religion, ethnicity, gender, age, disability, or pregnancy)

- eliminate any unfair or negative policies or practices

- take immediate action to eliminate discriminatory conduct, including inappropriate comments or behavior

- encourage diversity

- never retaliate against an employee for filing a discrimination complaint—it is illegal

Household employers struggle with their home being a personal residence, and at the same time, a workplace for others. Be aware of any discrimination laws in your state or locality and how they apply to you, then implement employment practices to avoid the inconvenience of arguments or a lawsuit.

The employment practices should be listed in the employee handbook.

Discrimination Checklist

- Know all discrimination laws and regulations that apply to the household workplace—federal, state, and local.

- Establish and enforce zero tolerance for unlawful activities and behaviors such as sexual harassment.

- Be prepared to respond to any complaint of sexual harassment. While your employee handbook covers your zero tolerance policy, be prepared on how you will handle this sensitive issue.

- Establish and implement procedures for dealing with illegal discrimination, and document them in the employee handbook.

- Keep in mind that many employment agencies are subject to equal employment opportunity law and may not legally discriminate on the employer's behalf.

- Be aware of the potential for document abuse and take care to verify a document's validity.

13

Termination, Resignation, and Saying Goodbye

All good things, and possibly some bad things, must come to an end. One of the most difficult aspects of being an employer is to face the end of an employee relationship, whether terminating an employee or dealing with a resignation.

There are certain ways to handle the end of a relationship, which should be provided in the household's employee handbook and the work agreement, and should be consistent with relevant laws. The best strategy that any employer can use when terminating an employee, accepting an employee's resignation, or saying goodbye to an employee is to address the situation as soon as possible and to be honest.

Always end an employee relationship professionally. Deal with it head-on and without delay. Often, an employer's first instinct to terminate an employee should be acted on, since it is seldom that the employer's perspective or situation changes.

At-Will Employment

Typically, an employee works at the will of the employer, known as at-will employment, unless a contract has been signed for a fixed term of employment. At-will employment means that the employer can fire the employee at any time, and that the employee can quit at any time.

Many employers ensure that they can apply at-will employment to their household by including as part of the job application an at-will employment statement, which the applicant usually initials or signs to acknowledge that he or she has read it and understands that he or she will be an at-will employee if hired. In addition, employers should include at-will employment language in job offer letters, employee handbooks, and termination letters. Without an at-will statement, the household employee's work agreement stipulates what was agreed on regarding when employment ends.

In the United States, at-will employees can be terminated for good, bad, or no cause. Three exceptions to the rule are the following:

1. the state's public policy was violated

2. an implied contract for employment was established

3. an implied covenant of good faith and fair dealing was established

In every U.S. state, except Montana, employment is presumed to be at-will. If you live in an at-will state, you do not need to give a warning before you terminate an employee, unless you have stipulated that you will do so in the work agreement or elsewhere. It is advisable, if the situation is not serious, to give the employee the chance to improve before making the final decision to stop employing them.

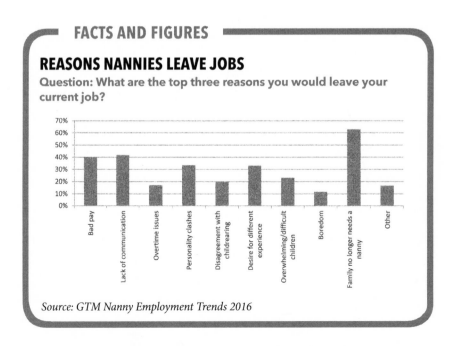

FACTS AND FIGURES

REASONS NANNIES LEAVE JOBS

Question: What are the top three reasons you would leave your current job?

Source: GTM Nanny Employment Trends 2016

Termination

Firing an employee is an uncomfortable situation for many employers and employees. Unless carefully done, firing an employee can be downright dangerous for the employer. Be prepared to show support and documentation to prove legitimate cause for termination—and take care that all employees are treated equally.

First, carefully review the initial offer letter, any employment contract, handbook, appraisals, and so on, for written agreements. Have the signed work agreement in hand. The work agreement should include detailed reasons for termination, as well as immediate termination clauses for any illegal or inappropriate behavior on the employee's part.

"It is best to terminate employees in a two-step process," said the president of an East Coast nanny placement agency. "First, talk to the employee about the issue, and give him or her time to improve or change. Explain that noncompliance can result in termination. Document the conversation, providing a copy to the employee. If the situation changes in a positive way, the employer avoids turnover. If the situation remains unchanged, termination is justified." Second chances, though, should never be considered if the employee has broken the law or has put the family home or household members in danger.

In addition, the employee handbook should have stipulated a progressive process for the employer to attempt to improve employee performance through the job performance evaluation. An employee who previously was made aware of unsatisfactory performance or incidents through *Incident Reports* (see Appendix E), and who knows his or her performance does not meet the employer's approval, also knows that he or she risks termination. The progressive discipline method works well and provides the employer with a record of the employee's performance issues. The progress usually entails a verbal warning, then a written warning if the problem persists, and last, termination. Not only does this method help protect the employer from legal action; it also provides the employee with fair warning about unsatisfactory job performance and possible termination if performance does not get better.

When an employee leaves employment, stipulate in a termination letter the exact time and date of termination, what is included in the final paycheck, when that paycheck will be issued, and other appropriate information. Also, some employers request that the employee return the employee handbook, which was stipulated in the statement release that was signed when the handbook was issued. (See Appendix E, for a sample *Termination of Employment to Household Employee Letter*.)

FACTS AND FIGURES
RED FLAGS WHEN ASSESSING TERMINATION

- Is it discriminatory?
- Is it on a whim?
- Is it to head off potential blackmail?
- Is it for financial hardship or difficulties?
- Is it because the employee is pregnant?
- Is it because the employee is involved with union activities?
- Is it because the employee is performing military service?
- Is it for any non-job-related activity?

FACTS AND FIGURES
TERMINATION BEST PRACTICE

Do

- Be prepared and be consistent
- Have an adult witness present
- Meet without children or dependents around
- Be concise and to the point
- Focus on measurable behavior (preferably written documentation)
- Allow for an employee response to avoid one-way communication

- State twice the decision to terminate

- Inform the employee of the severance policy and unemployment compensation option

- Avoid any lead time between firing and departing—the best time to set a termination meeting is at the end of the workday

- Reiterate the confidentiality agreement that the employee signed at the beginning of employment. Inform the employee that what he or she has learned about the family is very private, and that confidentiality was agreed on for the term of employment, as well as after employment ended

- Collect from the employee security codes, keys, car seats, and other family items

- Change home security codes after an employee has finished employment.

- Escort the employee from the premises

- Notify neighbors and school that your employee is no longer with your family (for security reasons)

- Make sure to pay for all time worked up to termination

- Provide a letter of reference for future work (if appropriate)

Do Not

- Delay—an employer's first hunch is usually the right one

- Apologize, ramble, or speak in generalities. You should speak directly and keep only to the facts

- Make it a one-way conversation—allow the employee to provide feedback

- Threaten an employee

- Be emotional and show your anger or distress

- Provide false hope—make the break clean

- Withhold financial or insurance benefits

- Hold a termination meeting in isolation or in public

- Have children present

- Provide prior notice of termination plans

- Allow the employee to depart with employer and/or house-hold belongings

Exit Interview or Termination Meeting

The best practice is to hold a termination meeting, during which the employer states the reason for termination, reviews any severance package offerings, and provides the employee with an opportunity to voice his or her views. Always have a concisely written letter prepared at the time of termination. (See Appendix E, for a sample *Termination of Employment to Household Employee Letter*.) Avoid lengthy explanations or apologies—be as straightforward as possible when explaining why the termination action is being taken. Keep your discussion short and to the point. Also, at the meeting have a prepared list of employer property and a deadline for its return. In some circumstances, unreturned property may be deducted from the final paycheck after the stated deadline has passed. Be sure to notify the employee that she or he may apply for unemployment insurance to determine whether she or he is eligible. Often it is suggested that a third party perform exit interviews, which may be a placement agency or a service such as GTM Household HR Helpdesk, or that a disinterested person be present. (See Appendix B, for a sample list of exit interview questions.)

An effective exit interview can provide constructive feedback to allow an employer to improve the employment environment for future employees. State laws vary on what constitutes legal practice when terminating an employee. (Go to www.dol.gov to determine which termination laws are enforced in specific states.) In addition, state laws vary in regard to when an employer is required to provide employees with their final paychecks, as well as whether the employer is mandated to pay an employee for unused vacation time, and so on. Contact the state labor department's wage and hour division for more information. Finally, consider offering the employee a severance package with a release of future claims contingency.

After the exit interview, the employer should write up what was discussed during the interview and file this with the termination letter in the employee's personnel file.

Severance

Severance for an employee that is leaving your household is discretionary. If the employee has behaved inappropriately and is being fired, then no severance is necessary. However, if the employee has been with the family for a long time, has been a good employee, and the reason for leaving is because of circumstances (e.g., the employee is retiring, the children are going to school, the family is moving away), then it is an acceptable gesture to provide some type of severance (if financially affordable) and as much notice before the end of the employment as you can (especially if the employee needs to look for another job). The amount you give as severance depends on the family finances, but also on how long the employee has worked for the family. Common severance is one week's pay for each year the employee has worked in the household, with a minimum of two weeks. For example, the New York Domestic Workers' Bill of Rights requires employers to provide two weeks' notice.

Mini-COBRA

Mini-COBRA allows employees and their families to continue health insurance coverage with small group carriers. Mini-COBRA closely mirrors the benefits required by the federal COBRA and has been adopted by many states, allowing small group coverage to be extended to those who would previously would have lost coverage. It is therefore more pertinent to household employees than COBRA, and employers should be aware of the differences between the two.

Although COBRA and mini-COBRA are very similar, some differences exist. While COBRA is a federal law, not enforced by the Division of Insurance, Mini-COBRA is a state law, enforced by the Division of Insurance. Generally, COBRA applies to health plans with 20 or more employees. Mini-COBRA generally applies to group health plans with 2-19 employees. Finally, COBRA applies to self-funded plans, but Mini-COBRA does not.

COBRA

Under the *Consolidated Omnibus Budget Reconciliation Act* (COBRA), employers with 20 or more employees who offer an employee health plan must offer employees and former employees the option of continuing their health care coverage if coverage is lost or reduced. This COBRA coverage is only available when coverage is lost because of certain events. While COBRA seldom applies to household employment because of the 20 or more employees stipulation, state and local laws may offer employees similar rights regardless of the number of employees. Under COBRA, coverage must be identical coverage provided to those beneficiaries not receiving COBRA. Employers need to be aware of their own state requirements and may contact their health plan administrator or their state insurance department to learn more.

Q & A

Q. How do I handle questions about a household employee who no longer works for me?

A. The norm is that most employers talk freely about their previous employees to agencies and other employers. However, when providing references, always stick to the facts—and only the facts. Avoid stating your opinion or hearsay or gossip. Use the personnel file to help you answer reference questions, such as dates of employment and the employee's title or position.

It is an accepted business practice to provide references with only a former employee's dates of employment and her or his title or position. However, this is not a common practice in household employment. Often families feel responsible to other families to provide references for the employee and insight into her or his job performance. When providing references, employers should remember that offering this information is generally at their discretion.

FACTS AND FIGURES
WHAT TO THINK ABOUT WHEN CONSIDERING TERMINATING AN EMPLOYEE

- Is the reason to terminate an employee job related?
- Does it relate to absenteeism?
- Is it due to work quality?
- Will it ensure the safety of the family and the household?
- Is it the result of the employee's failure to perform tasks?
- Is the reason to terminate related to misconduct?
- Is it the result of theft?
- Is it because the employee is regularly tardy for work?
- Is the employee neglecting her or his duties?
- Has the employee misused family or household property?

CASE STUDY

PAT CASCIO
EXPERIENCED AGENCY OWNER/OPERATOR
MORNINGSIDE NANNIES, LP
HOUSTON, TX

Pat Cascio of Morningside Nannies has a wealth of experience and a plethora of tales to tell regarding household employment. She lists one incident as "a classic case of the worst employer."

A nanny living outside the home, and who had been employed for seven months, slipped on her employer's kitchen floor while caring for the family's one-year-old child. Her injury, a broken ankle, was so significant that she called her employer, who arrived home in 15 minutes but refused to assist her. In fact, the nanny remained on the kitchen floor until her own son arrived to transport her to the hospital emergency room for treatment. (The nanny's ankle was set in a cast for three weeks, and then she required three weeks of physical therapy after the cast was removed.) The day after the injury, the employer, who had no workers' compensation insurance and was concerned about liability, fired the nanny over the telephone, offering no reason for the termination. In addition, the employer withheld payment for work the nanny performed during that pay period.

Upon intervention by the nanny's son, the employer paid the nanny for the two days she worked but refused to pay for the workday on which the nanny was injured, paid one week's severance (not two weeks', as stipulated in the signed employment agreement), and agreed to write a recommendation letter only after the nanny signed a statement saying she would not sue the employer.

The nanny, who had no health insurance, paid for all medical expenses without any assistance from the employer. As a result of the injury and termination, the nanny was unemployed for two months.

According to Cascio, employers need to be educated about the possible occurrence of injury to employees in their household. "I recommend they be willing to help with medical bills or provide health insurance," she said. "They should also be educated in regard to wrongful termination issues, as the nanny could have sued on both accounts."

Household employers must have a sound termination policy, which is outlined in the employee handbook. As an employer is not required to offer any explanation by law, it is helpful to provide closure to an employee, providing some items for her or him to improve upon for her or his next position, and preventing any future problems or retaliation due to a feeling of mistreatment, and so on.

Again, paying taxes, having the proper workers' compensation and unemployment insurance, and paying the employee for all work hours helps eliminate liability for the employer and employee.

—Guy

FACTS AND FIGURES

ELIGIBILITY FOR MINI-COBRA BY STATE

Eligibility for "mini-COBRA" by state	
State	Length of time eligible for COBRA
Arkansas	4 months
California	36 months
Colorado	18 months
Connecticut	30 months
Delaware	9 months
District of Columbia	3 months
Florida	18 months
Georgia	3 months
Illinois	24 months
Iowa	9 months
Kansas	18 months
Kentucky	18 months
Louisiana	12 months
Maine	12 months
Maryland	18 months
Massachusetts	36 months
Minnesota	36 months
Mississippi	12 months
Missouri	18 months

Nebraska	12 months
Nevada	36 months
New Hampshire	36 months
New Jersey	36 months
New Mexico	6 months
New York	36 months
North Carolina	18 months
North Dakota	36 months
Ohio	12 months
Oklahoma	6 months
Oregon	9 months
Pennsylvania	9 months
Rhode Island	18 months
South Carolina	6 months
South Dakota	36 months
Tennessee	15 months
Texas	36 months
Utah	12 months
Vermont	18 months
West Virginia	18 months
Wisconsin	18 months
Wyoming	12 months

Source: http://www.insure.com/health-insurance/cobra-by-state.html (2015)

Maximum Period of Continued Coverage and Its Extension

Under COBRA, continuation of health care coverage is mandated by the U.S. Department of Labor and available for a limited period of time, generally a maximum period of 18 or 36 months, as a result of a qualifying event. An employer may provide longer coverage periods, however, beyond the maximum period mandated by the federal government. The length of time depends on a second qualifying event's type.

To be eligible for an extension of the maximum period—generally from 18-36 months—an employee (or his or her qualified beneficiary) must be disabled or experience a second qualifying event.

- Disabled: If any member or beneficiary of the health plan coverage is disabled (as defined by the Social Security Association), all of the qualified beneficiaries already receiving coverage continuation (as a result of the first qualifying event) as stipulated by COBRA are entitled to an 11-month extension for a maximum total period of 29 months of continued coverage. The qualified beneficiary must meet requirements set forth by the U.S. Social Security Administration strictly for this disability extension. For in-depth information on COBRA, refer to the DOL booklet, "An Employee's Guide to Health Benefits under COBRA."

- Second qualifying event: An employee already receiving an 18-month period of continuation coverage may become entitled to another 18-month extension for a total maximum period of 36 months of continued coverage. A second qualifying event may be the death of a covered employee, divorce or legal separation of a covered employee and his or her spouse, an employee becoming entitled to Medicare, or a loss of a dependent child. The second qualifying event can be a second only if it would have caused lost coverage under the plan in the considered absence of the first qualifying event. Under COBRA, the cost of continued coverage via the extensions may be increased.

FACTS AND FIGURES

COBRA COVERAGE EXTENSION QUALIFYING EVENTS AND MAXIMUM TIME PERIOD OF CONTINUED COVERAGE

Qualifying Event	Qualifying Beneficiaries	Maximum Time Period of Continued Coverage
Termination (for reasons other than gross misconduct) or reduction in hours of employment	Employee Spouse Dependent child	18 months*
Employee enrollment in Medicare	Spouse Dependent child	36 months
Divorce or legal separation	Spouse Dependent child	36 months
Death of employee	Spouse Dependent child	36 months
Loss of dependent child (as defined by dependent child status under the plan)	Dependent child	36 months

*In certain circumstances, coverage may be extended.

Source: © 2015 U.S. Labor Department's An Employer's Guide to Group Health Continuation Coverage under COBRA.

Note: The U.S. Department of Labor offers an employer and employee hotline at 1-866-444-3272, and further information on COBRA and Mini-COBRA may be obtained at www.dol.gov/ebsa.

Termination Checklist

- Establish detailed information in the employee handbook regarding the employer's firing policy and practice. Also, detail termination procedures in the work agreement.

- When terminating an employee, have a prepared, concisely worded termination letter with information on final payment at the termination meeting.

- Be prepared to support your termination decision with materials kept in the employee's file—signed work agreement, performance reviews, history of absences, and so on.

- Provide the employee with a checklist and deadline to return employer property, such as keys and the employee handbook.

- Termination can be an uneasy, tense procedure, rife with potential damage. Ensure that all explanations are legitimate and that employer actions can be documented.

- Follow COBRA and mini-COBRA by offering the employee the option to continue her or his health insurance coverage. Even if exempt from COBRA requirements, consider extending to the employee an option for continued health insurance coverage.

Resignation

Employees should be guided by an employer's preference when they resign from their position. In business, common employment practice is for the employee to provide the employer with two weeks' notice. In household employment, 30 days' notice is often preferred, because of the lengthy time involved in hiring and replacing household help, and because there is not often other staff employed (unless part of a bigger household estate) so that someone else can pick up the resigned employee's duties while a replacement is found.

It would be advantageous for the employer to specify resignation expectations upon an employee's hire in the work agreement and the employee handbook. Be sure to include both employee and employer requirements to be followed when resigning.

FACTS AND FIGURES

ITEMS TO INCLUDE IN A RESIGNATION POLICY

- Specify the length of time preferred by the employer for the employee to give notice of resignation and if the employer will accept a verbal or written resignation (written is preferred).

- Detail what happens if an employee provides more than the minimum amount of notice. Let the employee know that you, as the employer, reserve the right to evaluate whether the additional notice is necessary and will confirm the final date of employment.

- Detail what happens if an employee provides little or no notice (e.g., ineligibility for rehire, no references will be provided).

- Specify conditions. For example, if an employee fails to report to work for a certain period of time (typically three days) without notifying the employer, the employer will consider that the employee's voluntary resignation.

- State whether the employee will be eligible for pay for unused accrued time off and provide information on when a final paycheck will be received, when benefits will end, and so on. (Typically, benefits end on the last day of the month in which termination becomes effective.)

Resignation Checklist

- Establish and document a resignation procedure in the employee handbook and the employee work agreement. The handbook should detail requirements for both the employee and employer to meet when an employee resigns.

- Establish the length of time that will be required when giving notice.

- Note if the employee is required to train the replacement.

- Inform the employee if he or she is eligible for re-employment.

- Obtain a written letter of resignation.

- Review with the employee benefits status and end dates.

- Notify the employee of his or her COBRA rights.

- Obtain or confirm forwarding address information to ensure benefits and tax information may be sent to the correct location and received by the employee in a timely manner.

Saying Goodbye

Some households make an employee's goodbye an event, involving the entire family in a dinner celebration or a night of reminiscing. Some employers provide the employee with an album with stories and photos, while others may provide a more businesslike gift, such as a watch or a plaque. The point is that some goodbyes are natural, and just because the employee is leaving, the household need not lose all contact with the employee. It is merely a change in the relationship; perhaps something that goes from full-time contact as an employee to occasional visits as a guest or a friend.

Of course, goodbyes affecting children have more of an impact. The household employer should be involved in communicating an employee's departure plans with the household. Household employers may want to work with a departing nanny or other household employee to explain to children why the employee is leaving employment, what his or her plans are, and how the change may affect the children and the household. Recognize that there can be a positive ending when one employee leaves, and take the necessary time to prepare the household for a new hire.

Goodbye Checklist

- Make sure you receive any items that were given to the employee during the course of his or her employment, including car and house keys, passes to any country clubs or pools, gas card, car seats, garage-door openers, cell phone, and so on.
- Discuss COBRA and Mini-COBRA with the employee.
- If the employee would like, provide a letter of reference.
- If the employee had worked with an agency, notify the agency of the situation.
- Conduct an exit interview.

About the Author

Guy Maddalone is founder and CEO of GTM Payroll Services Inc., which offers household payroll, human resources, insurance, and employee benefits services. Recognized in the United States household employment industry as the national expert, Maddalone has been operating businesses that attend to household employment for over 30 years. Starting with the placement of home health care and senior care services, Maddalone expanded his business to include nannies and other household staff, and named the company A New England Nanny. For 25 years, A New England Nanny has placed thousands of child care providers and nannies throughout upstate New York.

Maddalone founded GTM in 1991 to provide payroll and tax administration for household employers, the first in the industry. GTM is the nation's premier household payroll and tax service, and manages more than $1 billion annually in payroll, supporting more than 30,000 employees. GTM has also made the INC 5000 list eight times as one of the fastest-growing U.S. companies.

Maddalone conducts educational seminars throughout the country on the household employment industry, household human resources, household payroll taxes, IRS audits, tax compliance, and dependent care services for corporate employers. He is also a work-life dependent care consultant to GE, a licensed property and casualty broker specializing in Workers' Compensation, and a member of the Society of Human Resource Management (SHRM).

Involved with several prominent business organizations, including the Massachusetts Institute of Technology and Inc. magazine, Birthing of Giants, and former president of the Albany Chapter of the Young Entrepreneur's Organization, Maddalone also contributes greatly to the community in which he lives—from coaching youth sports teams to mentoring local college entrepreneurs and giving to many charities, including the Make-A-Wish Foundation. Maddalone is also heavily involved with industry associations, such as the Association of Premier Nanny Agencies and the International Nanny Association. The eldest son of 13 children, the importance of family is integral to Maddalone. He and his wife, Diane, reside in upstate New York with their three children.

Appendix A: Tax Calendar & Checklists

Useful tools for employers to have on hand include a tax calendar and IRS compliance and payroll checklists. The tax calendar lists important dates, such as due dates for quarterly tax filings and for tax form filings. The checklists are valuable resources in determining what needs to be done, in order, to remain compliant with the tax laws.

Employer Tax Responsibility Calendar

Month	Date	Event
JANUARY	15th	4th Quarter (Prior Year) Federal Estimated Taxes Due (Form 1040-ES)
	31st	4th Quarter (Prior Year) State Income Taxes Due
	31st	4th Quarter (Prior Year) Unemployment Taxes Due
	31st	W-2 form(s) mailed to employee(s)
	31st	W-3 and W-2 forms for the Prior Year to be filed with the Social Security Administration
FEBRUARY		No Deadlines
MARCH		No Deadlines
APRIL	15th	1st Quarter Federal Estimated Taxes Due (1040-ES)
	15th	Federal (Prior Year) Schedule H of Form Due with 1040
	30th	1st Quarter State Income Taxes Due
	30th	1st Quarter State Unemployment Taxes Due
MAY		No Deadlines
JUNE	15th	2nd Quarter Federal Estimated Taxes Due (1040-ES)
JULY	31st	2nd Quarter State Income Taxes Due
	31st	2nd Quarter State Unemployment Taxes Due
AUGUST		No Deadlines
SEPTEMBER	15th	3rd Quarter Federal Estimated Taxes Due (1040-ES)

OCTOBER	31st	3rd Quarter State Income Taxes Due
	31st	3rd Quarter State Unemployment Taxes Due
NOVEMBER		No Deadlines
DECEMBER		No Deadlines

14 Steps to Compliance

Mistakes or misinterpretations of the law can mean IRS audits, thousands of dollars in fines and penalties, or an employee lawsuit.

1	Obtain household employer tax IDs (federal and state)
2	File a new hire report with your state (if necessary)
3	Purchase workers' compensation insurance (if required in your state)
4	Adhere to all applicable tax, wage, and labor laws that pertain to household employment such as a Domestic Workers' Bill or Rights
5	Verify your employee's social security or tax identification number and complete Form I-9 for employment eligibility
6	Calculate employee tax withholdings
7	Prepare and distribute paystubs (even if paying by direct deposit)
8	File and remit quarterly state employment taxes
9	File and remit quarterly federal taxes using Form 1040-ES
10	Prepare and distribute Form W-2 to your employees by January 31
11	Prepare and file all year-end tax forms with your state and the Social Security Administration (Copy A of Form W-2 and Form W-3) by January 31
12	Prepare Schedule H and file with your federal income tax return (Form 1040)
13	Read and respond to government notices or alerts
14	Monitor changes to tax, wage, and labor laws that could potentially affect household employment

Household Payroll and Tax Checklist

BEFORE HIRING	
	Understand federal, state, and local tax, wage and labor laws including workers' compensation, disability insurance, and domestic workers' bill of rights
	Obtain your employer identification number
AT THE TIME OF HIRE	
	If you are withholding income taxes, provide your employees with Form W-4
	Obtain Form I-9 for employee eligibility verification
	Apply for a state unemployment ID number
	Apply for a state withholding number (if applicable)
	Apply for a state new hire report
	Obtain Form 1040-ES for estimated tax payments (if desired)
	Agree to a regular pay period schedule with your employee following any applicable state laws
ON PAY DAY	
	Withhold Social Security and Medicare taxes from your employee's gross pay
	Withhold federal and state income taxes (if agreed upon) from your employee's gross pay
ONGOING	
	Pay employer federal, state, and local taxes on time
	Keep records in a safe place for at least seven years
ANNUALLY	
	Provide your employees with Form W-2 (Wage and Tax Statement) on or before January 31
	Send Copy A of Form W-2 along with Form W-3 to the Social Security Administration by January 31

Appendix B: Interview Questions

The following are lists of questions to ask during a candidate interview. They cover a range of areas—from questions relating to general employment to questions regarding behavior and ethics. A prepared list of questions helps to keep the interview on track and helps to ensure that all questions and topics are covered. A list of interview questions is also beneficial when multiple candidates are interviewed, as it allows the employer to make fair and accurate comparisons and considerations by examining different candidates' answers and responses to the same questions.

Also included is a list of questions specific to job type: nanny, senior caregiver, housekeeper, and household manager.

Very similar to interview questions for job applicants, the exit interview questions help the employer keep on track and ensure all questions are answered. An exit interview is your opportunity to learn what works and what needs improving within the household, and how the employee viewed the job and the household. After the exit interview, the employer should write up his or her notes from the discussion and attach the completed exit interview questions form and write-up with the termination letter. Both are filed in the employee's personnel file.

Interview Questions

General:
- What made you choose this particular field of work?
- What motivates you at work? What is important to you about the household you work for? In the past, in what ways have you demonstrated that you care about the work you do?

- What do you feel is the greatest strength that you bring to your job or your work? What is an area(s) in which you need or would like to improve? How do you plan to address this?

- How would you describe your ideal working conditions?

- What are your career plans for the future?

- How would you describe your personality?

- What kinds of things do you like doing when you are off work? What are your hobbies or interests?

Educational Background:

- What is your educational background?

- How would you rate yourself academically?

- What are you doing now to develop your knowledge or talents? What have you done in the past to expand your knowledge in your field?

- What do you do to keep informed in your field?

- Tell me about a mistake you have made, in your current or previous positions, and what you did to resolve it.

Work History:

- Why are you leaving your current position (or why did you leave your most recent position)?

- Of your previous positions, which did you like the best and why? Which did you like the least? Which motivated you the most?

- Describe your relationship with the last household. What do you think that your employer or manager would say about your job performance?

- At work, what have been your major work accomplishments? What are you most proud of with regard to past experience and why?

- Describe your working relationships with others.

Behavior:

- Name a specific problem you faced on the job. How did you resolve it?

- Describe a time when you had to go above and beyond the call of duty to get the job done.
- What frustrates you about your job? Give an example. How did you handle it and what was the result?
- What was the toughest decision that you had to make recently in your job? Why was it difficult, and how did you handle the situation?
- Describe how you solved a problem in a unique way.

Ethical:

- What process do you use to resolve an ethical dilemma? What, if anything, would you have done differently?
- Tell us when it was necessary to make an exception to the rules to get something accomplished.

Learning Orientation:

- What do you feel is a specific weakness of yours and how did you overcome it? Be specific.

Results Focused:

- What is an accomplishment that you are especially proud of?

Change Orientation:

- Describe a time when you were faced with a change in your work environment. What was it and how did you handle it?
- Think of a situation in which you were provided with very little instruction on how to perform a task. How did you proceed?

Specific Job Requirements:

- Would you be able to work flexible hours if necessary?
- Which children's ages do you like the best and why?
- How would you handle an emergency? Have you ever had to do so in the past?
- How would you discipline my child if he or she misbehaves?
- What are your favorite activities to do with children?

Additional application questions to use when hiring a **nanny**

- Do you have an educational background in child development?

- How many years of child care experience do you have?

- What age will you care for?

- How many children will you care for?

- Have you experience in caring for multiples?

- Would you care for sick children?

- Would you care for children with special needs?

- Will you assist with homework?

- Will you tutor science?

  - Reading?

  - Foreign language?

- What child care tasks are you willing to perform?

- Why are you interested in working in child care?

- With respect to child care, what activities would you organize on a daily or weekly basis?

- What is your philosophy on discipline?

- If you were a parent looking for a child care provider, what characteristics would you look for in a provider? What would be most important to you in hiring a nanny or child care provider?

- What are the most important characteristics you believe lend to a successful relationship between a child care provider and the parents?

- Briefly tell us about your family life (e.g., your parents, siblings, children you have raised).

Additional application questions to use when hiring a **senior caregiver**

- Do you have experience working with an elderly or disabled person? How many years?

- Do you have experience working in a private household? How many years?
- What senior care responsibilities are you willing to perform?
- What household responsibilities are you willing to perform or assist with?
- Are you able to lift heavy objects (fifty pounds or more)?
- Have you had medical training in transferring?
- Are you able to transfer someone from a wheelchair into a car?
- Are you able to transfer someone from a wheelchair into a bed?
- How do you handle someone who is angry, fearful, or upset?
- How do you handle someone who is downcast or depressed?
- Do you have experience caring for someone with mental problems, such as depression, dementia, or loss of memory? Please explain.
- Why do you want to work in senior care?

Additional application questions to use when hiring a **housekeeper**

- What formal experience do you have as a housekeeper?
- How many years' experience do you have in a private household?
- What is the largest property you have ever cleaned (square feet)?
- Which housekeeping tasks are you willing to perform?
- Which laundry tasks are you willing to perform?
- Which ironing tasks are you willing to perform?
- Check one of the following that best describes your house-keeping standards:

    _____ I have sloppy housekeeping standards

    _____ I am a messy but happy housekeeper

    _____ My housekeeping standards are average

    _____ I am a neat and orderly housekeeper

- What are your housekeeping standards?

  ____ I must have orderliness to function

  ____ I always perform every task scrupulously and thoroughly.

- Please rate yourself on the following skills, using a 0-10 scale with 10 being the highest or best and 0 being the lowest or worst.

  ____ Computer use

  ____ Cooking

  ____ Communication

  ____ Problem solving

  ____ Organizational

- Will you prepare meals for (please check all that apply):

  ____ My employer's children only

  ____ My employer's immediate family living within the household

  ____ My employer's immediate family and household staff

  ____ My employer's children and their playmates

  ____ My employer's guests

  ____ Any person within the household at that meal time, excluding vendors, service professionals, and repair people

  ____ Anyone my employer requests me to feed

- Are you willing to work in a home with a child?

  - What ages?

  - How many?

- What is your personal style of service?

Additional application questions to use when hiring a **household manager**

- Do you have formal experience as a household manager?

- How many years' experience do you have in a private household?
- What is the largest property you have ever managed (sq. ft.)?
- What is the largest size of household staff you have managed?
- What household management tasks are you willing to perform?
- Please rate yourself on the following skills, using a 0–10 scale with 10 being the highest or best and 0 being the lowest or worst.

  ____ Communication

  ____ Problem solving

  ____ Formal service

  ____ Social etiquette

  ____ Personnel management

  ____ Leadership

  ____ Fiscal management

  ____ Negotiating skills

- Please describe your computer skills and list which programs you are proficient with.
- Are you willing to work in a home with a child?
  - What ages?
  - How many?
- What is your personal style of service?
- What is your style of management?
- Please describe any experience you have working with contractors.
- Please describe the kinds of household duties you are not willing to perform.

Exit Interview Questions

Today's date_____
Date employment began_____
Date employment ended_____

Why are you leaving your household position?

What will you be doing when you leave your position?

If you are to be employed in another household position, please explain why.
How would you rate the job?
Excellent   Good   Average   Fair   Poor
If average or less, why?

How would you rate the family?
Excellent   Good   Average   Fair   Poor
If average or less, why?

Did you have a written job description?
Yes   No

Did you have a written work agreement?
Yes   No

What were your duties?

What problem(s) did you encounter in the job or household?

If you were in the same situation again, would you accept a position with this family?
Yes   No
If no, why not?

Would you recommend that other household employees work for this family?
Yes   No
If no, why not?

Would you consider working as a household employee again in the future if applicable?
Yes   No

What would you suggest the household improve upon?

Other Comments:

Household Employee Signature _____

Date _____

Workdays/schedule_____

Name of household employer_____

Appendix C: Resources

What follows are links and telephone numbers where you can find a wealth of information on various topics, including hiring and discrimination laws, payroll taxes and wages, unemployment insurance, and state and federal requirements for hiring household help. In addition, there are links to several organizations that provide information on nanny tips and practices as well as agency information.

Resources and References

Websites

GTM Payroll Services Inc.
www.gtm.com
Association of Premier Nanny Agencies
www.theapna.org
Americans with Disabilities Act
www.ada.gov
Consumer Product Safety Commission
www.cpsc.gov
Internal Revenue Service
www.irs.gov
International Guild of Professional Butlers
www.butlersguild.com
International Nanny Association
www.nanny.org
I-9 Central (USCIS)
www.uscis.gov/i-9central
Social Security Administration
www.ssa.gov

U.S. Citizenship and Immigration Services
www.uscis.gov
U.S. Equal Employment Opportunity Commission
www.eeoc.gov
U.S. Department of Labor
www.dol.gov
U.S. Department of Labor Wage and Hour Division
www.dol.gov/whd

Telephone Numbers

GTM Payroll Services Inc.
1-800-929-9213
American with Disabilities Act Information Line
1-800-514-0301
Internal Revenue Service (IRS) Business
1-800-829-4933
Internal Revenue Service (IRS) Tax Questions
1-800-829-1040
IRS Taxpayer Advocate
1-877-777-4778
Social Security Service
1-800-772-1213
U.S. Citizenship and Immigration Services
1-800-375-5283
U.S. Equal Employment Opportunity Commission
1-800-669-4000 (call is automatically directed to the nearest EEOC Field Office)
U.S. Department of Labor Wage and Hour Toll-Free Information and Helpline
1-866-4USWAGE (1-866-487-9243)

Appendix D: Sample Hiring Forms

The following forms may be helpful in your household help hire. Use them as they are or adapt them to serve your household. Please ensure you are aware of any requirements for overtime, personal and sick time, and other wage and hour stipulations in your state and amend the forms accordingly.

Offer Letter for Household Employment

Confidential

(Date)

Mary Poppins

123 Main Street

Chicago, IL, 12345

Dear Mary,

To confirm our conversation of earlier today, _____ (date), I am pleased to offer you the full-time position of nanny with our family. We would like you to start work on _____ (date). Your hours will be Monday through Friday, 8:15 a.m. until 5:30 p.m. Your compensation package is as follows.

- Compensation:

  $10 per hour

  Overtime $15 per hour

  $493.75 gross per week for 46.25 hours

  Paid weekly through GTM's EasyPay® service

- Benefits (after 60 days of employment):

  Paid health insurance for a single individual of either major medical, HMO, or PPO

  Health Reimbursement Account

  Guardian dental insurance coverage

  IRA retirement plan participation, 3 percent family contribution

- Vacation:

  Two weeks paid vacation after 60 days of employment

  One week—employer choice

  One week—employee choice

- Personal and Sick Time:

  Three paid personal days and two sick days per year after 60 days of employment

- Holidays:

   Six paid holidays plus three floating (family choice) after 60 days of employment

We are happy you have accepted our offer, and we look forward to you joining our family. Please call us with any questions. Otherwise, we look forward to seeing you to finalize some customary paperwork on _____ (date). Please return this letter to the address noted above to confirm your acceptance of this position.

Sincerely,

Household Employer (s)

   Accepted by

   _____ _____

   Candidate Name   Date

All household employees are employed at-will. This employment is at the discretion of the employer and the employee. Employment may terminate with or without notice or cause. Employees are also free to end employment at any time, for any reason, with or without notice.

Rejection Letter to Candidate

[Date]

Dear _____,

Thank you for your interest in employment with our household. We have reviewed your application and carefully considered your qualifications. At this time, we have selected another candidate for the position.

   We will retain your application and if we need additional information concerning your qualifications, we will contact you.

Sincerely,

Household Employer

Nanny Job Description

Summary

To provide child care to the _____ household's children, in a loving, secure, positive, and responsible manner following the parents' ideologies of discipline and child rearing as requested.

Essential Functions

Interact with the children keeping in mind developmental issues.

Read interesting and stimulating stories.

Respond with thoughtful answers to questions.

Help the children solve problems.

Maintain the children's cleanliness (e.g., hands and face, soiled clothing).

Be able to handle emergency situations calmly and swiftly, and with reassurance.

Provide daily communication with the parents regarding the children: good occurrences and any problems or concerns.

Keep the children safe at all times inside and outside the house.

Manage the home, including light housework and picking up after the children and in their play area.

Provide nutritional meal planning, including snacks for the children and, on occasion, for the family.

Provide exhilarating, thought-provoking learning recreation.

Provide teaching methods to children.

Be dependable and flexible with schedule. Notify the family well in advance of any needed time off.

Take direction from the parents and maintain a patient, understanding, and cheerful demeanor with a good sense of humor.

Adhere to the Employer and/or Household Employee Work Agreement.

Nonessential Functions

Assist in managing the home by helping with family laundry, housekeeping, including vacuuming and dusting, and family meal preparation.

Purchase children's clothing.

Assist with errands such as grocery shopping or picking up or dropping off dry-cleaning.

Knowledge, Skills, Abilities

Basic knowledge of CPR and first aid.

Knowledge of child development issues, such as age-appropriate activities and nutrition.

Basic reading and writing skills.

Ability to follow written and oral instructions.

Ability to be active with the children (e.g., standing, walking, bending, kneeling, lifting, climbing stairs).

Knowledge of operating home electronics and kitchen appliances.

Safe driving skills and child seat safety.

Supervisory Responsibilities

None

Working Conditions

The job will be performed at the primary residence of the _____ household.

(Use this section to give guidelines and describe your home and its layout, provisions for food, any pets in the house, whether or not a vehicle will be provided to use while working, and so on.)

Minimum Qualifications

A high school diploma or equivalent preferred.

Must be at least 18 years old.

Must have a valid driver's license.

Previous child care experience with references.

Success Factors

A warm, caring, and compassionate personality with a love of children.

Follows directions well but also takes initiative when needed.

Possesses schedule flexibility.

Housekeeper Job Description

Summary

To do anything necessary to maintain an impeccable appearance in the _____ home and to ensure the value of the possessions trusted in your care.

Essential Functions

Conduct a scheduled cleaning of the house.

Vacuum and clean the floors, carpets, and area rugs.

Dust and polish all surfaces.

Do all family laundry and ironing.

Coordinate the drop off and pick up of dry cleaning.

Schedule all linen changes.

Keep a household maintenance report.

Track inventory of all household cleaning products.

Nonessential Functions

Care and maintenance of fine china, silver, and crystal.

Assist with serving responsibilities for dinner parties or other events in the home.

Keep floral arrangements fresh throughout the house.

Run errands.

Conduct household shopping.

Knowledge, Skills, Abilities

Have knowledge of and understand the need for quartering/zoning a home.

Have the ability to track which rooms must be detail-cleaned several times a month and which may be detail-cleaned only once a month.

Possess knowledge of various cleaning products and know which work most effectively on specific surfaces.

Have the ability to follow a schedule and work efficiently and effectively.

Have strong communication skills.

Supervisory Responsibilities

None

Working Conditions

The job will be performed at the primary residence of the _____ household.

(Here you can describe your home—its layout and square footage, additional residences to be managed, housing accommodations, and so on.)

Minimum Qualifications

Previous experience working in private service as a housekeeper.

Professional references.

Success Factors

Meticulous attention to detail.

Follows direction well and takes initiative to ensure the highest standards are met.

Senior Caregiver and/or Companion Job Description

Summary

Assist senior in maintaining an independent life and provide the best care when independent living is no longer possible.

Essential Functions

Assist in preparing and serving meals.

Light cleaning duties.

Driving.

Bathing.

Helping to dress.

Run errands.

Grocery shopping.

Nonessential Functions

Accompanying senior to events and appointments.

Traveling with senior.

Knowledge, Skills, Abilities

Basic nursing skills.

Knowledge of first aid and CPR.

Ability to perform everyday activities and movements (e.g., lifting, standing, walking, bending, kneeling, climbing stairs).

Safe driving skills.

Knowledge of operating home electronics and kitchen appliances.

Knowledge of medication administration (e.g., following dosage schedule and amount).

Supervisory Responsibilities

None

Working Conditions

The job will be based from the primary residence of the _____ household. (Here you can describe your home—its layout and square footage, additional residences to be managed, housing accommodations, etc.).

Minimum Qualifications

Degree in social work or related field, or equivalent field experience. First-aid and CPR certification or training.

Success Factors

Possess a calming and accommodating personality.
Patience and ability to be flexible.
Warm and friendly disposition.

Maintenance Worker Job Description

Summary

Responsible for the performance of specialized maintenance and repair operations. Expected to plan details of projects and carry them out to completion.

Essential Functions

Provides maintenance in such areas as skilled and semiskilled electrical, plumbing, painting, roof repair, carpentry, etc.

Inspects safety of all equipment, machinery, and tools.

Operates power-driven and motorized equipment.

Performs skilled work in the maintenance, repair, alteration, and remodeling of the residence.

Performs rough and finished carpentry.

Performs bench carpentry using shop equipment and power tools such as drills, saws, sanders, planers, air nailers, routers, and radial arm saws.

Assembles, installs, and repairs pipes, fittings, and fixtures of water, heating, and drainage systems.

Performs preventative maintenance and minor repairs on cooling and air distribution systems.

Pours concrete to make floors, walkways, pads, or other projects.

Repairs or replaces leaking and defective roofing.

Repairs doors, door checks, and locks.

Repairs window frames, tables, chairs, and other related objects.

Mixes prepared paint and paints a variety of surfaces both inside and outside the residence using brushes, spray guns, and rollers.

Makes routine electrical repairs such as replacing lighting fixtures, electrical outlets, appliances, light switches.

Estimates and orders materials and supplies.

Ensures the proper inventory controls are in place for various materials and supplies.

Cleans equipment and work areas.

Nonessential Functions

Assists in the maintenance of grounds.

Knowledge, Skills, Abilities

Knowledge of methods, practices, tools, and materials used in building maintenance, and repair work.

Knowledge of occupational hazards and necessary safety precautions applicable to maintenance work.

Knowledge of the general repair of large equipment, and experience in repairing such equipment.

Skill in the use and care of tools and equipment necessary to perform various maintenance and repair tasks.

Ability to operate, install, and repair all equipment in a safe and efficient manner.

Ability to plan and organize the proper performance of a variety of construction, maintenance, and repair tasks.

Uses graphic instructions such as blueprints, layouts, or other visual aids.

Ability to follow oral and written instructions, working independently while performing major repairs and overhauls.

Calculates cost, labor, and material estimates by performing arithmetic functions such as addition, subtraction, multiplication, division, and algebra.

Establishes priorities for own workload based on such factors as need for immediate action, work objectives, work schedule, and knowledge or future needs, etc.

Supervisory Responsibilities

Directs the work of other skilled or semiskilled staff for specified projects.

Working Conditions

While performing the duties of this job, the employee is frequently exposed to fumes or airborne particles and toxic or caustic chemicals.

Employee may be exposed to excessive dust, mold, or mildew.

Duties to be performed are both outside and inside in varying conditions, including extreme heat, extreme cold, and wet and/or humid, etc.

While performing the duties of this job, the employee is regularly required to stand, walk, use hands and arms to operate tools and equipment, climb, crouch or stoop, and lift and/or carry objects weighing up to 40 pounds.

Minimum Qualifications

Successful completion of a standard high school program supplemented by trade school courses.

Three years of skilled level experience in building maintenance and repair work, with a high level of proficiency in at least two of the building trades.

Any reasonable combination of knowledge, skills, abilities, training, and experience may be supplemented.

Success Factors

Listens and asks for clarification, when needed. Responds well to questions.

Demonstrates accuracy and thoroughness.

Follows policies and procedures.

Completes tasks correctly and on time.

General Application for Employment

Name Last	First	Middle	Previous Name(s) if any

Address Number	Street	City	State	Zip Code

Telephone	Email address

Driver's License #	State

Education

Name/Location of School	Degree Earned (Y/N)	Type	Year Graduated	Major
Grade School				
High School				
Vocational School				
College				
Graduate School				

Courses in Child Development, Education

Extracurricular Activities _____

Employment History

(Starting with current to most recent, list all previous positions. Explain any gap between employment in the space provided.)

DATES	EMPLOYED	EMPLOYER PHONE	POSITION HELD

Explanation of any gaps in employment

Background

A. Have you ever been convicted of a crime? [ ] No [ ] Yes

If yes, explain the nature of the offense, date and court location.

_____

B. Have you had any traffic citations, (including speeding tickets, DWI or DUI convictions) in the past five years? [ ] No [ ] Yes

If yes, list all traffic citations for the past five years, including speeding tickets, DWI or DUI convictions.

_____

Is your driver's license currently valid, not under a suspension or revoked? [ ] Yes [ ] No

_____

Explain: _____

In what other states have you had a driver's license?

_____

State   License numbers (if known)

C. List all addresses you have lived at for the past five years.

ADDRESS   COUNTY   STATE   DATES

_____

_____

_____

_____

_____

Availability/Compensation

When can you start work? _____

Are you willing to make a one-year commitment? [ ] Yes [ ] No

What days and hours are you available to work? _____

_____

Gross hourly rate requested $ _____   per _____

What benefits do you desire? _____

Statement

I have not withheld any information a reasonable person would expect a prospective candidate to provide. I have been honest in revealing and explaining any undesirable background information. I do certify that all information noted here is true to the best of my knowledge.

I authorize full disclosure and release to any duly authorized agent of the Household Employer of all information and records both public and private, including, but not limited to, criminal and financial history, as required to conduct a complete background investigation. I hereby release all persons and agencies from any liability associated with such disclosure. I understand such information may be duplicated and given to any prospective client seeking to hire me, and I hereby authorize this.

I also specifically request that all agencies and references fully cooperate with this investigation and provide the requested information.

_____   _____
Applicant Signature   Date

Paycheck and Payroll Earnings Statement

Household Employer
123 Main Street
New York, NY 10028

Dummy Account For EV   11
                         1000

Check Date 7/29/2016   Check Number 10021

Pay *Six Hundred Eighty-Three Dollars and Sixty-Four Cents*

$******683.64

To the Order of: 0001   10021

Alice Nelson
123 Main Street
New York, NY 10028

Authorized Signature

⑈010021⑈ ⑆011000138⑈ 12345⑈

Alice Nelson			Household Employer					123 Main Street New York, NY 10028 518-373-5555	
Company Household	Period Begin 7/18/2016	Division	Personal 32.000000-2.000000= 30.000000 HOUR						
Number 0001	Period End 7/31/2016	Branch	Sick 11.000000-0.500000= 10.500000 HOURS						
Social Security #	Check Date 7/29/2016	Department	Vacation 55.000000-10.000000= 45.000000 HOU						
Hire Date 1/1/2004	Check Number 10021	Tears							

Earnings							Deductions		
Description	Location / Job	Rate	Hours	Current	Year To Date	Description		Current	Year To Date
Hourly Rate 1		12.00	80.00	960.00	960.00	Fed (S/1) (910.00)		82.32	82.32
Milage Reimb		12.00	0.00	13.44	13.44	OASDI (960.00)		59.52	59.52
Memos				25.00		Medicare (960.00)		13.92	13.92
HRA			0.00	25.00	25.00	NY (S/1) (910.00)		26.18	26.18
						New York City Res.(910.00)		17.86	17.86
						Life Insurance		10.00	10.00
						Health Insurance		30.00	30.00
						Simple IRA		50.00	50.00
Total Earnings			80.00	973.44	973.44	Total Deductions		289.80	289.80
NET PAY		683.64	Total Direct Deposits		0.00	Check Amount		683.64	683.64

Check Date   Check Number

$************

Pay _____

To the Order of: _____

_____
Authorized Signature

Company   Period Begin   Division

Appendix E: Sample Employment Forms

This appendix contains various forms that you may use in the course of your household employment.

For IRS forms, up-to-date forms can be found at www.irs.gov.

Form I-9: Employment Eligibility Verification

https://www.uscis.gov/sites/default/files/files/form/i-9.pdf

Employment Eligibility Verification	USCIS
Department of Homeland Security U.S. Citizenship and Immigration Services	**Form I-9** OMB No. 1615-0047 Expires 08/31/2019

▶**START HERE:** Read instructions carefully before completing this form. The instructions must be available, either in paper or electronically, during completion of this form. Employers are liable for errors in the completion of this form.

ANTI-DISCRIMINATION NOTICE: It is illegal to discriminate against work-authorized individuals. Employers **CANNOT** specify which document(s) an employee may present to establish employment authorization and identity. The refusal to hire or continue to employ an individual because the documentation presented has a future expiration date may also constitute illegal discrimination.

Section 1. Employee Information and Attestation *(Employees must complete and sign Section 1 of Form I-9 no later than the first day of employment, but not before accepting a job offer.)*

Last Name *(Family Name)*	First Name *(Given Name)*		Middle Initial	Other Last Names Used *(if any)*
Address *(Street Number and Name)*	Apt. Number	City or Town		State	ZIP Code
Date of Birth *(mm/dd/yyyy)*	U.S. Social Security Number	Employee's E-mail Address	Employee's Telephone Number

I am aware that federal law provides for imprisonment and/or fines for false statements or use of false documents in connection with the completion of this form.

I attest, under penalty of perjury, that I am (check one of the following boxes):

☐ 1. A citizen of the United States

☐ 2. A noncitizen national of the United States *(See instructions)*

☐ 3. A lawful permanent resident   (Alien Registration Number/USCIS Number):

☐ 4. An alien authorized to work   until (expiration date, if applicable, mm/dd/yyyy):
Some aliens may write "N/A" in the expiration date field. *(See instructions)*

*Aliens authorized to work must provide only one of the following document numbers to complete Form I-9:
An Alien Registration Number/USCIS Number OR Form I-94 Admission Number OR Foreign Passport Number.*

1. Alien Registration Number/USCIS Number: _____
   OR
2. Form I-94 Admission Number: _____
   OR
3. Foreign Passport Number: _____
   Country of Issuance: _____

QR Code - Section 1
Do Not Write In This Space

Signature of Employee	Today's Date *(mm/dd/yyyy)*

Preparer and/or Translator Certification (check one):
☐ I did not use a preparer or translator.   ☐ A preparer(s) and/or translator(s) assisted the employee in completing Section 1.
(Fields below must be completed and signed when preparers and/or translators assist an employee in completing Section 1.)

I attest, under penalty of perjury, that I have assisted in the completion of Section 1 of this form and that to the best of my knowledge the information is true and correct.

Signature of Preparer or Translator	Today's Date *(mm/dd/yyyy)*
Last Name *(Family Name)*	First Name *(Given Name)*
Address *(Street Number and Name)*	City or Town	State	ZIP Code

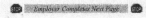

STOP *Employer Completes Next Page* STOP

Employment Eligibility Verification
Department of Homeland Security
U.S. Citizenship and Immigration Services

USCIS
Form I-9
OMB No. 1615-0047
Expires 08/31/2019

Section 2. Employer or Authorized Representative Review and Verification

(Employers or their authorized representative must complete and sign Section 2 within 3 business days of the employee's first day of employment. You must physically examine one document from List A OR a combination of one document from List B and one document from List C as listed on the "Lists of Acceptable Documents.")

Employee Info from Section 1	Last Name (Family Name)	First Name (Given Name)	M.I.	Citizenship/Immigration Status

List A Identity and Employment Authorization	OR	List B Identity	AND	List C Employment Authorization
Document Title		Document Title		Document Title
Issuing Authority		Issuing Authority		Issuing Authority
Document Number		Document Number		Document Number
Expiration Date (if any)(mm/dd/yyyy)		Expiration Date (if any)(mm/dd/yyyy)		Expiration Date (if any)(mm/dd/yyyy)
Document Title				
Issuing Authority		Additional Information		QR Code - Sections 2 & 3 Do Not Write In This Space
Document Number				
Expiration Date (if any)(mm/dd/yyyy)				
Document Title				
Issuing Authority				
Document Number				
Expiration Date (if any)(mm/dd/yyyy)				

Certification: I attest, under penalty of perjury, that (1) I have examined the document(s) presented by the above-named employee, (2) the above-listed document(s) appear to be genuine and to relate to the employee named, and (3) to the best of my knowledge the employee is authorized to work in the United States.

The employee's first day of employment (mm/dd/yyyy): _____ (See instructions for exemptions)

Signature of Employer or Authorized Representative	Today's Date(mm/dd/yyyy)	Title of Employer or Authorized Representative
Last Name of Employer or Authorized Representative	First Name of Employer or Authorized Representative	Employer's Business or Organization Name
Employer's Business or Organization Address (Street Number and Name)	City or Town	State	ZIP Code

Section 3. Reverification and Rehires (To be completed and signed by employer or authorized representative.)

A. New Name (if applicable)			B. Date of Rehire (if applicable)
Last Name (Family Name)	First Name (Given Name)	Middle Initial	Date (mm/dd/yyyy)

C. If the employee's previous grant of employment authorization has expired, provide the information for the document or receipt that establishes continuing employment authorization in the space provided below.

Document Title	Document Number	Expiration Date (if any) (mm/dd/yyyy)

I attest, under penalty of perjury, that to the best of my knowledge, this employee is authorized to work in the United States, and if the employee presented document(s), the document(s) I have examined appear to be genuine and to relate to the individual.

Signature of Employer or Authorized Representative	Today's Date (mm/dd/yyyy)	Name of Employer or Authorized Representative

LISTS OF ACCEPTABLE DOCUMENTS
All documents must be UNEXPIRED

Employees may present one selection from List A
or a combination of one selection from List B and one selection from List C.

LIST A	LIST B	LIST C
Documents that Establish Both Identity and Employment Authorization	**Documents that Establish Identity**	**Documents that Establish Employment Authorization**
1. U.S. Passport or U.S. Passport Card	1. Driver's license or ID card issued by a State or outlying possession of the United States provided it contains a photograph or information such as name, date of birth, gender, height, eye color, and address	1. A Social Security Account Number card, unless the card includes one of the following restrictions:
2. Permanent Resident Card or Alien Registration Receipt Card (Form I-551)		(1) NOT VALID FOR EMPLOYMENT
3. Foreign passport that contains a temporary I-551 stamp or temporary I-551 printed notation on a machine-readable immigrant visa	2. ID card issued by federal, state or local government agencies or entities, provided it contains a photograph or information such as name, date of birth, gender, height, eye color, and address	(2) VALID FOR WORK ONLY WITH INS AUTHORIZATION
4. Employment Authorization Document that contains a photograph (Form I-766)	3. School ID card with a photograph	(3) VALID FOR WORK ONLY WITH DHS AUTHORIZATION
5. For a nonimmigrant alien authorized to work for a specific employer because of his or her status:	4. Voter's registration card	2. Certification of Birth Abroad issued by the Department of State (Form FS-545)
a. Foreign passport; and	5. U.S. Military card or draft record	3. Certification of Report of Birth issued by the Department of State (Form DS-1350)
b. Form I-94 or Form I-94A that has the following:	6. Military dependent's ID card	4. Original or certified copy of birth certificate issued by a State, county, municipal authority, or territory of the United States bearing an official seal
(1) The same name as the passport; and	7. U.S. Coast Guard Merchant Mariner Card	
(2) An endorsement of the alien's nonimmigrant status as long as that period of endorsement has not yet expired and the proposed employment is not in conflict with any restrictions or limitations identified on the form.	8. Native American tribal document	5. Native American tribal document
	9. Driver's license issued by a Canadian government authority	6. U.S. Citizen ID Card (Form I-197)
	For persons under age 18 who are unable to present a document listed above:	7. Identification Card for Use of Resident Citizen in the United States (Form I-179)
6. Passport from the Federated States of Micronesia (FSM) or the Republic of the Marshall Islands (RMI) with Form I-94 or Form I-94A indicating nonimmigrant admission under the Compact of Free Association Between the United States and the FSM or RMI	10. School record or report card	8. Employment authorization document issued by the Department of Homeland Security
	11. Clinic, doctor, or hospital record	
	12. Day-care or nursery school record	

Examples of many of these documents appear in Part 8 of the Handbook for Employers (M-274).

Refer to the instructions for more information about acceptable receipts.

Form SS8: Determination of Worker Status for Purposes of Federal Employment Taxes and Income Tax Withholding

https://www.irs.gov/pub/irs-access/fss8_accessible.pdf

Form **SS-8** (Rev. May 2014) Department of the Treasury Internal Revenue Service	**Determination of Worker Status for Purposes of Federal Employment Taxes and Income Tax Withholding** ▶ Information about Form SS-8 and its separate instructions is at www.irs.gov/formss8.	OMB. No. 1545-0004 **For IRS Use Only:** Case Number: **Earliest Receipt Date:**

Name of firm (or person) for whom the worker performed services	Worker's name

Firm's mailing address (include street address, apt. or suite no., city, state, and ZIP code)	Worker's mailing address (include street address, apt. or suite no., city, state, and ZIP code)

Trade name	Firm's email address	Worker's daytime telephone number	Worker's email address

Firm's fax number	Firm's website	Worker's alternate telephone number	Worker's fax number

Firm's telephone number (include area code)	Firm's employer identification number	Worker's social security number	Worker's employer identification number (if any)

Note. If the worker is paid for these services by a firm other than the one listed on this form, enter the name, address, and employer identification number of the payer. ▶

Disclosure of Information

The information provided on Form SS-8 may be disclosed to the firm, worker, or payer named above to assist the IRS in the determination process. For example, if you are a worker, we may disclose the information you provide on Form SS-8 to the firm or payer named above. The information can only be disclosed to assist with the determination process. If you provide incomplete information, we may not be able to process your request. See *Privacy Act and Paperwork Reduction Act Notice* in the separate instructions for more information. **If you do not want this information disclosed to other parties, do not file Form SS-8.**

Parts I–V. All filers of Form SS-8 must complete all questions in Parts I–IV. Part V must be completed if the worker provides a service directly to customers or is a salesperson. If you cannot answer a question, enter "Unknown" or "Does not apply." If you need more space for a question, attach another sheet with the part and question number clearly identified. Write your firm's name (or worker's name) and employer identification number (or social security number) at the top of each additional sheet attached to this form.

Part I	**General Information**

1 This form is being completed by: ☐ Firm ☐ Worker; for services performed _____ to _____
                                                  (beginning date)   (ending date)

2 Explain your reason(s) for filing this form (for example, you received a bill from the IRS, you believe you erroneously received a Form 1099 or Form W-2, you are unable to get workers' compensation benefits, or you were audited or are being audited by the IRS). _____

3 Total number of workers who performed or are performing the same or similar services: _____

4 How did the worker obtain the job? ☐ Application ☐ Bid ☐ Employment Agency ☐ Other (specify) _____

5 Attach copies of all supporting documentation (for example, contracts, invoices, memos, Forms W-2 or Forms 1099-MISC issued or received, IRS closing agreements or IRS rulings). In addition, please inform us of any current or past litigation concerning the worker's status. If no income reporting forms (Form 1099-MISC or W-2) were furnished to the worker, enter the amount of income earned for the year(s) at issue $ _____

    If both Form W-2 and Form 1099-MISC were issued or received, explain why. _____

6 Describe the firm's business. _____

For Privacy Act and Paperwork Reduction Act Notice, see the separate instructions.   Cat. No. 16106T   Form **SS-8** (Rev. 5-2014)

Form SS-8 (Rev. 5-2014)   Page **2**

| Part I | **General Information** (continued) |

7   If the worker received pay from more than one entity because of an event such as the sale, merger, acquisition, or reorganization of the firm for whom the services are performed, provide the following: Name of the firm's previous owner:

Previous owner's taxpayer identification number: _____ Change was a: ☐ Sale ☐ Merger ☐ Acquisition ☐ Reorganization
☐ Other (specify) _____
Description of above change: _____

Date of change (MM/DD/YY): _____

8   Describe the work done by the worker and provide the worker's job title. _____

9   Explain why you believe the worker is an employee or an independent contractor. _____

10 Did the worker perform services for the firm in any capacity before providing the services that are the subject of this determination request?
☐ Yes   ☐ No   ☐ N/A
If "Yes," what were the dates of the prior service? _____
If "Yes," explain the differences, if any, between the current and prior service. _____

11 If the work is done under a written agreement between the firm and the worker, attach a copy (preferably signed by both parties). Describe the terms and conditions of the work arrangement. _____

| Part II | **Behavioral Control** (Provide names and titles of specific individuals, if applicable.) |

1   What specific training and/or instruction is the worker given by the firm? _____

2   How does the worker receive work assignments? _____

3   Who determines the methods by which the assignments are performed? _____
4   Who is the worker required to contact if problems or complaints arise and who is responsible for their resolution? _____

5   What types of reports are required from the worker? Attach examples. _____

6   Describe the worker's daily routine such as his or her schedule or hours. _____

7   At what location(s) does the worker perform services (for example, firm's premises, own shop or office, home, customer's location)? Indicate the appropriate percentage of time the worker spends in each location, if more than one. _____

8   Describe any meetings the worker is required to attend and any penalties for not attending (for example, sales meetings, monthly meetings, staff meetings). _____

9   Is the worker required to provide the services personally? . . . . ☐ Yes   ☐ No
10 If substitutes or helpers are needed, who hires them? _____
11 If the worker hires the substitutes or helpers, is approval required? . . . . ☐ Yes   ☐ No
If "Yes," by whom? _____
12 Who pays the substitutes or helpers? _____
13 Is the worker reimbursed if the worker pays the substitutes or helpers? . . . . ☐ Yes   ☐ No
If "Yes," by whom? _____

Form **SS-8** (Rev. 5-2014)

Form SS-8 (Rev. 5-2014)   Page 3

Part III   Financial Control (Provide names and titles of specific individuals, if applicable.)

1   List the supplies, equipment, materials, and property provided by each party:
    The firm: _____
    The worker: _____
    Other party: _____
2   Does the worker lease equipment, space, or a facility? . . . . □ Yes □ No
    If "Yes," what are the terms of the lease? (Attach a copy or explanatory statement.) _____

3   What expenses are incurred by the worker in the performance of services for the firm? _____

4   Specify which, if any, expenses are reimbursed by:
    The firm: _____
    Other party: _____
5   Type of pay the worker receives: □ Salary   □ Commission   □ Hourly Wage   □ Piece Work
    □ Lump Sum   □ Other (specify) _____
    If type of pay is commission, and the firm guarantees a minimum amount of pay, specify amount. $ _____
6   Is the worker allowed a drawing account for advances? . . . . □ Yes □ No
    If "Yes," how often? _____
    Specify any restrictions. _____

7   Whom does the customer pay? . . . . □ Firm   □ Worker
    If worker, does the worker pay the total amount to the firm? □ Yes   □ No   If "No," explain. _____

8   Does the firm carry workers' compensation insurance on the worker? . . . . □ Yes □ No
9   What economic loss or financial risk, if any, can the worker incur beyond the normal loss of salary (for example, loss or damage of equipment, material)? _____
    _____

10 Does the worker establish the level of payment for the services provided or the products sold? . . . . □ Yes □ No
    If "No," who does? _____

Part IV   Relationship of the Worker and Firm

1   Please check the benefits available to the worker: □ Paid vacations   □ Sick pay   □ Paid holidays
    □ Personal days   □ Pensions   □ Insurance benefits   □ Bonuses
    □ Other (specify) _____
2   Can the relationship be terminated by either party without incurring liability or penalty? . . . . . . □ Yes □ No
    If "No," explain your answer. _____

3   Did the worker perform similar services for others during the time period entered in Part I, line 1? . . □ Yes □ No
    If "Yes," is the worker required to get approval from the firm? . . . . □ Yes □ No
4   Describe any agreements prohibiting competition between the worker and the firm while the worker is performing services or during any later period. Attach any available documentation. _____
    _____
5   Is the worker a member of a union? . . . . □ Yes □ No
6   What type of advertising, if any, does the worker do (for example, a business listing in a directory or business cards)? Provide copies, if applicable. _____

7   If the worker assembles or processes a product at home, who provides the materials and instructions or pattern? _____

8   What does the worker do with the finished product (for example, return it to the firm, provide it to another party, or sell it)? _____

9   How does the firm represent the worker to its customers (for example, employee, partner, representative, or contractor), and under whose business name does the worker perform these services? _____

10 If the worker no longer performs services for the firm, how did the relationship end (for example, worker quit or was fired, job completed, contract ended, firm or worker went out of business)? _____

                                                                                    Form SS-8 (Rev. 5-2014)

Form SS-8 (Rev. 5-2014)   Page **4**

| **Part V** | **For Service Providers or Salespersons.** Complete this part if the worker provided a service directly to customers or is a salesperson. |

1   What are the worker's responsibilities in soliciting new customers?

2   Who provides the worker with leads to prospective customers?

3   Describe any reporting requirements pertaining to the leads.

4   What terms and conditions of sale, if any, are required by the firm?

5   Are orders submitted to and subject to approval by the firm? . . . . ☐ Yes ☐ No

6   Who determines the worker's territory?

7   Did the worker pay for the privilege of serving customers on the route or in the territory? . . . . ☐ Yes ☐ No

If "Yes," whom did the worker pay?

If "Yes," how much did the worker pay? . . . . $

8   Where does the worker sell the product (for example, in a home, retail establishment)?

9   List the product and/or services distributed by the worker (for example, meat, vegetables, fruit, bakery products, beverages, or laundry or dry cleaning services). If more than one type of product and/or service is distributed, specify the principal one.

10   Does the worker sell life insurance full time? . . . . ☐ Yes ☐ No

11   Does the worker sell other types of insurance for the firm? . . . . ☐ Yes ☐ No

If "Yes," enter the percentage of the worker's total working time spent in selling other types of insurance . . . . . %

12   If the worker solicits orders from wholesalers, retailers, contractors, or operators of hotels, restaurants, or other similar establishments, enter the percentage of the worker's time spent in the solicitation . . . . %

13   Is the merchandise purchased by the customers for resale or use in their business operations? . . . . ☐ Yes ☐ No

Describe the merchandise and state whether it is equipment installed on the customers' premises.

Sign Here ▶

Under penalties of perjury, I declare that I have examined this request, including accompanying documents, and to the best of my knowledge and belief, the facts presented are true, correct, and complete.

_____ Title ▶ _____ Date ▶ _____
Type or print name below signature.

Form **SS-8** (Rev. 5-2014)

Form W-4: Employee's Withholding Allowance Certificate

https://www.irs.gov/pub/irs-pdf/fw4.pdf

Form W-4 (2016)

Purpose. Complete Form W-4 so that your employer can withhold the correct federal income tax from your pay. Consider completing a new Form W-4 each year and when your personal or financial situation changes.

Exemption from withholding. If you are exempt, complete only lines 1, 2, 3, 4, and 7 and sign the form to validate it. Your exemption for 2016 expires February 15, 2017. See Pub. 505, Tax Withholding and Estimated Tax.

Note: If another person can claim you as a dependent on his or her tax return, you cannot claim exemption from withholding if your income exceeds $1,050 and includes more than $350 of unearned income (for example, interest and dividends).

Exceptions. An employee may be able to claim exemption from withholding even if the employee is a dependent, if the employee:

• Is age 65 or older,

• Is blind, or

• Will claim adjustments to income; tax credits; or itemized deductions, on his or her tax return.

The exceptions do not apply to supplemental wages greater than $1,000,000.

Basic instructions. If you are not exempt, complete the **Personal Allowances Worksheet** below. The worksheets on page 2 further adjust your withholding allowances based on itemized deductions, certain credits, adjustments to income, or two-earners/multiple jobs situations.

Complete all worksheets that apply. However, you may claim fewer (or zero) allowances. For regular wages, withholding must be based on allowances you claimed and may not be a flat amount or percentage of wages.

Head of household. Generally, you can claim head of household filing status on your tax return only if you are unmarried and pay more than 50% of the costs of keeping up a home for yourself and your dependent(s) or other qualifying individuals. See Pub. 501, Exemptions, Standard Deduction, and Filing Information, for information.

Tax credits. You can take projected tax credits into account in figuring your allowable number of withholding allowances. Credits for child or dependent care expenses and the child tax credit may be claimed using the **Personal Allowances Worksheet** below. See Pub. 505 for information on converting your other credits into withholding allowances.

Nonwage income. If you have a large amount of nonwage income, such as interest or dividends, consider making estimated tax payments using Form 1040-ES, Estimated Tax for Individuals. Otherwise, you may owe additional tax. If you have pension or annuity income, see Pub. 505 to find out if you should adjust your withholding on Form W-4 or W-4P.

Two earners or multiple jobs. If you have a working spouse or more than one job, figure the total number of allowances you are entitled to claim on all jobs using worksheets from only one Form W-4. Your withholding usually will be most accurate when all allowances are claimed on the Form W-4 for the highest paying job and zero allowances are claimed on the others. See Pub. 505 for details.

Nonresident alien. If you are a nonresident alien, see Notice 1392, Supplemental Form W-4 Instructions for Nonresident Aliens, before completing this form.

Check your withholding. After your Form W-4 takes effect, use Pub. 505 to see how the amount you are having withheld compares to your projected total tax for 2016. See Pub. 505, especially if your earnings exceed $130,000 (Single) or $180,000 (Married).

Future developments. Information about any future developments affecting Form W-4 (such as legislation enacted after we release it) will be posted at www.irs.gov/w4.

Personal Allowances Worksheet (Keep for your records.)

A Enter "1" for **yourself** if no one else can claim you as a dependent . . . . **A** ____

B Enter "1" if:
  • You are single and have only one job; or
  • You are married, have only one job, and your spouse does not work; or
  • Your wages from a second job or your spouse's wages (or the total of both) are $1,500 or less. **B** ____

C Enter "1" for your **spouse.** But, you may choose to enter "-0-" if you are married and have either a working spouse or more than one job. (Entering "-0-" may help you avoid having too little tax withheld.) . . . . **C** ____

D Enter number of **dependents** (other than your spouse or yourself) you will claim on your tax return . . . . . **D** ____

E Enter "1" if you will file as **head of household** on your tax return (see conditions under **Head of household** above) . **E** ____

F Enter "1" if you have at least $2,000 of **child or dependent care expenses** for which you plan to claim a credit . . . **F** ____
  (Note: Do **not** include child support payments. See Pub. 503, Child and Dependent Care Expenses, for details.)

G **Child Tax Credit** (including additional child tax credit). See Pub. 972, Child Tax Credit, for more information.
  • If your total income will be less than $70,000 ($100,000 if married), enter "2" for each eligible child; then **less** "1" if you have two to four eligible children or **less** "2" if you have five or more eligible children.
  • If your total income will be between $70,000 and $84,000 ($100,000 and $119,000 if married), enter "1" for each eligible child . . **G** ____

H Add lines A through G and enter total here. **(Note:** This may be different from the number of exemptions you claim on your tax return.) ▶ **H** ____

For accuracy, complete all worksheets that apply.
  • If you plan to **itemize or claim adjustments to income** and want to reduce your withholding, see the **Deductions and Adjustments Worksheet** on page 2.
  • If you are **single and have more than one job** or **are married and you and your spouse both work** and the combined earnings from all jobs exceed $50,000 ($20,000 if married), see the **Two-Earners/Multiple Jobs Worksheet** on page 2 to avoid having too little tax withheld.
  • If **neither** of the above situations applies, **stop here** and enter the number from line H on line 5 of Form W-4 below.

-------- Separate here and give Form W-4 to your employer. Keep the top part for your records. --------

Form W-4
Department of the Treasury
Internal Revenue Service

Employee's Withholding Allowance Certificate

▶ Whether you are entitled to claim a certain number of allowances or exemption from withholding is subject to review by the IRS. Your employer may be required to send a copy of this form to the IRS.

OMB No. 1545-0074

2016

1 Your first name and middle initial	Last name	2 Your social security number

Home address (number and street or rural route)

3 ☐ Single ☐ Married ☐ Married, but withhold at higher Single rate.
Note: If married, but legally separated, or spouse is a nonresident alien, check the "Single" box.

City or town, state, and ZIP code

4 If your last name differs from that shown on your social security card, check here. You must call 1-800-772-1213 for a replacement card. ▶ ☐

5 Total number of allowances you are claiming (from line H above or from the applicable worksheet on page 2) **5** ____

6 Additional amount, if any, you want withheld from each paycheck . . . . **6** $ ____

7 I claim exemption from withholding for 2016, and I certify that I meet **both** of the following conditions for exemption.
  • Last year I had a right to a refund of **all** federal income tax withheld because I had **no** tax liability, **and**
  • This year I expect a refund of **all** federal income tax withheld because I expect to have **no** tax liability.
  If you meet both conditions, write "Exempt" here . . . . ▶ **7** ____

Under penalties of perjury, I declare that I have examined this certificate and, to the best of my knowledge and belief, it is true, correct, and complete.

Employee's signature
(This form is not valid unless you sign it.) ▶

Date ▶

8 Employer's name and address (Employer: Complete lines 8 and 10 only if sending to the IRS.)	9 Office code (optional)	10 Employer identification number (EIN)

For Privacy Act and Paperwork Reduction Act Notice, see page 2.　　Cat. No. 10220Q　　Form **W-4** (2016)

Form W-4 (2016)   Page 2

Deductions and Adjustments Worksheet

Note: Use this worksheet *only* if you plan to itemize deductions or claim certain credits or adjustments to income.

1	Enter an estimate of your 2016 itemized deductions. These include qualifying home mortgage interest, charitable contributions, state and local taxes, medical expenses in excess of 10% (7.5% if either you or your spouse was born before January 2, 1952) of your income, and miscellaneous deductions. For 2016, you may have to reduce your itemized deductions if your income is over $311,300 and you are married filing jointly or are a qualifying widow(er); $285,350 if you are head of household; $259,400 if you are single and not head of household or a qualifying widow(er); or $155,650 if you are married filing separately. See Pub. 505 for details . . .	1	$
2	Enter: { $12,600 if married filing jointly or qualifying widow(er) $9,300 if head of household $6,300 if single or married filing separately }	2	$
3	**Subtract** line 2 from line 1. If zero or less, enter "-0-"	3	$
4	Enter an estimate of your 2016 adjustments to income and any additional standard deduction (see Pub. 505)	4	$
5	**Add** lines 3 and 4 and enter the total. (Include any amount for credits from the *Converting Credits to Withholding Allowances for 2016 Form W-4 worksheet in Pub. 505.*)	5	$
6	Enter an estimate of your 2016 nonwage income (such as dividends or interest)	6	$
7	**Subtract** line 6 from line 5. If zero or less, enter "-0-"	7	$
8	**Divide** the amount on line 7 by $4,050 and enter the result here. Drop any fraction	8	
9	Enter the number from the **Personal Allowances Worksheet**, line H, page 1	9	
10	**Add** lines 8 and 9 and enter the total here. If you plan to use the **Two-Earners/Multiple Jobs Worksheet**, also enter this total on line 1 below. Otherwise, **stop here** and enter this total on Form W-4, line 5, page 1	10	

Two-Earners/Multiple Jobs Worksheet (See *Two earners or multiple jobs* on page 1.)

Note: Use this worksheet *only* if the instructions under line H on page 1 direct you here.

1	Enter the number from line H, page 1 (or from line 10 above if you used the **Deductions and Adjustments Worksheet**)	1	
2	Find the number in **Table 1** below that applies to the **LOWEST** paying job and enter it here. **However,** if you are married filing jointly and wages from the highest paying job are $65,000 or less, do not enter more than "3"	2	
3	If line 1 is **more than or equal to** line 2, subtract line 2 from line 1. Enter the result here (if zero, enter "-0-") and on Form W-4, line 5, page 1. **Do not** use the rest of this worksheet	3	

Note: If line 1 is **less than** line 2, enter "-0-" on Form W-4, line 5, page 1. Complete lines 4 through 9 below to figure the additional withholding amount necessary to avoid a year-end tax bill.

4	Enter the number from line 2 of this worksheet	4	
5	Enter the number from line 1 of this worksheet	5	
6	**Subtract** line 5 from line 4	6	
7	Find the amount in **Table 2** below that applies to the **HIGHEST** paying job and enter it here	7	$
8	**Multiply** line 7 by line 6 and enter the result here. This is the additional annual withholding needed . .	8	$
9	Divide line 8 by the number of pay periods remaining in 2016. For example, divide by 25 if you are paid every two weeks and you complete this form on a date in January when there are 25 pay periods remaining in 2016. Enter the result here and on Form W-4, line 6, page 1. This is the additional amount to be withheld from each paycheck	9	$

Table 1				Table 2			
Married Filing Jointly		**All Others**		**Married Filing Jointly**		**All Others**	
If wages from LOWEST paying job are—	Enter on line 2 above	If wages from LOWEST paying job are—	Enter on line 2 above	If wages from HIGHEST paying job are—	Enter on line 7 above	If wages from HIGHEST paying job are—	Enter on line 7 above
$0 - $6,000	0	$0 - $9,000	0	$0 - $75,000	$610	$0 - $38,000	$610
6,001 - 14,000	1	9,001 - 17,000	1	75,001 - 135,000	1,010	38,001 - 85,000	1,010
14,001 - 25,000	2	17,001 - 26,000	2	135,001 - 205,000	1,130	85,001 - 185,000	1,130
25,001 - 27,000	3	26,001 - 34,000	3	205,001 - 360,000	1,340	185,001 - 400,000	1,340
27,001 - 35,000	4	34,001 - 44,000	4	360,001 - 405,000	1,420	400,001 and over	1,600
35,001 - 44,000	5	44,001 - 75,000	5	405,001 and over	1,600		
44,001 - 55,000	6	75,001 - 85,000	6				
55,001 - 65,000	7	85,001 - 110,000	7				
65,001 - 75,000	8	110,001 - 125,000	8				
75,001 - 80,000	9	125,001 - 140,000	9				
80,001 - 100,000	10	140,001 and over	10				
100,001 - 115,000	11						
115,001 - 130,000	12						
130,001 - 140,000	13						
140,001 - 150,000	14						
150,001 and over	15						

Privacy Act and Paperwork Reduction Act Notice. We ask for the information on this form to carry out the Internal Revenue laws of the United States. Internal Revenue Code sections 3402(f)(2) and 6109 and their regulations require you to provide this information; your employer uses it to determine your federal income tax withholding. Failure to provide a properly completed form will result in your being treated as a single person who claims no withholding allowances; providing fraudulent information may subject you to penalties. Routine uses of this information include giving it to the Department of Justice for civil and criminal litigation; to cities, states, the District of Columbia, and U.S. commonwealths and possessions for use in administering their tax laws; and to the Department of Health and Human Services for use in the National Directory of New Hires. We may also disclose this information to other countries under a tax treaty, to federal and state agencies to enforce federal nontax criminal laws, or to federal law enforcement and intelligence agencies to combat terrorism.

You are not required to provide the information requested on a form that is subject to the Paperwork Reduction Act unless the form displays a valid OMB control number. Books or records relating to a form or its instructions must be retained as long as their contents may become material in the administration of any Internal Revenue law. Generally, tax returns and return information are confidential, as required by Code section 6103.

The average time and expenses required to complete and file this form will vary depending on individual circumstances. For estimated averages, see the instructions for your income tax return.

If you have suggestions for making this form simpler, we would be happy to hear from you. See the instructions for your income tax return.

Work Agreement Sample

This Agreement is made and entered into on _____ (date), between
_____ (employer) residing at
_____ and _____(employee) residing at _____

Recitals

Employer is an individual and a "Household Employer," resident of
_____ (state), and over the age of 18.

Employee is an individual, resident of _____ (state), and over the
age of 18.

Employee is willing to be employed by Employer, and Employer is willing to employ Employee, on the terms and conditions set forth in
this Agreement.

A. Employment

Employment under this agreement is to begin on _____ and continue unless sooner terminated as provided herein.

Subject to the supervision and control of Employer, Employee shall
perform the usual and customary duties of _____,
including but not limited to that of those described in the written
job description.

Employee shall work at the convenience of Employer, arriving and leaving at times to be specified by Employer. Employee shall not be
required to work more than ____ hours per week, but may consent
to do so.

B. Compensation

Subject to the following provisions of this agreement, the Employer
agrees to pay the Employee a gross compensation hourly rate of
$_____.

Employer shall deduct and withhold appropriate amounts from
Employee's gross pay as required by federal and state laws.

Employer shall pay Employee on a (weekly _____) basis on the Friday of each week.

Employee shall receive an overtime wage of 1.5 times the usual gross hourly rate for each hour worked exceeding 40 hours per week. At the Employer's option, the Employer may compensate Employee by either paying overtime or by giving Employee compensatory time off, during the same pay period.

Employer, at its own discretion, may agree to increase Employee's hourly gross compensation from time to time in writing.

C. Benefits

Employee is entitled to _____ days of paid vacation annually. The vacation must be scheduled 30 days in advance and agreed to by employer. Vacation is based upon normal payment for a 40-hour workweek.

Employee will receive _____ days per year as paid sick time. Sick time may not be accumulated from year to year. Sick time benefits cannot be taken in cash compensation and are forfeited on termination of employment.

D. Terms and Conditions of Employment

Employee may not drink alcohol, use illegal drugs, or smoke while on duty for the employer.

Employer shall provide Employee with a petty cash fund for job-related expenses. Employer shall reimburse Employee upon providing Employer with a complete expense report with related receipt(s). Reimbursements will be made weekly.

Employment with the Household Employer lends itself to intimate and sensitive information. Therefore, Household Employee agrees to treat household information as private and confidential both during and after his/her employment tenure. Household Employee agrees that no information pertaining to the household, such as the home's security system code or a password for child care drop offs, is to be repeated inside or outside of the worksite. This applies to any information that is discussed by parties within the household, as well. In addition, Household Employee agrees not to discuss his or her salary and benefits with other household employees. Household Employee acknowledges that a violation of this rule of conduct will be grounds for early dismissal.

E. Termination of Agreement

Employer may terminate employment by Employee for violation of paragraph D-1.

Employer may terminate employment by Employee for failure to perform the duties set forth in the job description and employee handbook.

Termination means that benefits in paragraph C cease as of the date of termination.

Work agreement may be ended by mutual agreement.

Employment is at the discretion of Employer and Employee. Either party may terminate this agreement with or without notice or cause.

F. Modification and Interpretation

The job description may change by mutual consent.

Each party expects that Employee will conform to the custom and practice of the _____ (household employment, e.g., chef, nanny, butler).

G. Applicable Laws

The provisions of this agreement shall be construed in accordance with the laws of the state of _____.

_____   _____

Household Employer   Date

_____   _____

Household Employee   Date

(NOTICE: the information in this sample is designed to provide an outline that you can follow when formulating personnel plans. Because of the variances of many local, city, county, and state laws, we recommend that you seek professional legal counseling before entering into any agreement.)

Confidentiality and Nondisclosure Agreement

This Agreement ("Agreement") is made effective as of _____,
20__, by and between _____,
("Household Employer"), of _____, [address]
of the _____ Household and _____,
("the Household Employee").

Household Employer is a private household with an employment position.

Household Employer desires to have services of the Household Employee.

Household Employee is willing to be employed by Household Employer.

Therefore, the parties agree as follows:

CONFIDENTIALITY. Employment with the Household Employer lends itself to intimate and sensitive information. Therefore, Household Employee agrees to treat household information as private and confidential both during and after his/her employment tenure. Household Employee agrees that no information pertaining to the household, such as the home's security system code or a password for child care drop-offs, is to be repeated inside or outside of the worksite. This applies to any information that is discussed by parties within the household, as well. In addition, Household Employee agrees not to discuss his or her salary and benefits with other household employees. Household Employee acknowledges that a violation of this rule of conduct will be grounds for early dismissal.

UNAUTHORIZED DISCLOSURE OF INFORMATION. If it appears that Household Employee has disclosed (or has threatened to disclose) Information in violation of this Agreement, Household Employer shall be entitled to a Court injunction to restrain Household Employee from disclosing, in whole or in part, such Information, or from providing any services to any party to whom such Information has been disclosed or may be disclosed. Household Employer shall not be prohibited by this provision from pursuing other remedies, including a claim for losses and damages.

CONFIDENTIALITY AFTER TERMINATION OF SERVICES. The confidentiality provisions of this Agreement shall remain in full force and effect for a one-year period after the termination of Household Employee's services.

APPLICABLE LAW. The laws of the State of _____ shall govern this Agreement.

Household Employer

By Date _____   Date _____

AGREED TO AND ACCEPTED.

Household Employee

By _____   Date _____

Employee Handbook Acknowledgment Receipt

Date: _____

I acknowledge that I have received a copy of the household employee handbook, and that I am responsible for reading and understanding the information set forth within the handbook. I understand that I am responsible for returning the employee handbook to my employer upon my resignation or termination of employment.

Employee Name (please print): _____

Employee Signature: _____

Expense Report of Household Employee and Mileage Reimbursement Worksheet

EXPENSE REPORT OF HOUSEHOLD EMPLOYEE

DATE	Day	Meals	Food & Grocery	Transport & Travel	Supplies	Equipment & Tools	Entertainment	Other
Totals								

Mileage Reimbursement Worksheet

	Sun	Mon	Tues	Wed	Thurs	Fri	Sat
Date							
No. of Miles							
Reimbursement Rate (_¢/mile)							
Total							

SUBTOTAL $
Less advance $
Less prepaid expenses $
Total due employee $

REMEMBER: Attach Travel Authorization form and itinerary.

Approved by:

_____   _____

Household employee   Household employer

Medical Care Release Form

I, _____ (parent/guardian), authorize the following household employee, _____, to act on my behalf in the care of my dependent(s). The above person has my authority to request emergency health and/or medical services for my dependent in case of a health emergency.

Primary Physician: _____

Dependent Name: _____ DOB _____

Known Allergies _____

Dependent Name: _____ DOB _____

Known Allergies _____

Dependent Name: _____ DOB _____

Known Allergies _____

Parent/Guardian Signature Telephone   Date

Medication Permission

I give my permission that _____

___, who is caring for my dependent, give my dependent the following medication.

Dependent's name:

_____

_____

Medication:

_____

_____

Condition for which medication is prescribed:

_____

_____

Instructions for use:

Dosage _____

Time(s) _____

_____

Prescribing physician's name:

_____

Telephone:

_____

Possible side effects to be aware of:

_____

_____

_____

Parent/Guardian Signature   Date

_____   _____

Attendance Record of Household Employee

Employee: _____   Date hired: _____

Vacation due: _____

Sick/personal leave due: _____

For the month of: _____   year: _____

Date	Day of the Week	Present (Hours)	Vacation (Hours)	Sick (Hours)	Comments
1					
2					
3					
4					
5					
6					
7					
8					
9					
10					
11					
12					
13					
14					
15					
16					
17					
18					
19					
20					
21					
22					
23					
24					
25					
26					
27					
28					
29					
30					
31					

Time Off Request Form

Household Employee: _____

Personal Time Off Requests

Paid Time Off: Begins to accrue after 90 days of employment.

Requests for PTO of two or more days must be submitted at least two weeks in advance.

Bereavement Leave: Up to three days of paid leave is available for a death in the immediate family.

	Start date	End date	Hours
Personal time off			
Bereavement			
Jury duty/witness			
Military service			
		Total paid time off	

Vacation Requests

Vacation Instructions: Please submit your vacation request at least four weeks in advance of START DATE.

	Start date	End date	Hours	Employer approval
1st choice				
2nd choice				
3rd choice				
		Total paid time off		

Household Employee   Date: _____
Name: _____

Employer Name: _____   Date: _____

Performance Evaluation Form

(To be used quarterly during a one-on-one performance review meeting)

Household Employee Name: _____

Date: _____

Projects, issues, etc.	Date Addressed	Estimated Date of Completion	Assistance Needed, Issues to Resolve, etc.
Current Items			
1			
2			
3			
Items Completed			
A			
B			
C			
Areas where I can help you improve your skill set or improve your job performance			
A			
B			
Personal job-centered growth items completed last month, and future plans for personal job-related growth			
A			
B			

Tuition Reimbursement Request Form

Current position held: _____

Employee name: _____

Household employer: _____

Title of course no. 1: _____

Course description: _____

Dates of course: _____

Name of school/entity: _____

Reason for taking course: _____

Required Coursework: It is defined as necessary for degrees, certificates, or an individual course that a household employer required an employee to complete in order to meet performance standards or to keep pace with new development in the current job. Tuition will be paid at ____ percent (tuition or tuition and books), upon receipt of fee statements and course transcript. For reimbursement, employees must achieve a passing grade as defined by the educational organization and as approved by the household employer.

Job-Related Coursework: It is the responsibility of the employee to document the relationship of the reimbursed coursework to the household's employment needs and to obtain approval from the household employer. Tuition will be paid at ____ percent (tuition or tuition and books), upon receipt of fee statements and course transcript.

For reimbursement, employees must achieve a passing grade as defined by the educational organization and as approved by the household employer.

NOTE: You are required to submit the course description, proof of successful course completion along with receipts for tuition, and grades to the household employer before reimbursement will be made.

Household employee _____ Date _____

Household employer _____ Date _____

Incident Report

Household employee name _____

Employee position/title _____

Today's date _____

Incident time _____

Incident date _____

Incident location _____

Description of the incident that occurred

_____

_____

Witnesses to the incident (if applicable)

_____

_____

Corrective or disciplinary action to be taken

[ ] Verbal [ ] Written [ ] Probation [ ] Suspension

[ ] Other (explain below)

_____

(If on probation, period begins _____ and ends _____.)

Corrective action(s)/improvement(s) to be achieved

_____

Consequences for failure to improve future performance or correct behavior

_____

Household Employee Statement

I acknowledge that I have read and understand the above information and consequences.

_____   _____

Household employee   Date

_____   _____

Household employer   Date

_____   _____

Witness   Date

Termination of Employment to Household Employee Letter

Date _____

Dear _____,

As we have discussed, your employment with our household will terminate at the close of business on _____. You are entitled to the following benefits, per our household's policy:

1. Your salary will be continued through _____.

2. Your health insurance benefits will continue through _____.

Beyond that date, your rights to continue coverage under COBRA will be provided to you under separate cover.

3. You will be paid for your unused, accrued vacation, and personal time.

4. You may be entitled to unemployment insurance. It's your responsibility to contact the local office of unemployment to understand your entitled benefits, if any.

Should you have further questions, you may contact _____ at _____.

Sincerely,

Household Employer

All household employees are employed at will. This employment is at the discretion of the employer and the employee. Employment may terminate with or without notice or cause.

Employees are also free to end employment at any time, for any reason, with or without notice.

(NOTE: Certain states require "service letters," which must also include a reason for the termination. If this is the case in your state, or if you wish to document the reason for termination, make sure to include only verifiable facts.)

Glossary

A

At-Will Employment. At-will employment allows an employer to hire an employee any time, and the employee can quit at any time.

Au Pair. An au pair is a foreign national living in the United States as part of the host family who receives a small stipend in exchange for babysitting and help with housework. Legally authorized to live and work in the United States for up to one year in order to experience American life, an au pair may or may not have previous child care experience.

Affordable Care Act. The Patient Protection and Affordable Care Act (PPACA), commonly called the Affordable Care Act (ACA) or Obamacare, is a United States federal statute enacted by President Barack Obama on March 23, 2010. The aim of the act is that hospitals and primary physicians would transform their practices financially, technologically, and clinically to drive better health outcomes, lower costs, and improve their methods of distribution and accessibility.

B

Babysitter. A babysitter provides supervisory, custodial care of children on an irregular basis. No special training or background is expected.

Butler. According to the International Guild of Professional Butlers Household Employee Definitions, a butler uses his or her skills and attitude to provide service to his employer. Attitude is defined as energy, commitment, and attention to detail while striving for perfection. The butler role fills myriad services, including overseeing and scheduling all household help and contracted vendors; keeping household budgets; managing inventories; greeting callers; managing household, family, and estate security; organizing and overseeing events and parties held in the household; serving meals and drinks; and many other supervisory and hands-on tasks to operate the household professionally and efficiently.

C

Certified Nursing Assistants (CNA). A CNA generally assists with bathing and personal care.

Companions. These employees offer company or supervision to people who cannot be left alone. They may prepare meals, and some may stay through the night. They are generally available through home care agencies or are independently hired.

Consolidated Omnibus Reconciliation Act (COBRA). The federally mandated COBRA requires employers with 20 or more employees to offer an option of continued health care coverage after an employee and/ or his plan beneficiaries experience a qualifying event, such as if an employee is terminated from his or her position, COBRA allows he or she to continue health coverage through his or her present plan. (Please also see Mini-COBRA.)

Cook. In contrast to the chef, a cook is self-taught, typically very talented in the local cuisine, and not responsible for creating the menu. Prepared meals are often house favorites. A cook cleans and serves as a chef does.

D

Disability Insurance. Disability benefits are temporary cash benefits paid to an eligible earner and are for injuries or illness occurring *off* the job. It is a form of insurance that insures the beneficiary's earned income against the risk that a disability will make earning impossible.

Domestic Couples. Domestic couple teams are generally inside-outside teams: one partner may cook and clean while the other handles all outside work. The tasks involved incorporate aspects of the maid, housekeeper, houseman, house manager, and gardener roles.

Doula. Doula, a word from ancient Greek, today refers to a person experienced in childbirth who provides continuous support to the mother before, during, and for several weeks after childbirth.

Driver. A licensed professional who drives the employer to and from all specified destinations. A driver may also be responsible for maintenance of the employer's vehicles.

E

Earned Income Credit (EIC). EIC, which is claimed on an employee's federal income tax return, reduces his or her tax or allows him or her to receive a payment from the IRS.

Exclusive Provider Organization (EPO). An EPO is an insurance plan that is a network of individual medical care providers or groups of medical care providers who have entered into written agreements with an insurer to provide health insurance to subscribers.

Employee Handbook. A document that explains the household workplace's rules, practices, and policies, and is given to the employee at the start of their hire.

Estate Manager or Executive Estate Manager. A true estate manager is typically responsible for a substantial property(ies) and aircraft, yachts, and other employer personal interests. Management authority over inside and outside staffs and operations is held at varying degrees, depending on the employer. The executive estate manager refers to the highest level in this category, and, in complex situations, is similar to the chief executive officer in the corporate world. Some key tasks include developing personnel and financial management plans, as well as written position descriptions, standards of quality, and operating manuals; providing overall leadership to household service staff; organizing, planning, and evaluating all estate job activities; providing primary human resources for estate employees; coordinating and monitoring all property, buildings development, and maintenance; coordinating and monitoring all contracted services such as security, outside cleaning services; and effectively communicating with employer.

F

Flexible Spending Account (FSA). This plan allows the employee to set aside a portion of his or her pretax salary in an account, which is deducted from the employee's paycheck over the course of the year and can be used for eligible medical care expenses.

G

Gardener. A gardener tends to the landscaping, lawn, and outside environment of the employer's property.

Gentleman's Gentleman. The gentleman's gentleman provides similar services as the butler, but with service focused on the gentleman employer.

Governess. Traditionally an educated person (minimum bachelor's degree), the governess is employed by families for the full- or part-time at-home education of school-age children. A governess functions as a teacher and is not usually concerned with domestic work or the physical care of younger children.

Gross Pay. The wage paid to the employee *before* the necessary withholding taxes (Social Security, Medicare, state and federal) are deducted.

H

Health Insurance Portability and Accountability Act of 1996 (HIPPA). HIPPA amended the Employee Retirement Income Security Act (ERISA) to provide new rights and protections for participants and beneficiaries in group health plans.

Health Maintenance Organization (HMO). A health maintenance organization (HMO) is a plan that provides medical services to its members for a fixed, prepaid premium and requires members to use only the plan's participating (or networked) providers.

Health Reimbursement Arrangement (HRA). A contribution program for health-related expenses which is sponsored by the employer and reimburses an employee for eligible medical care expenses, as defined by the IRS.

Home Health Care. Home health care is professional health care, provided under the direction of a physician and in the patient's home, and is a viable and often preferable alternative for those people who do not need 24-hour supervision or an extended hospitalization to recover.

Homemakers. For people who are unable to perform daily household duties and who have no available help, homemakers clean, shop, launder, and prepare meals and are available through home care agencies or are independently hired.

House Manager Couples. House manager couples are less hands-on than domestic couples and more managerial. While they may handle cooking and/or service, house manager couples manage service delivery per house standards. Often, one partner performs personal assistant duties while the other handles butler or house manager tasks.

Household Employer. Per the IRS, a household employer is an individual who employs housekeepers, maids, gardeners, and others who work around that individual's private residence.

Household Manager. The household manager is another term for a butler, with a few subtle differences, such as that a butler is knowledgeable and sophisticated in the finer details of privilege and wealth, particularly in the area of wines and food. A household manager usually oversees staff in one residence, greets callers, assists in staff training, schedules and coordinates staff, plans and organizes parties and events in the home, serves meals and drinks, and may be involved in many more functions akin to a butler's responsibilities.

Hours Worked. According to the U.S. Fair Labor Standards Act, in general, hours worked include all time an employee must be on duty, on the employer's premises, or at any other prescribed workplace.

Housekeeper. The housekeeper handles general cleaning, laundry, ironing, mending, and other basic household functions.

I

Independent Contractor. A person who is hired to do work for another person but who is not an employee or agent of that person. The hiring person is not responsible for the actions of the independent contractor, nor does he or she owe the independent contractor the same legal duties that an employer owes to an employee under labor and employment laws.

Individual Health Plan. An individual health plan is for people not connected to an employer, such as self-employed people who have no other employees.

Immigrant. Per the U.S. Justice Department, an immigrant is a foreign national who is authorized to live and work permanently in the United States.

In-Home Child Care. A situation in which a caregiver cares for children in his or her home.

Individual Retirement Account (IRA) and the Roth IRA. An IRA is a special savings plan authorized by the federal government to help people accumulate funds for retirement. Traditional IRAs and Roth IRAs allow individual taxpayers to contribute 100 percent of their earnings up to the IRA's plan-specified maximum dollar amount. Traditional IRA contributions may be tax deductible, whereas Roth IRA contributions are not. Roth IRA principal and interest accumulate tax-free (Roth contributions have already been taxed).

M

Maids. Parlor maids, scullery maids, kitchen maids, laundry maids, housemaids, and ladies' maids are various positions in a staffed home. A maid performs specialized tasks, primarily care and cleaning duties, and is often associated with a particular area of the home.

Migrant Worker. A worker who travels from one area to another in search of work.

Mini-COBRA. Mini-COBRA (Consolidated Omnibus Reconciliation Act) allows employees and their families to continue health insurance coverage with small group carriers, for firms with two to nineteen employees. (Please see COBRA.)

N

Nanny. Live-in or live-out, a nanny works in the household to undertake all tasks related to the care of children. Duties are generally restricted to child care and the domestic tasks related to child care. A nanny may or may not have had any formal training, though often has a good deal of actual experience. Nanny's workweek ranges from 40-60 hours per week, and a nanny usually works unsupervised.

Nanny Share (or Share Care). A situation in which two (or more) families engage the services of a single nanny to care for their children at the same time.

Net Pay. The wage paid to the employee *after* the necessary withholding taxes (Social Security, Medicare, state and federal) are deducted.

Noncitizen. A person who comes from a foreign country.

Nonimmigrant. A nonimmigrant is a foreign person who seeks entry into the United States or who has already been admitted for a specific purpose for a temporary period of time.

Nursery Nurse. The nursery nurse is a title used in Great Britain for a person who has received special training and preparation in caring for young children, in or out of the home. The nursery nurse may be live-in or live-out, works independently, and is responsible for everything related to child care. Duties are generally restricted to child care and the domestic tasks related to child care, and the workweek is usually 50-60 hours per week. In addition to specialized training, the nursery nurse successfully passed Great Britain's certification examination of the National Nursery Examination Board.

P

Parent's or Mother's Helper. Lives in or lives out and works to provide full-time child care and domestic help for families in which one parent is home most of the time. The parent's or mother's helper may be left in charge of the children for brief periods of time and may or may not have previous child care experience.

Personal Assistant. The personal assistant is a key position in the private life of the household employer and performs a broad category of services.

Generally, the personal assistant focuses on handling the employer's correspondence and communications, staff coordination, travel planning, errands, and odd jobs.

Personal Attendant. An employee that assists with personal care and accompanies clients to medical appointments and recreational and social activities.

Personal Care (also called Custodial Care). A nonskilled service or care that includes help with dressing, bathing, eating, transferring, walking, toileting, and so on.

Personal Time Off. Personal time off (PTO) refers to all the time offered to the employee for time off or work benefits.

Permanent Resident or Immigrant (also known as Green Card Holder). A foreign-born person who has been sponsored by a qualifying family member or employer, and who has approval to reside permanently in the United States as a lawful permanent resident. This person holds a Resident Alien Card, known often as a green card.

Preferred Provider Plan (PPO). A preferred provider plan (PPO) is a managed care health plan that contracts with providers. Plan members are offered a financial incentive to use providers on the plan's network but are able to see non-network providers as well.

Private or Personal Chef. A private or personal chef is professionally trained and seasoned in various cuisines and caters to the preferences, tastes, and diets of his or her employers. The private or personal chef performs or cooks in the home, as well as on a family-owned yacht and aircraft; may serve meals and refreshments; and cleans the kitchen and related facilities such as coolers and freezers.

S

Sandwich Generation. A generation of people, typically in their thirties or forties, responsible for simultaneously bringing up their own children and for caring for their aging parents.

Security Professional. An individual who is responsible for household security, including household property and personal security.

Senior Caregiver (also called Eldercare Provider). A generic term referring to someone who helps an elderly person with daily care, health care, financial matters, companionship, and social activity. A senior caregiver may offer assistance for payment or voluntarily.

T

Temporary to Hire. When an employment agency offers a program where the agency screens and selects the employee and employs them for an initial time period so the family can 'try out' the employee. The family pays the agency as part of the employee's hourly wage and then hires the employee after the time period has ceased.

U

U.S. Citizen. Per the U.S. Justice Department, citizens include people who are born in the United States, Puerto Rico, Guam, the Northern Mariana Islands, and the U.S. Virgin Islands, as well as others who obtain U.S. citizenship.

U.S. National. Per the U.S. Justice Department, U.S. nationals include people born in America Samoa, including Swains Island.

W

Workers' Compensation. An insurance policy that provides compensation to an employee for medical expenses resulting from work-related illness or injury.

Workweek. According to the U.S. Fair Labor Standards Act, a workweek is a period of 168 hours during seven consecutive 24-hour periods.

Index